A.S.A. MONOGRAPHS

General Editor: MICHAEL BANTON

1

The Relevance of Models
for Social Anthropology

A.S.A. MONOGRAPHS

Published under the auspices of the Association of Social
Anthropologists of the Commonwealth

General Editor: Michael Banton

Michael Banton, editor

1. *The Relevance of Models for Social Anthropology*
2. *Political Systems and the Distribution of Power*
3. *Anthropological Approaches to the Study of Religion*
4. *The Social Anthropology of Complex Societies*

Edmund Leach, editor

5. *The Structural Study of Myth and Totemism*

Raymond Firth, editor

6. *Themes in Economic Anthropology*

I. M. Lewis, editor

7. *History and Social Anthropology*

THE RELEVANCE OF
MODELS FOR
SOCIAL ANTHROPOLOGY

Edited by Michael Banton

TAVISTOCK PUBLICATIONS
London · New York · Sydney · Toronto · Wellington

First published in 1965
by Tavistock Publications Limited
11 New Fetter Lane, London EC4

Second impression 1968
Third impression 1969
SBN 422 71370 8
1.3

First published as a Social Science Paperback in 1968 ✓
Second impression 1969
SBN 422 72490 4
1.2

Printed by photolithography by
Bookprint Limited, Crawley, Sussex

This volume derives from material presented at a Conference on 'New Approaches in Social Anthropology' sponsored by the Association of Social Anthropologists of the Commonwealth, held at Jesus College, Cambridge, 24-30 June 1963

Distributed in the U.S.A.
by Barnes & Noble Inc.

IN MEMORIAM

A. R. RADCLIFFE-BROWN

FIRST CHAIRMAN AND LIFE PRESIDENT

OF THE ASSOCIATION OF SOCIAL ANTHROPOLOGISTS

OF THE COMMONWEALTH

Contents

Contents

Max Gluckman and Fred Eggan

Introduction

The several disciplines of modern anthropology – prehistoric archaeology, physical anthropology, social or sociological anthropology, cultural anthropology, and psychological anthropology – have separated out of a general anthropology which in the second half of the nineteenth century and into the twentieth century aimed to study man both as a biological and as a social being. There are still many general anthropologists, mainly in the United States but also in Europe; and the various aspects of anthropology are still taught in many universities as a combined degree. Nevertheless, by the 1930s the different disciplines were beginning to separate from one another, though some scholars were still eminent in more than one discipline. As each anthropological discipline separated out, its practitioners turned to other subjects, whose techniques and modes of analysis were more appropriate to their problems than were those of their erstwhile colleagues. Physical anthropologists depended more on the biological sciences; psychological anthropologists (who studied the interaction of culture and personality) on psychology, especially depth·psychology, and psychiatry; and social anthropologists on sociology, history, political science, law, and economics. Cultural anthropologists alone continued to draw on the biological, psychological, and sociological sciences.

Outwardly the common mark of social, cultural, and psychological anthropology was that they all continued to be comparative and cross-cultural in outlook, with an emphasis on the small-scale tribal societies of the world; and for many years the study of such a society was virtually the initiation ceremony which admitted a scholar into the ranks of anthropology. Hence all anthropologists felt they had something in common, besides their joint membership in such organizations as the

American Anthropological Association and the Royal Anthropological Institute of Great Britain and Ireland.

We believe they had something more in common, drawn from their traditional unity, besides their previous, almost unique, concentration on the tribal societies. This was a continuing focusing of interest on *customs*, as having an interrelated dependence on one another, whether in forming cultural patterns, or in operating within systems of social relations, or in the structuring of various types of personality in different groups. This focus on customs in interdependence has continued to distinguish the disciplines of anthropology from the other subjects with which each branch is increasingly associated. The analysis of custom remains one of the distinctive contributions of all anthropological studies to the human sciences.

The extent to which anthropologists specialized in one or other aspect of the general subject varied in different countries. In Great Britain, the trend has steadily moved more and more to distinctive specialization as an archaeologist, a physical anthropologist, or a sociological-social anthropologist. In Oxford and Cambridge, where anthropology has been longest taught, regulations provide for general anthropological qualifications, but it is possible for students to qualify entirely in social anthropology and other social sciences, or at most to have minimal tuition in other types of anthropology. Compulsory training on the biological side is perhaps strongest for social anthropological specialists at University College, London. At other London colleges, and at the other British universities where social anthropology has been established since the last war, the subject has usually been placed in social science faculties or departments, with sociology, economics, and political science. In a few universities only are links strong with geography or psychology within a combined Honours degree.

The British Honours degree necessarily leads, except for the Cambridge Tripos system, to a reduction in the types of other subjects that can be taken by undergraduates specializing in social anthropology. This process does not operate in the American undergraduate schools of anthropology, and hence at that level students who wish to become social anthropologists take a much greater variety of subjects, and the anthropology they are taught tends to continue to cover several branches of the subject. This naturally influences graduate schools of anthropology, since their products have to be able to teach in more than one branch of anthropology, if they are appointed to small colleges (see Mandelbaum, Lasker, and Albert, 1963).

Nevertheless, in the United States most anthropologists are becoming as specialized as they are in British universities, and are correspondingly associating with various cognate disciplines according to their type of specialization. Owing to the greater size of the country, and the far greater number of universities and of anthropologists, there is in the United States a greater variety of types of anthropologist than in the British Commonwealth. It is in the States that cultural and psychological anthropology flourish in addition to the social anthropology, physical anthropology, linguistics, and prehistoric archaeology that are represented in Britain. The flourishing of these several branches of anthropology in the States is probably fertilized, too, by the absence of the Honours degree system: there is a more varied interdisciplinary contact, which continues beyond the undergraduate level.

The increasing specialization of British social anthropologists with a decreasing interest on their part in prehistoric archaeology, physical anthropology, and cultural anthropology, in 1946 led the practitioners of the subject in Britain – then under a score – to form the Association of Social Anthropologists of the (British) Commonwealth. Though they wished still to support the Royal Anthropological Institute, they considered that they had specific and limited interests, sufficiently distinct from those of general anthropology, to require the support of a specific organization. This has meant, for example, that social anthropologists in Britain have had an organized means of giving evidence on their own problems to commissions advising the British Government on higher education and research, besides evidence given by the Royal Anthropological Institute for anthropology in general. The process of *partial* separation from general anthropology continued until, in 1960, the social anthropologists joined with sociologists and social psychologists to form a new Sociology Section of the British Association for the Advancement of Science. Two of the five presidents of the Section to date have been social anthropologists. Social anthropologists still participate in the older Anthropology and Archaeology Section, but they submit more papers to, and attend in greater numbers at, meetings of the new section.

Between 1946 and 1962 the Association of Social Anthropologists of the (British) Commonwealth increased its membership from under a score to over one hundred and fifty, even though election to membership required normally both the holding of a teaching or research post in the Commonwealth and the attainment of either a post-graduate degree (usually a doctorate) or substantial publication. Meetings of the Association in Britain ceased to be small gatherings of perhaps a dozen people, and were attended by between thirty and sixty members.

In 1962 Professor Raymond Firth, then Chairman of the Association, proposed that it should try to raise the funds to invite a dozen American social anthropologists to one of its meetings. He suggested that since the milieux in which American social anthropologists worked were so much more varied than the milieu of British social anthropologists, it would be profitable to see what was common between us and where we differed, in a series of papers on 'New Approaches in Social Anthropology'. He pointed out that though there were many individual contacts between some members of the Association and American colleagues, many British and Americans had not met one another: moreover, we had never had a joint, organized stocktaking. He further suggested that papers should be read only by scholars who had entered the subject since the war: so the phrase 'new approaches' signifies that the papers collected in these four volumes present the problems and views of a younger generation of anthropologists.

When the Association enthusiastically adopted Firth's proposal, there was no corresponding organization of social anthropologists in the U.S.A. with whom there could be discussions and arrangements. The Association therefore more or less thrust on Professor Fred Eggan of the University of Chicago the task of representing American social anthropologists. It did so for several reasons, besides his own standing as a social anthropologist. The late Professor A. R. Radcliffe-Brown, who had been for the first years of the Association's existence its Life President, and to whose memory this series of A.S.A. Monographs is dedicated, had taught at Chicago from 1931 to 1937. Eggan had succeeded, so to speak, to Radcliffe-Brown's position, and under the Roman rule of universal succession might be regarded as representing him. Above all, under Radcliffe-Brown's influence there had developed in Chicago perhaps the strongest single group of *social* anthropologists in the U.S.A. Eggan agreed to help organize the meeting, but insisted, of course, that his British colleagues should select the dozen American scholars whom they wished to hear. With great difficulty, the British, eventually by vote, chose a dozen from the large number they would have liked to invite. If there seems a bias to Chicago, or Chicago-trained Americans (as one or two of the others rather ironically suggested), the British are responsible, and not Eggan. The American Anthropological Association agreed to sponsor a request for support, and the National Science Foundation generously financed the Americans' journey to Britain.

The programme, to which twice as many British as Americans contributed papers, was divided into four main sections. Two to three papers were presented in a group, and discussion was then opened by either an American or a British anthropologist – again, those opening the discussions were selected from the post-war generation, though more senior anthropologists were allowed to join in the general discussion. But these Monographs are not a report on the proceedings of the Conference. They embody theoretical papers by twenty younger anthropologists, who have amended their arguments, where they felt it necessary, after listening to the comments of their colleagues. Effectively the papers present, therefore, growing-points in social anthropology as seen by a new generation of practitioners.

Two years passed between the time when Firth, as Chairman of the Association, made his original proposal, and the meeting itself, which was held in Jesus College, Cambridge, in June 1963. By that time Gluckman had succeeded Firth as Chairman, and on him, and the yet-again conscribed Eggan, has fallen the task of introducing the Monographs. It has been a difficult task: the papers cover a range of ethnographic areas and of problems which they cannot themselves compass competently.

Hence this Introduction makes no attempt to assess the substantive problems and solutions suggested in the papers. Instead, it tries to pull together the kinds of issue which crop up as interesting the contributors in several of the papers.

There was also a major technical difficulty. The papers are published in four separate volumes, covering, respectively:

1. The relevance of models for social anthropology;
2. Political systems and the distribution of power;
3. Anthropological approaches to the study of religion;
4. The social anthropology of complex societies.

Since the Introduction was planned to cut across all four volumes, we decided to write a single text and print it in each volume. Various readers may approach the series through any of the four. The arabic figures 1, 2, 3, and 4 indicate in which of the monographs is located an essay referred to in the Introduction.

SPECIALIZATION AND SPREAD: LINKS WITH THE SOCIAL SCIENCES

The specialization of social anthropologists in a separate discipline, and the extent to which they have turned to sociology and political science, are particularly marked in these monographs. This is not surprising in the volumes on political problems (2) and on complex societies, including both peasantries and urban areas (4), where the problems dealt with are common to the three disciplines. As it happens, the other disciplines that are commonly grouped in the social sciences – economics and law – are not cited.

This is partly a matter of chance. We could provide for only a limited number of papers, and arrangements had been made to have a paper on the use of economic models in social anthropology by Mrs Lorraine Baric; but at the crucial time she went to Yugoslavia to do field-research.

Two papers do deal with 'economic problems', in the widest but not the technical sense of 'economics'. The first is by Marshall Sahlins, 'On The Sociology of Primitive Exchange', in monograph 1. Though by its title this might be thought to deal with economic problems, its actual emphasis is on 'sociology'. It considers types of exchange in terms of degrees of reciprocity as these alter along a scale of contexts of tribal social relations, from the most personal to the least personal – if we reduce a complex analysis to a single sentence. Sahlins makes no reference to economic theorizing as such, and indeed part of the discussion of his paper turned on this point.

Eric Wolf carries out a somewhat similar analysis of morphological changes in 'Kinship, Friendship, and Patron-Client Relations in Complex Societies' (4). In this essay, Wolf examines the kinds of situation in terms of ecological and economic situations in which kinship, friendship, and patron-client relationships respectively are dominant outside the nuclear family. No more than with Sahlins, would one expect this problem to lead Wolf into the use of economic theory as such. Save for one citation from Schumpeter, he does not rely on the economists.

The absence of reference to economic theory in the papers hence means that one approach, whether it be new or old, is not covered in these four monographs. We think it is true to say that technical economics has had less influence on social anthropological research than other social sciences have had, possibly because of its highly abstract nature. In the Register of the Association of Social Anthropologists less than 3 in a 100 members list 'economics' among their special interests, and there are also few specialists in the U.S.A. Yet before the war, among other senior anthropologists, Firth, originally trained as an economist, had used the technical concepts of economics to good effect for a tribal society in his *Primitive Polynesian Economy* (1939) and, after the War, for a peasant society in his *Malay Fishermen* (1946). More recently, a number of younger anthropologists, some with training in economics, have used this training impressively. But this is perhaps more marked among those who have studied peasant societies, than among those who have studied tribes, as is shown, perhaps, in *Capital, Saving and Credit in Peasant Societies* (Firth & Yamey (eds.), 1964), a symposium containing essays by nine younger British social anthropologists, by four Americans, and by one Norwegian who was trained partly in Britain.

The Association of Social Anthropologists hopes in the near future to publish a Monograph in which the use of theoretical economics in recent work by British scholars will be considered.

When these symposia were planned, arrangements had also been made to have at least one paper on problems in the field of law. Illness prevented P. J. Bohannan from preparing this. The absence of any treatment of tribal law, and more generally of processes of social control, does not reflect the extent to which these problems have interested social anthropologists in recent decades, particularly since the publication of Llewellyn and Hoebel's *The Cheyenne Way: Conflict and Case Law in Primitive Jurisprudence* (1941). That book, and Hoebel's earlier work, inspired a number of studies on jurisprudential problems, particularly on juristic method in the judicial or arbitral process, among both American and British social anthropologists. This work has drawn largely, if sometimes indirectly, on American sociological jurisprudence. This field of research is therefore not covered in the Monographs.

Here, then, are two social sciences not drawn on for this symposium.

References outside those to the work of social anthropologists are clearly most numerous to sociologists – for example, to sociometric work and to the work of the sociologists Ginsberg, Homans, and W. F. Whyte, by Adrian Mayer in his treatment of 'The Significance of Quasi-Groups in the Study of Complex Societies' (4). J. Clyde Mitchell in the same volume discusses 'Theoretical Orientations in African Urban Studies' and he begins by stating that 'differences in behaviour as between people in the town and in the country have for long been the topic of study of sociologists and other social scientists in Europe and America. . .'. Though Mitchell cites only a few of these sociologists, their work clearly has influenced not only Mitchell, but also the numerous other anthropologists who have studied urban areas in Africa and who are cited by Mitchell.

But it would seem that, leaving aside Durkheim, whose school's influence on social anthropology has always been marked, the influence of Weber on younger social anthropologists in recent years has been considerable. If anything, that influence is under-represented in these essays: it has been very marked in a number of monographs, as in L. A. Fallers's *Bantu Bureaucracy* (no date: about 1956). With the influence of Weber – and partly inspired by his writings – goes the influence of Talcott Parsons among modern sociologists.

Perhaps the most cited and influential of modern sociologists in these monographs is R. K. Merton. His discussions of levels of theory, and of the distinction between manifest and latent functions, have always been exploited by anthropologists; and Melford Spiro uses them in his essay on religion in Monograph 3. But generally it is the increasing interest in the more meticulous analysis of social roles (referred to below) which inspired the writers to draw on Merton's treatment of role-sets – Ward Goodenough in 'Rethinking "Status" and "Role"' (1), Aidan Southall on roles in different political systems (2), and Ronald Frankenberg in an essay on the changing structure of roles in different types of British communities (4), use Merton, appreciatively and critically.

Parsons too has influenced anthropologists' thinking about this key concept. There are also indications of a growing importance here of the work of Erving Goffman – himself influenced by the work of social anthropologists – on how people operate their roles. Goodenough has drawn markedly on Goffman's books on *The Presentation of Self in Everyday Life* (1959) and *Encounters* (1961). Frankenberg argues that there is a convergence between the ideas of Goffman and those developed in British social anthropology, especially by Barnes, Gluckman, and Turner.

These references must be sufficient to show how much social anthropologists are now drawing on the cognate subject of sociology. The essays thus reflect, in research and analysis, the tendency in both countries for social anthropology and sociology to be taught either in one department or in closely linked departments.

The references above are to certain types of sociology. No essay makes use of demographic analysis – but Mitchell's and a couple of other essays refer to the importance of demographic analysis, which in general has been inadequately used by social anthropologists in their reports on communities. However, it is worth noting here that anthropologists such as Mitchell and

J. A. Barnes have, in their treatment of suitable problems, been contributing to theory in demographic studies.

In their Introduction to *African Political Systems* (1940), Fortes and Evans-Pritchard wrote that: 'We have not found that the theories of political *philosophers* [italics added] have helped us to understand the societies we have studied and we consider them of little scientific value . . .' (at p. 5). At least one reviewer asked why they did not draw on the work of political *scientists*. Since Fortes and Evans-Pritchard, with *African Political Systems*, virtually established 'political anthropology', their successors have turned increasingly to political scientists for assistance in their analysis. We have already cited Fallers's use of Weber's hypotheses in his study of Soga bureaucracy, and many other monographs on political problems have used Weberian ideas as well as works by those who are more specifically political scientists or constitutional historians. Every essay in Monograph 2 refers to works in political science. The most-cited work is Easton's study of *The Political System* (1953), and his article on 'Political Anthropology' in *Biennial Review of Anthropology* (1959). Easton, in Lloyd's words (4), 'took time from his studies of modern societies to examine the progress made by social anthropologists. [Easton] castigates the failure of the anthropologists to develop any broad theoretical orientation to politics, ascribing this to their preoccupation with general problems of social control, conflict, and integration and their reluctance to define the respective limits of political and other – social, religious, economic – systems. Easton offers a classification of African political systems which is based upon the differentiation in political roles. . . .'

We are tempted to point out that in the kinds of societies traditionally studied by social anthropologists political, economic, religious, and social systems are in fact often not differentiated, and to reply that political scientists have not themselves made so clear a definition of political systems. But, reviewing the essays under consideration, Easton's own suggestion about the classification of political systems in terms of differentiation in roles fits in with a main concern of recent anthropology – marked in Aidan Southall's essay on 'A Critique of the Typology of States and Political Systems' (2).

For the rest, the social anthropologist in his analysis of political problems seems to turn to whatever source, outside of anthropology, he feels can assist his specific analysis. Thus when F. G. Bailey considers 'Consensus as a Procedure for Taking Decisions in Councils and Committees: with special reference to village and local government in India' (2), he uses work by Morris-Jones, a political scientist, on India; Wheare's now classic survey of *Government by Committee* (1955); a study of contemporary parties and politics in Japan; and F. M. Cornford's witty analysis of Cambridge University politics, *Microcosmographia Academica* (1908). Nicholas, in a comparative analysis of 'Factions' (2), equally uses a small number of political science studies. We are not suggesting that these writers use all – or even the most important – relevant sources from political science: indeed, we ourselves know of others they might have used. We indicate here only that there is a readiness to turn to political science, and Bailey's essay has more references to works by political scientists than to works by other anthropologists. Political anthropology, at least, is linking up with its cognate discipline: and this clearly is not difficult, since the concepts and analytic framework of political science are not too diverse from those of social anthropology. No new techniques have to be learned to master them.

SPECIALIZATION AND SPREAD: LINKS WITH BIOLOGY, PSYCHOLOGY, AND CULTURAL ANTHROPOLOGY

In contrast to this turn towards sociology of various kinds and to at least some fields of political science, plus the under-represented use of economics and law, we note relatively few references to cultural anthropology, psychological anthropology, psychology, and the biological sciences. In the volume on religion (3) there are references to the work of Margaret Mead, partly in the particular ethnographic context of Bali in which she worked with Gregory Bateson. This is in Clifford Geertz's essay on 'Religion as a Cultural System'. He begins by stating that the detailed studies of religion in particular societies which have characterized social anthropology are in 'a state of general stagnation', suffering under what 'Janowitz has called the dead hand of competence'. Geertz summarizes the achievements of anthropological study of religion as: 'Yet one more meticulous case-in-point for such well-established propositions as that ancestor worship supports the jural authority of elders, that initiation rites are means for the establishment of sexual identity and adult status, that ritual groupings reflect political oppositions, or that myths provide charters for social institutions and rationalizations of social privilege may well finally convince a great many people, both inside the profession and out, that anthropologists are, like theologians, firmly dedicated to proving the indubitable.'

We do not believe that these summary statements at the opening of Geertz's essay are quite fair assessments of the acute and complicated analyses actually made by social anthropologists of ancestor cults, initiation ceremonies, political rituals, and the social context of myths, exemplified in the three essays on religion in specific societies in the same volume – by V. W. Turner on 'Colour Classification in Ndembu Ritual', by R. Bradbury on 'Fathers, Elders, and Ghosts in Edo Religion', and by E. Winter on 'Traditional Groupings and Religion among the Iraqw'. Geertz has himself written a notable analysis (1960) of a single society's religions.

Geertz is clearly being critical of his own, as well as of his colleagues', work, in order to plead for a much wider treatment of the general 'cultural dimension of religious analysis'. And he is not unique among younger anthropologists in feeling that the social anthropological analysis of religion by itself is inadequate. We take it that this mode of analysis is restricted to examining the role of religion, with emphasis on custom, rite, and belief, in social relations; and we believe that those who follow this procedure realize that they are not explaining 'the whole of religion'. They accept that they are analysing religion in only one of its dimensions, and that other dimensions have to be analysed by other types of discipline, using different techniques and perhaps examining other types of data. Clearly any set of phenomena as complicated as religion – indeed any social complex – for total understanding has to be subjected to investigation by several disciplines.

We believe that most social anthropologists would accept this. Melford Spiro in his essay on 'Religion: Problems of Definition and Explanation' (3) states in his 'Conclusion' to his argument 'that an adequate explanation for the persistence of religion requires both psychological (in this instance, psycho-analytical) and sociological variables'. Religion, or family structure, or motivations, can be taken variously as independent or dependent variables. Spiro continues: 'But many studies of religion, however, are concerned not with the explanation of religion, but with the role of religion in the explanation of society. Here, the explanatory task is to discover the contri-butions which religion, taken as the independent variable, makes to societal integration, by its satisfaction of sociological wants. This is an important task, central to the main concern of anthropology, as the science of social systems. We seriously err, however, in mistaking an explanation of society for an explanation of religion which, in effect, means confusing the sociological functions of religion with the bases for its perform-ance.' In his introductory paragraphs to his essay on Iraqw ritual (3) Winter makes the same clarification.

We have cited Spiro at length because it is in the study of religion that some social anthropologists have manifested a reluctance to accept that a specifically social anthropological analysis, giving an admittedly limited explanation, provides anything like an adequate explanation. The essays by Geertz and Spiro exhibit some of this feeling, which has appeared also in work published elsewhere, by Britons as well as Americans. Where they invoke psychology, not all of them follow Spiro in calling for some form of depth-psychology. The psychic frame-work employed may be an intellectualist one, in which the ex-planatory value for the observers is emphasized, as in the claim that the difference between tribal and universalistic rituals stems from the way people in tribal societies construct their model of the universe on the model they abstract from their own social relations (Horton, 1964).

Spiro and Winter clarify the issues involved. To understand religion, in a commonsense use of 'understand', [at least] both sociological and psychological explanations are required. The sociological – that is, the social anthropological – analysis alone is an explanation of the role of religion in social relations; and a psychological analysis alone is an explanation of the role of religion in the functioning of the personality. Nevertheless, we note that there is this dissatisfaction with the limited extent of social anthropological analysis in this field, which does not show in the treatment of political and a number of other problems.

Spiro's remains a general, abstract essay. Geertz's, interestingly enough after his castigatory opening, is largely taken up with a penetrating analysis of a specific situation in Java. With all respect, we believe that there is not 'a state of general stagnation' in the subject: the evidence of several monographs shows that social anthropological understanding of religion and ritual in specific societies continues to advance. Geertz calls for a study of symbols: we consider this is illuminatingly achieved in Turner's essay on colour symbolism among the Ndembu. Geertz 'slights' such well-established propositions as that 'ancestor worship supports the jural authority of elders': we consider that Bradbury's essay on the role of ghosts and spirits among the Edo, in a comparative background, and Winter's similar attempt to illuminate the specific variants of spirit-cult organization among the Iraqw, show by contrast how steady, deep, and wide is the penetration of the subject's understanding here.

Moreover, a discipline may advance by the working out logically of basic theoretical propositions, some of which are perhaps based on observation. This applies to theoretical economics and to some aspects of Parsons's theory of action in sociology. Social anthropology has not shown a corresponding development, save perhaps in some of Lévi-Strauss's analyses. Advance may also be achieved by the formulation of a series of propositions, based on observation. In the natural sciences, a number of these propositions have been cumulatively brought under a hierarchy of increasingly embracing laws. Social anthropology, like sociology and political science, has numerous propositions at the first level. It may lack widely embracing laws to cover many of these, but, like sociology and political science, it does have some theories of the middle range, as Merton (1958), with others, has phrased the situation. These middle-range theories are applied within a 'general orientation towards substantive materials' (ibid, pp. 87-88).

The kind of general approach to their data which social anthropologists have developed is illustrated throughout these essays: an insistence by most that there are interdependencies between both social relations and customs, and further associations between these interdependencies. Analysis of these interdependencies is often set in an evolutionary framework, even if it be a morphological rather than a temporal one, as the essays by Sahlins on primitive exchange (1), Wolf on kinship, friendship, and patron-client relations (4), and Mitchell and Frankenberg on the rural to non-rural continuum (4) well illustrate. The same framework is used by Lloyd and Southall, to some extent, in their essays on the typology of political systems (2). Yet social anthropology, judging by these essays, still lacks the kind of fundamental orientation found, for example, in Marxist sociology.

Individual propositions, stated baldly out of the context of this orientation, and of both field situation and corpus of allied propositions, may appear to be truistic – and hence banal. But the skill of anthropologists, like that of practitioners of the cognate disciplines, lies to a large extent still in their ability to apply, and weigh the application of, selected propositions to specific situations. This may be done within a single situation, with comparative checking implicit, or it may be done with occasional explicit comparison, or it may be done outright as a comparative study. On the whole, these procedures, and attempts to develop them with refinement of the basic propositions, appear to us to dominate these essays on 'new approaches' in the subject. The striving is after clarification; elimination of muddles; clearing away of concepts that, though once useful, now appear to be too gross and to block analysis; and the formulation of better theories of the middle range. These tendencies are marked in the essays by Geertz and Spiro, though these are also the only essays which press for, and aim at, much higher-level theories.

One attempt to formulate further theories of the middle range is appropriately referred to in this section on links with psychology and cultural anthropology. Wolf's analysis of the contexts in which kinship, friendship, and patron-client relations are respectively dominant in complex societies (4), is in some respects complementary to Sahlins's essay on the changing contexts of exchange in tribal societies (1): basically, it is *social* anthropological in tackling its problems, with the emphasis on making a living, handling relations with authorities, etc. But at the end of the essay, Wolf suggests that the varying texture of relations with kin, friends, and patrons or clients may have 'a point of encounter with what has sometimes been called the national character approach'. Examining works in this field, he is struck by the fact that 'they have utilized – in the main – data on the interpersonal sets discussed in [his] paper, and on the etiquettes and social idioms governing them'. Wolf cites three instances, and concludes: 'It is obvious that such descriptions and analyses do not cope with the institutional features of national structure. Yet it is equally possible that complex societies in the modern world differ less in the formal organization of their economic or legal or political systems than in the character of their supplementary inter-personal sets. Using the strategy of social anthropology, moreover, we would say that information about these sets is less meaningful when organized in terms of a construct of homogeneous national character, than when referred to the particular body of social relations and its function, partial or general, within the supplementary or parallel structure underlying the formal institutional framework. . . . The integration of the great society requires the knitting of these interstitial relations.'

We have cited Wolf at length because he appears to us explicitly to map in outline common ground between several of the essays which deal with what can be the social anthropological contribution to the study of complex societies. It is clearly accepted that a study of large-scale institutional frameworks such as the economic, or the administrative and political, falls to the lot of economists, political scientists, and sociologists. With this acceptance, goes the assumption, to quote Wolf again, of a possibility 'that complex societies of the modern world differ less in the formal organization of their economic or legal or political system than in the character of their supplementary interpersonal sets'. Anthropologists of all kinds have always been fascinated by the variety of human behaviour, even when they have sought uniformity and generality in that variety. So that aside from their interest in the small-scale, which fits with their techniques of observation, they tend to concentrate on those features of complex – as of tribal – societies where there are some distinctive sets of customs which require to be explained. We think this tendency shows in Bailey's treatment of committees and Nicholas's of factions in modern India (2).

This tendency is particularly marked in Monograph 4, specifically devoted to complex societies. In his essay on 'Theoretical Orientations in African Urban Studies' Mitchell begins by stating that 'in Africa, as elsewhere, urban studies raise the same questions'. He continues by stating that 'the focus of sociological interest in African urban studies must be on the way in which the behaviour of town-dwellers fits into, and is adjusted to, the social matrix created by the commercial, industrial, and administrative framework of a modern metropolis – having regard to the fact that most African town-dwellers have been born and brought up in the rural hinterland of the city, in which the cultural background is markedly dissimilar from that of the city'. After discussing social surveys and intensive studies, he distinguishes between 'historical' or 'processive' change to cover overall changes in the social system, and 'situational change', which covers changes in behaviour 'following participation in different social systems'. In dealing with both these types of change, Mitchell emphasizes the importance of relations of kinship and friendship – thus he faces the same problems as Wolf. He is then concerned to distinguish structural from categorical relationships, before passing to emphasize the importance of studying 'the network of personal links which individuals have built around themselves in towns'. Seeing problems very similar to those seen by Wolf, he suggests that the study of networks may show 'the way in which norms and values are diffused in a community, and how the process of "feedback" takes place.' In these studies, gossip, joking relations, historical antecedents, can all be taken into account.

In Monograph 4 Adrian Mayer treats, with technical detail, a similar set of problems, in an essay on 'The Significance of

Quasi-Groups in the Study of Complex Societies'. He too emphasizes the importance of networks and action-sets of relations, as against groups, and tries to clarify and refine those concepts. He applies them to an Indian electoral stuggle. He concludes: 'It may well be that, as social anthropologists become more interested in complex societies and as the simpler societies themselves become more complex, an increasing amount of work will be based on Ego-centred entities such as action-sets and quasi-groups, rather than on groups and sub-groups' – the latter being, presumably, what Wolf calls 'the formal organization' of complex societies.

Burton Benedict, in the same monograph, considers 'Sociological Characteristics of Small Territories' such as Mauritius. He sets his task as an assessment of the relation between the scale of society and: the number, kinds, and duration of social roles; types of values and alternatives; magico-religious practices; jural relations; political structure; and economic development. The first three are traditionally in the field of social anthropology. What is more significant is that in handling the last two sets of problems, Benedict emphasizes that the elites involved are small, and, though not explicitly, we are back with the problems of quasi-groups, networks, and action-sets.

Frankenberg's discussion (also in 4) of changes in the structure of social roles and role-sets in a range of British 'communities', from the truly rural to the housing-estate, hinges again on changes, in both groups and quasi-groups, which determine the structure of individuals' varied roles; but he illustrates too the urgent need to study custom, belief, and ceremonial as our specific contribution.

We see here, then, a common orientation, and a drive towards a common set of concepts, as social anthropologists tackle the problems of urban societies and of changing tribal and peasant communities. Some of them argue explicitly that these concepts developed to handle 'complex' situations, would also illuminate studies of tribal societies. These studies deal with problems which social anthropologists share with sociologists and political scientists, rather than with other types of anthropologists, and it may be that the *social* part of the title 'social anthropology' will begin to outweigh the *anthropology*. Yet there remain specific interests derived from the common tradition of *anthropology*.

Only in the study of religion do any of the contributors argue for the essential place of some psychological treatment. As it happens, the studies of kinship relations included occur only in the volume on 'the relevance of models': the whole fruitful field of study in psychological anthropology, represented by Lewinson, Linton, Mead, Whiting, and many others, is not referred to. This may be partly a reflection of who was asked to contribute, and what those invited decided to write on. Yet these essays show that there is a whole dimension of marital and parental relations which, it is accepted, can be studied without reference to psychological concomitants.

Strikingly, the feeling that it is justifiable for social anthropologists to work without reference to studies in psychology, is shown in Joe Loudon's essay on 'Religious Order and Mental Disorder' in a South Wales community (4). Loudon is a qualified medical, who later turned to anthropology. He has been trained in psychiatry, and has worked for the British Medical Research Council on the position of the mentally ill in a community, and the community's reaction to such people. His research is into attitudes, yet he works with the same basic concepts as his colleagues: he analyses social roles in terms of class and social status, religious affiliation, length of residence in the district, etc., in relation to conscious attitudes, involving the allocation of culpability, assumption that mental disorder is illness, and so forth. So too in studying the religious order he is concerned with statements about the role of crises in personal relations, in so far as these affect reactions to mental disorder. He looks also at patterns of social mobility, and at the effect of these on individuals' social networks. His general mode of analysis 'fits' with the analyses we have just discussed: significantly, to handle social attitudes, he does not turn to work in social psychology.

GENERAL ORIENTATIONS

In this background of realignment with cognate disciplines, the essays show two main trends. The first is an insistence that certain concepts that were acceptable in preceding decades are now too gross to be useful, and have to be refined, or that they may even block further analysis. The second is the feeling that more work should be done to pull together, in a comparative framework, observations that are discrete in terms of subject-matter or of ethnographic milieu. Obviously, these are the two possibilities that offer themselves, aside from carrying out studies that repeat what has been done before – and we do not regard such studies as useless. One can either penetrate more deeply into an area of problems, or pull together what has already been done.

There are many new ideas in these essays, but no author has tried to put forward an altogether new theoretical approach – or even to recast the basic orientations of the subject. In making the statement, we do so with full allowance for Spiro's insistence (3) that to study religion, as against studying society, a psychological approach is as essential as a social anthropological one. Geertz pleads (3) for a new look – via philosophy, history, law, literature, or the 'harder' sciences – at religion, but he nevertheless considers that 'the way to do this is not abandon the established traditions of social anthropology in this field, but to widen them'. He still looks to Durkheim, Weber, Freud, and Malinowski as 'inevitable starting-points for any useful anthropological theory of religion'. The specific problems he deals with – suffering, evil, chance, the bizarre, ethics – are not in themselves new fields of problems, though his proffered solutions to the problems may be new.

The basic orientation in these essays is therefore still the acceptance that the events which comprise human behaviour exhibit regularities whose forms are mutually interdependent, over and above their interdependence in the personality-behaviour systems of each individual actor. As Radcliffe-Brown put it, there are social systems whose structures can be analysed. An interdependence of cultural institutions, each of which has an elaborate structure, would perhaps be the parallel Malinowskian formulation. Given this general orientation, it seems to us that these social anthropologists have a much looser idea of a social system, or of a complex of institutions, than Radcliffe-Brown or Malinowski had. A social system is not seen in analogy with an organic system, whose structure is maintained by some customary procedure, as it was by Radcliffe-

Brown. Nor is there acceptance of Malinowski's ideas of the function of institutions in relation to a hierarchy of needs: Spiro (3) specifically criticizes this approach.

These 'tight' models of social systems or cultures were abandoned by the inter-war generation of social anthropologists (see Redfield, 1955). But those anthropologists continued to worry about the nature of social systems and cultures, or the structure of social fields. On the evidence of these essays, the younger anthropologists no longer consider this worry justified: at least none of them has dealt with that kind of problem at length, or as basic to his analysis. Geertz (3) goes to some pains to discuss 'culture'. Spiro (3) has some discussion of what a system is. David Schneider, in an essay on 'Some Muddles in the Models: or, How the System Really Works' (1) considers the competing, and hotly argued, opposed views of two sets of anthropologists on descent and affinity: and he states that one cause of their disputation is that they need to be clearer about whether the theory is advanced to cover the structure of a social system, or whether it is about how the individual finds his way in that system. He feels that the argument will get nowhere, unless this point is clarified. That is, he asks for clarity on problems set, and he is not concerned with the epistemology of the subject. We hope that our younger colleagues feel that earlier disputation on the nature of social systems and social fields, or on the nature of culture, clarified the issues, if only through the substantive work done; and that the disputation was not always meaningless.

When we say there seems to be no new general orientation shown, but a determination to get on with the job with established orientations, we must mention the 'new' evolutionary school of Leslie White, represented here by Sahlins's essay on primitive exchange in Monograph 1. The evolutionary argument is not marked in this particular essay, and on the whole Sahlins's analysis is similar in structure to the arguments of Wolf about kinship, friendship, and patron-client relations (4), of Frankenberg about the association of role types with forms of British community (4), of Benedict about the characteristics of small-scale territories (4), and of Lloyd and Southall about the typology of African political systems (2). The type of argument is shown in the cautious hypothesis about primitive money which, among others, is advanced, by Sahlins: 'it [primitive money] occurs in conjunction with unusual incidence of balanced reciprocity in peripheral social sectors. Presumably it facilitates the heavy balanced traffic'. This is precisely the sort of hypothesis about an association between social variables which is commonly sought by anthropologists, and is well illustrated in the four other essays just cited. But Sahlins continues: 'The conditions that encourage primitive money are most likely to occur in the range of primitive societies called tribal and are unlikely to be served by band or chiefdom development . . . Not all tribes provide circumstances for monetary development and certainly not all enjoy primitive money, as that term is here understood. For the potentiality of peripheral exchange is maximized only by some tribes. Others remain relatively inner-directed.'

We consider that, despite the turning against the simple evolutionary theories of the nineteenth century, some kind of evolutionary, or morphological, framework has been implicit in most comparative work in social anthropology. We say, 'or morphological', because many scholars have avoided an outright evolutionary statement in order to evade temporal implications. Radcliffe-Brown did this, but he believed strongly in social evolution. The result is that, aside from their important theses on the relation between use of energy and social forms, the new evolutionists, as Sahlins's essay shows, are trying to handle associations of concomitant variations, rather than items of culture, in somewhat similar ways to their colleagues. Nevertheless, we note that this new evolutionary theorizing is here represented only in the interstices, rather than in the central part, of Sahlins's essay.

REFINEMENT OF CONCEPTS

We have said that one main line of approach in these monographs, represented in several essays, is the refinement of standard concepts, in hopes of penetrating more deeply into the structure of social life. This tendency is marked in the several discussions of social roles. Even before Linton in 1936 advanced his definitions of 'status' and 'role', the handling of these phenomena was important in social anthropology: one has only to think of Radcliffe-Brown's concern with social personality and persona. But Linton's formulation, with the increasing interest of social anthropologists in sociological studies, focused attention more sharply on social structures as systems of roles (see, for example, Nadel, 1957). The work on social roles of Merton and Parsons, and later Goffman, as already cited, became influential. Some of the essays accept that, for certain purposes, 'role' can be used in analysis, as a general concept: but it is also subjected to a closer reexamination than almost anything else in the monographs.

This tone is set by the very first essay, Goodenough's 'Rethinking "Status" and "Role": Toward a General Model of the Cultural Organization of Social Relationships' (1). Goodenough is dissatisfied with the impasse into which we have run through the use of status and role as, to use our own shorthand, 'global' concepts, covering types of facts which need to be clearly differentiated. At the same time, he is dissatisfied with the present tendency to look at structural relationships apart from their cultural content. Drawing analogies from structural linguistics, he therefore attempts to construct a means of establishing both vocabularies and a syntax of the rules of 'roles.' To do this, he aims at a clearer specification of terms to describe the attributes of individuals and the relationships between them. He suggests, therefore, that status should not be, as he says Linton treated it, a means of reference to categories or kinds of persons, but that it should be confined to combinations of right and duty only. Social 'positions' in a categorical sense he calls 'social identities'. Each person has several social identities, and in specific situations one is selected as appropriate: this Goodenough terms 'the selector's *social persona* in the interaction'.

We are not, in this Introduction, summarizing any of the essays, and the preceding sketch is intended only to indicate the drive for the refinement of concepts which in the past have been illuminatingly employed, in order to secure more penetrating analysis. Having specified his terms, Goodenough proceeds to outline different types of situation in which these clarify relations between various egos and alters. On the cultural content side, he distinguishes the ranges of rights and duties, as against privileges and immunities – following here the terminology of the jurist, Hohfeld, which Hoebel has tried to get anthropologists to adopt. Goodenough thereupon proposes a technique by use of scalograms, to work out whether there are right-duty/ privilege-immunity clusters in particular identity relationships as seen *by single informants*. Varied cultural demands – such as 'sleeping in the same house', 'joking sexually in public' – are taken, and the informant is asked whether each demand applies in a particular identity relationship. These combine to give specific composite pictures of duty-scales. Goodenough argues that owing to limitations on the cognitive power of individuals – here is another example of an author citing psychological research – the demands, each forming a 'status dimension', must be limited in number to seven or less. He suggests that these duty-scales can be powerful instruments of social analysis, since (as he demonstrates by examples) they will allow objective measurement of anger, insult, flattery, and the gravity of offences. The last point is illustrated by a situation where breach of norm on the part of one identity justifies severe breach of duty by another. This will lead to precision in the study of single societies, and in the comparison of different societies.

This summary does not set out all the intricacies of the argument; but we have discussed this essay in order to illustrate what we mean when we say several authors see one line of advance in an increasing refinement of established concepts, and specification of others, to replace single concepts which, in their traditional global form, have outlived their usefulness. Goodenough's essay is the most explicit treatment of 'status' and 'role' in this way; but it seems to us that similar procedures are at least implicit in those parts of Lloyd's and Southall's essays on political systems (2) which aim to relate changes in role patterns with changes in macroscopic political structures. The explicit reformulation of the ideas involved in social roles emerges again in Frankenberg's essay (4) on changes in roles with 'movement' from British rural areas, through villages and small towns, into cities. Like Goodenough, he concerns himself with patterns of interaction – and he turns to cybernetics for ideas to handle these patterns. Both of them find in Goffman's searching study of *The Presentation of the Self in Everyday Life* (1959) and *Encounters* (1961) stimulus in handling the nuances involved in the complexity of daily social interaction, as against the more formal earlier analysis of roles in structural frameworks.

The same drive towards the breaking up of established concepts in order to examine more meticulously both the framework of social relations and the interaction between individuals shows in other fields. It is present in Sahlins's essay on types of primitive exchange (1) and Wolf's treatment of relations of kinship, friendship, and patronage *vis-à-vis* clientship (4), which have been considered by us in other contexts. It occurs as explicitly as in Goodenough's essay on status and role, in Mayer's article on 'The Significance of Quasi-Groups in the Study of Complex Societies' (4). Goodenough discusses the history of the concepts 'status' and 'role' and the ambiguities in their use, with difficulties that have arisen in applying them. Mayer looks equally closely at the way in which J. A. Barnes (1954) and E. Bott (1957) used the idea of 'the social network' – an idea which Barnes advanced in its present general form, and whose importance was stressed by Redfield (1955, p. 28) in a Huxley Memorial Lecture delivered shortly afterwards.

Mayer is concerned to clarify the different kinds of networks and action-sets that have to be distinguished, and also procedures for measuring their form and ramifications. As stated above, the same theme is present in essays by Mitchell, Benedict, and Loudon in Monograph 4 on the study of complex societies, and in Bailey's essay on committees and Nicholas's on factions in Monograph 2. These scholars are finding that theories based on concepts of groups, groupings and associations, and dyadic relationships, are inadequate for their problems: the network, and other forms of quasi-groups, which are ego-centred, are becoming more significant in bridging the gap between structural framework and individual action. There is clearly a close fit here with attempts to improve on the concepts of status and role. We note here too Mitchell's (4) distinction between structural and categorical relationships (i.e. between relationships set in associations and institutions, and relationships based on common attributes, such as race, tribe, and class).

The urge to clarify and refine appears also in a different context in Barbara Ward's essay 'Varieties of the Conscious Model' (1), where she considers the situation of a group of boat-dwelling fisherman in Hong Kong. These people consider themselves to be Chinese; and, Ward asks, by what model can their Chinese identity be assessed? Her starting-point is Lévi-Strauss's distinction 'between culturally produced models and observer's models. The former, constructs of the people under study themselves, he calls conscious models; the latter, unconscious, models'. Ward argues that to understand her field situation, she had to take into account several conscious models – that of Chinese society held by Chinese literati, that of the group under study held by themselves, those of this group held by other groups of Chinese – as well as the unconscious, the anthropologist's, model. She examines the relationship between these models, as set in the context of different areas of Chinese society, to assess where 'the uniformity and continuity of the traditional Chinese social system' lay; and she finds it in family structures.

The demand for rethinking, clarification, and refinement runs through all the essays in Monograph 1, that on 'models'. We have cited it from the essays by Goodenough, Sahlins, and Ward. It appears as strikingly in the other essays: by Ioan Lewis on 'Problems in the Comparative Study of Unilineal Descent' and David Schneider on 'Some Muddles in the Models'. Lewis argues that if correlations are to be established in comparative work, it is necessary to measure the intensity of such a principle as unilineal descent. He attempts to do this by applying various criteria to four patrilineal societies. He comes to the conclusion after his survey that by these principles involved in unilineal descent, various societies scale differently, and hence he suggests that this kind of classification is difficult and probably unfruitful. He argues that the functional significance of descent varies too much, hence canons of descent may not be fruitful criteria. 'The lumping together of societies on the basis of patriliny or matriliny alone can only lead to confusion. The functional implications of descent are much more significant than whether descent is traced in the patri – or matri-line' – an argument advanced by Leach in *Rethinking Anthropology* (1961).

Since Lewis does not suggest alternative criteria, we take his essay to be an example of that important class of work which aims to prove that a particular line of research is fruitless. The implications of the final sentence are clear: more refined, multiple variables must be sought.

Schneider's essay is much more difficult to delineate. It deals with a heated controversy between anthropologists about relationships of descent, and relationships of marriage or alliance. The argument is complex, and difficult to follow without detailed knowledge of the background literature which is discussed – and at least one of us, a political anthropologist, frankly confesses his difficulties here. Nevertheless, for present purposes it is clear that Schneider is trying to clarify the terminological and other muddles that he considers obstruct agreement: he points out to the contestants where they are talking in fact about different things, when they appear to be talking about the same thing. For, he says, there are two categories of anthropologists involved, and though there may be differences between the members of each category, they are distinctive from the others. There are the descent theory anthropologists (Fortes, Gluckman, Goody), who look for actual groups of people who intermarry with one another, and alliance theory anthropologists (Lévi-Strauss, Leach, Needham), who are primarily interested in 'that construct or model which is fabricated by the anthropologist and which is presumed to have, as its concrete expression, the norms for social relations and the rules governing the constitution of social groups and their interrelations'. Schneider argues that aside from weaknesses in each theory, they both contain contradictions and obscurities in their formulations. Most of the disputants are not clear in their arguments with one another on how far they are erecting conceptual models, which do not refer to real segments of the society, and how far they are referring to actual segments, based mainly on ownership of property and other jural rights. He suggests that this is because each of the theories is elaborated for a different type of society. The alliance theory is formulated for systems (which Schneider calls segmental) in which marriages of women proceed always from one segment to another; the descent theory for systems (which Schneider calls segmentary) in which men in one segment can marry into a number of other segments.

Schneider feels that each protagonist is driven by the polemical situation to defend 'his type', and that leads to the 'propagation of whole-system, over-simple typologies'. His own plea is for the use of typologies for specific problems, 'not for sorting of concrete societies into unchangeable, inherent, inalienable categories'. Selection of various elements, rigorously defined, and examination of combinations, permutations, and recombinations of these elements in many constellations, will prove more profitable.

SPECIFICATION OF CONTEXT

Schneider's essay contains also a plea for the clearer specification of more limited and varying contexts of relations, in order to assess the association of variables. Similar demands are present in a number of other essays on various subjects. They appear in every essay of the Monograph 2 on political problems. Bailey, in examining the alleged value, or rather 'the mystique', of 'consensus' in committees, distinguishes what he calls elite and arena councils, the size of councils, forms of external relationships. Nicholas places factional disputes in various types of situation. Lloyd looks at a limited political problem, by classifying three polities in terms of modes of recruitment of the elite and analysing their association with four other important variables. Southall argues for 'partial analysis of partial systems', and takes as his criterion for classifying political systems the differentiation of political roles. In Monograph 3, Bradbury looks at the contexts in which Edo cults of the dead, as against ancestral cults, may be significant; while Winter, in analysing Iraqw religion stresses, much as Schneider does, that there are with reference to this problem at least two types of society in Africa.

THE SEARCH FOR THE BROAD HYPOTHESIS OR THEORY

It seems, then, that most of the contributors to this volume favour clarification, the breaking down, and the refinement, of standard concepts, together with closer specification of narrower social contexts, as likely to be a more fruitful line of advance than the search for sweeping generalizations. This is explicitly stated in a few essays, and is implicit in others. Since contributors were asked to write papers indicating where they thought new approaches would be fruitful, we believe we may assume that the essays in this series reflect the feeling of our younger colleagues, and that they did not merely submit to us essays on a problem on which they happened to be working. There was, of course, in the discussion on the papers, argument on this point: as there was plenty of abstract argument about scientific method. But it must be significant that perhaps only two out of a score of papers can be seen as arguing for a much wider treatment of a specific problem – and we are not sure that this is a correct interpretation of Geertz's paper (3) when taken in its entirety, or of Spiro's essay at clarifying the various dimensions involved in the study or religion. Both of them emphasize the close and meticulous analyses of facts in restricted contexts: their plea is rather for an increase in the disciplines whose techniques and concepts should be employed in analysis by social anthropologists.

All the essays in fact show that social anthropologists are ready to turn where they feel they can get help to solve a specific problem. But the one difference we find between British and American contributors is that the British on the whole confine themselves to a narrower range of other disciplines – those commonly grouped as the social sciences. As stated above, Loudon's essay on 'Religious Order and Mental Disorder' (4) illustrates this restriction. Turner, in his analysis of Ndembu colour classification (3), is aware of how closely his problems raise issues treated by the psycho-analysts, but he eschews involvement in psycho-analytic interpretations. The American anthropologists are readier to move outside the restricted range of the social sciences to draw on disciplines which employ quite different techniques and concepts.

CONCLUSION

Overall, then, these essays, whether they consider a single society or make surveys over several societies, show the continuing balancing of detailed, meticulous analysis of limited social fields with comparative checking that has long characterized the subject. The meticulous analysis of a single situation dominates in Turner's essay on colour classification, as it does in Bradbury's on Edo and Winter's on Iraqw religion. It forms too a core to Geertz's paper (all in Monograph 3). The comparative survey dominates Sahlins's analysis of exchange (1) and Wolf's of kinship, friendship, and patronage. Both types of analysis are strongly present in all the essays.

We have not attempted in this Introduction to discuss the argument of each essay or to assess its merits. The field covered by the essays shows that, even setting aside ethnographic specialization, a social anthropologist now will find it difficult to be competent on political problems, economic problems, domestic life, religious action, etc. – particularly as more and more is drawn from cognate disciplines. Therefore we are not competent to assess more than a few of the essays, and to do that would have been invidious. Instead, we have tried to delineate what we see as common in these new approaches, spread over a variety of problems and printed in four Monographs. Our own essay may be at least a guide to where readers can find the new leads that are being pursued by a younger generation of social anthropologists.

ACKNOWLEDGEMENTS

Finally, we have to thank, for our colleagues and ourselves, a number of people on whom this symposium has depended. Professor Raymond Firth conceived the plan and pushed through the preliminary arrangements, with Professor Fred Eggan. The Executive Board of the American Anthropological Association was kind enough to sponsor a request to the National Science Foundation which provided the financial support to enable the Americans to travel to Britain. Dr Michael Banton, as Honorary Secretary of the Association, organized the conference, and has acted as editor of the Monographs. The Fellows and domestic staff of Jesus College, Cambridge, provided a setting in which we met in great comfort amidst pleasant surroundings; and this side of our foregathering was admirably handled by Mr G. I. Jones, Lecturer in Social Anthropology in Cambridge University and Fellow of Jesus College. Mr John Harvard-Watts and Miss Diana Burfield of Tavistock Publications have been invaluable and generous in help over publication.

A number of anthropologists worked hard in preparing openings to the discussion of each section. Some of the Americans who presented papers undertook this double duty. The following British anthropologists filled the role: Dr M. Banton, Dr P. Cohen, Dr J. Goody, and Professor P. M. Worsley. We had also the pleasure of the company of Professor G. C. Homans of Harvard, a sociologist who has worked with social anthropologists, and who effectively prevented us from developing too great ethnocentricity. He travelled especially from America to attend the meeting.

Finally, Gluckman insists, on behalf of the Association of Social Anthropologists of the British Commonwealth, on thanking Fred Eggan. As Firth inspired the meeting, Eggan, though acting as an individual, made it possible. In many ways, including his own presence as an American elder, supported only by the happy chance of Professor Sol Tax being in Britain, he contributed to what was a memorable occasion in the history of social anthropology – which is permanently encapsulated in these four volumes. And Eggan wishes, on behalf of the American group, to express their appreciation of the fine hospitality of their hosts which went beyond the strict requirements of the occasion, and to thank Max Gluckman for the excellence of his chairmanship and for assuming the task of drafting this introduction. To the authors of the essays, our joint thanks are due.

REFERENCES

BARNES, J. A. 1954. Class and Committees in a Norwegian Island Parish. *Human Relations* **7**: 39-58.

BOTT, E. 1957. *Family and Social Network*. London: Tavistock Publications.

CORNFORD, F. M. 1908. *Microcosmographia Academica: Being a Guide for the Young Academic Politician*. Cambridge: Heffer (reprinted 1953).

EASTON, D. 1953. *The Political System*. New York: Knopf.

—— 1959. Political Anthropology. In B. J. Siegel (ed.), *Biennial Review of Anthropology*. Stanford: Stanford University Press.

FALLERS, L. A. No date: about 1956. *Bantu Bureaucracy: A Study of Integration and Conflict in the Politics of an East African People*. Cambridge: Heffer, for the East African Institute of Social Research.

FIRTH, R. 1939. *Primitive Polynesian Economy*. London: Routledge.

—— 1946. *Malay Fishermen: Their Peasant Economy*. London: Kegan Paul, Trench, Trubner.

FIRTH, R. & YAMEY, B. S. 1964. *Capital, Saving and Credit in Peasant Societies*. London: Allen & Unwin.

FORTES, M. & EVANS-PRITCHARD, E. E. (eds.). 1940. *African Political Systems*. London: Oxford University Press, for the International African Institute.

GEERTZ, C. 1960. *The Religion of Java*. Glencoe, Ill.: The Free Press.

GOFFMAN, E. 1959. *The Presentation of the Self in Everyday Life*. New York: Doubleday Anchor Books.

—— 1961. *Encounters: Two Studies in the Sociology of Interaction*. Indianopolis: Bobbs-Merrill.

HORTON, R. 1964. Ritual Man in Africa. *Africa* **34**.

LEACH, E. R. 1961. *Rethinking Anthropology*. London: Athlone Press.

LINTON, R. 1936. *The Study of Man*. New York: Appleton-Century.

LLEWELLYN, K. & HOEBEL, E. A. 1941. *The Cheyenne Way: Conflict and Case Law in Primitive Jurisprudence*. Norman: University of Oklahoma Press; London: Allen & Unwin.

MANDELBAUM, D., LASKER, G. W. & ALBERT, E. M. 1963. *The Teaching of Anthropology*. American Anthropological Association, Memoir 94.

MERTON, R. K. *Social Theory and Social Structure*. 1957 (revised and enlarged edition). Glencoe, Ill.: The Free Press.

NADEL, S. F. 1957. *The Theory of Social Structure*. London: Cohen & West; Glencoe, Ill.: The Free Press.

REDFIELD, R. 1955. Societies and Cultures as Natural Systems. *Journal of the Royal Anthropological Institute* **85**: 19-32.

WHEARE, K. C. 1955. *Government by Committee*. Oxford: Clarendon Press.

Ward H. Goodenough

Rethinking 'Status' and 'Role'
Toward a General Model of the Cultural Organization of Social Relationships

INTRODUCTORY COMMENT

This examination of the concepts 'status' and 'role' arises from my concern with a problem in ethnographic description.[1] It is the problem of developing methods for processing the data of field observation and informant interview so as to enhance the rigor with which we arrive at statements of a society's culture or system of norms such that they make social events within that society intelligible in the way that they are intelligible to its members. My thinking about this problem has been inspired largely by structural linguistics, a discipline that has achieved a high degree of rigor in formulating descriptive statements of the normative aspects of speech behavior. I have found it useful to look upon the cultural content of social relationships as containing (among other things) 'vocabularies' of different kinds of forms and a 'syntax' or set of rules for their composition into (and interpretation as) meaningful sequences of social events.

This orientation was explicit in my account of the social organization of Truk (Goodenough, 1951). Out of it developed my later work with 'componential analysis' in what might be called descriptive or structural semantics (Goodenough, 1956, 1957),[2] representing an approach to constructing valid models of the categorical aspects of social norms. Here, I shall elaborate another analytical method that was first suggested in my Truk report, one aimed at a grammatical aspect of normative behavior. Hopefully it will enable us to make systematic and exhaustive descriptions of the cultural domain embraced by the expressions 'status' and 'role'.

THE POINT OF DEPARTURE

Ralph Linton (1936, pp. 113-114) defined statuses as 'the polar

1

positions . . . in patterns of reciprocal behavior'. A polar position, he said, consists of 'a collection of rights and duties'; and a role is the dynamic aspect of status, the putting into effect of its rights and duties.

Unfortunately, Linton went on to discuss statuses not as collections of rights and duties but as categories or kinds of person. All writers who do not treat status as synonymous with social rank do much the same thing,[3] including Merton (1957, pp. 368-370) in his important refinement of Linton's formulation. All alike treat a social category together with its attached rights and duties as an indivisible unit of analysis, which they label a 'status' or 'position' in a social relationship. This lumping together of independent phenomena, each with organizations of their own, accounts, I think, for our apparent inability to exploit the status-role concepts to our satisfaction in social and cultural analysis.[4] For example, my brother is my brother, whether he honors his obligations as such or not. A policeman's conduct in office may lead to social events that formally remove him from office, but it does not determine in any direct way whether he is a policeman or not. Other social transactions determine what his social category or identity actually is. Furthermore, there are legislative transactions that can serve to alter the rights and duties that attach to the category policeman in its dealings with other categories without the defining characteristics of the category being in any way altered. What makes him legally and formally a policeman need not have been affected.

These considerations have led me to break with established sociological practice. I shall consistently treat statuses as combinations of right and duty only. I shall emphasize their conceptual autonomy from social 'positions' in a categorical sense by referring to the latter as *social identities*. I would, for example, speak of ascribed and achieved identities where Linton (1936, p. 115) speaks of 'ascribed' and 'achieved' statuses. In accordance with Linton's original definition, then, the formal properties of statuses involve (1) what legal theorists call rights, duties, privileges, powers, liabilities, and immunities (Hoebel, 1954, pp. 48-49) and (2) the ordered ways in which these are distributed in what I shall call *identity relationships*.

2

RIGHTS AND DUTIES

Rights and their duty counterparts serve to define boundaries within which the parties to social relationships are expected to confine their behavior. Privileges relate to the areas of option within these boundaries. For example, when I am invited out to dinner, it is my hostess's right that I wear a necktie; to wear one is my duty. It is also her right that its decoration be within the bounds of decency. But she has no right as to how it shall be decorated otherwise; it is my privilege to decide this without reference to her wishes. For status analysis, the boundaries (the rights and duties) command our attention and not the domain of idiosyncratic freedom (privileges). As for powers, they and their liability counterparts stem from privileges, while immunities result from rights and the observance of duties. None of them needs to be treated as a feature of status relationships that requires analysis independent of the analysis of rights and duties.

As used in jurisprudence, rights and duties are two sides of the same coin. In any relationship A's rights over B are the things he can demand of B; these same things are what B owes A, B's duties in the relationship. Therefore, whenever we isolate either a right or a duty, we isolate its duty or right counterpart at the same time.[5]

A great deal of social learning in any society is learning one's duties to others, both of commission and omission, and the situations in which they are owed. They are matters that informants can talk about readily; they have words and phrases for them. The methods of descriptive semantics (componential analysis), referred to above, should provide a suitable means for describing the actual content of specific rights and duties with considerable rigor. But even without this, once we have established the existence of a duty for which our informants have a word or expression in their language, we can explore its distribution in identity relationships without our necessarily having its exact content clearly defined. The informant knows what he is talking about, if we as investigators do not.

SOCIAL IDENTITIES

A social identity is an aspect of self that makes a difference in how one's rights and duties distribute to specific others. Any aspect

3

of self whose alteration entails no change in how people's rights and duties are mutually distributed, although it affects their emotional orientations to one another and the way they choose to exercise their privileges, has to do with personal identity but not with social identity. The utility of this distinction is clear when we consider the father-son relationship in our own society. The status of the social identity 'father' in this relationship is delimited by the duties he owes his son and the things he can demand of him. Within the boundaries set by his rights and duties it is his privilege to conduct himself as he will. How he does this is a matter of personal style. We assess the father as a person on the basis of how he consistently exercises his privileges and on the degree to which he oversteps his status boundaries with brutal behavior or economic neglect. But as long as he remains within the boundaries, his personal identity as a stern or indulgent parent has no effect on what are his rights and duties in this or any other relationship to which he may be party.

Every individual has a number of different social identities. What his rights and duties are varies according to the identities he may appropriately assume in a given interaction. If John Doe is both my employer and my subordinate in the National Guard, then the duties I owe him depend on whether I assume the identity of employee or of company commander in dealing with him. We tend to think of duties as things we owe to individual alters, but in reality we owe them to their social identities. In the army, what we *owe* a salute is 'the uniform and not the man'. Furthermore, what duties are owed depends on ego's and alter's identities taken together and not on the identity of either one alone, as Merton (1957, p. 369) has observed. In our society, for example, a physician's rights and duties differ considerably depending on whether he is dealing with another physician, a nurse, a patient, or the community and its official representatives. If a status is a collection of rights and duties, then the social identity we label 'physician' occupies a different status in each of these identity relationships. Failure to take account of the identities of alters and to speak in general terms of the status of a chief or employer has been responsible for much of the apparent lack of utility of the status-role concepts.[6]

Another source of difficulty has been a tendency for many

analysts to think of the parties to status relationships as individual human beings. This mistake invites us to overlook the identity of the alter in those relationships where the alter is a group and not an individual. Obviously, communities, tribes, and nations become parties to status relationships when they make treaties with one another and when they enter into contracts with individuals and subgroups within their memberships. Criminal law, as it is usually defined, concerns the duties that individuals and corporations[7] owe the communities of which they are members. Animals, inanimate objects, and purely imaginary beings may also possess rights and/or owe duties.

IDENTITY SELECTION

As Linton (1936, p. 115) aptly observed, some identities are 'ascribed' and some 'achieved'. He was talking about how one comes to possess a particular social identity as a matter of social fact. How is it that one comes to *be* a professor or a married man, for example? Everyone has many more identities, however, than he can assume at one time in a given interaction. He must select from among his various identities those in which to present himself.[8]

As regards some identities, of course, there is no choice. Having reached a certain age, I have a duty as a member of my society to present myself as an adult and as a man in all social interactions to which I may be party. However, I am under no obligation to present myself as a professor of anthropology in all interactions. Quite the contrary.

Several considerations govern the selection of identities.

An obvious consideration is an individual's (or group's) qualifications for selecting the identity.[9] Does he in fact possess it? He may masquerade as a policeman, for example, donning the symbols that inform others of such an identity, and yet not be one. People often pretend to social identities for which they are not personally qualified, but such pretence is usually regarded as a serious breach of one's duties to fellow-members of one's peace group, duties that attach to one's identity as a member of a human community.

Another consideration is the occasion of an interaction. For

5

any society there is a limited number of culturally recognized types of activity. The legitimate purposes of any activity provide the culturally recognized reasons for interactions, and they in turn define occasions. The same individuals select different identities in which to deal with one another depending on the occasion. For example, I may call upon someone who is in fact both my physician and my personal friend because I wish to be treated for an illness or because I wish to invite him to dinner. The purpose that specifies the occasion for the interaction determines whether I assume the identity of 'patient' or 'personal friend' in approaching him.[10]

The setting, as distinct from the occasion, might also seem to be an obvious consideration in identity selection. For example, the same individual may or may not assume the identity of chairman of a meeting depending on what other persons are present, but here we are really dealing with the factor of qualifications for assuming an identity, already mentioned. Or again, when I invite my physician friend to dinner, how I approach him depends on whether or not one of his patients is a witness to the transaction, but this is not so much a matter of identity selection as it is a matter of choosing among alternative ways of honoring one's duties and exercising one's privileges. I suspect that settings are more likely to affect how one conducts oneself in the same identity relationship than to govern the selection of identities, but this is a matter requiring empirical investigation.

An important consideration is that, for any identity assumed by one party, there are only a limited number of matching identities available to the other party. If two people enter an interaction each assuming an identity that does not match the one assumed by the other, they fail to establish a relationship. The result is ungrammatical, and there is social confusion analogous to the semantic confusion that results from story-completion games in which no one is allowed to know anything but the last word that his predecessor in the game has written down. We take care to employ various signs by which to communicate the identities we wish to assume, so that others may assume matching ones and we can interact with mutual understanding.[11] Any pair of matching identities constitutes an *identity relationship*.

It is noteworthy that different identities vary as to the number of identity relationships that are grammatically possible for them within a culture. But in all cases the number appears to be quite limited. Thus in my culture the identity relationships 'physician-physician', 'physician-nurse', 'physician-patient' are grammatical, but there is no such thing as a 'physician-wife' relationship or a 'physician-employee' relationship. The physician must operate in the identity 'husband' with his wife and in the identity 'employer' with his employees.

Finally, we must consider that the parties to a social relationship do not ordinarily deal with one another in terms of only one identity-relationship at a time. The elderly male physician does not deal with a young female nurse in the same way that a young male physician does, and neither deals with her as a female physician does. In other words, identities such as old, adult, young adult, man, and woman are as relevant as are the identities physician and nurse. Some identities are relevant to all social interactions. In my culture, for example, I must always present myself to others as an adult and as a male. This means that I am ineligible for any identity that is incompatible with being adult and male. Among the various identities that I do possess and that are compatible with these two, not all are compatible with one another, nor are they always mutually exclusive as to the occasions for which they are appropriate. The result is that for any occasion I must select several identities at once, and they must be ones that can be brought together to make a grammatically possible composite identity. In order to avoid confusion I shall reserve the term identity for anything about the self that makes a difference in social relationships, as defined earlier. The composite of several identities selected as appropriate to a given interaction constitutes the selector's *social persona* in the interaction.[12]

The selection of identities in composing social relationships, then, is not unlike the selection of words in composing sentences in that it must conform to syntactic principles governing (1) the arrangement of social identities with one another in identity relationships, (2) the association of identities with occasions or activities, and (3) the compatibility of identities as features of a coherent social persona.

7

IDENTITY RELATIONSHIPS
AND STATUS RELATIONSHIPS

For each culturally possible identity relationship there is a specific allocation of rights and duties. The duties that ego's identity owes alter's identity define ego's duty-status and alter's right-status. Conversely, ego's right-status and alter's duty-status are defined by the duties that alter's identity owes ego's identity. As we shall see, one cannot deduce alter's duties from a knowledge of only ego's, except when both identities in a relationship are the same. In two separate identity relationships, ego may have the same duty-status and different right-statuses or the same right-status and different duty-statuses. When we examine the distributions of rights and duties among a society's identity relationships, we must look at every relationship twice and observe how the rights and duties are allocated from the point of view of each participating identity independently.

Every pair of reciprocal duty-statuses (or corresponding right-statuses) constitutes a *status relationship*. As we shall see, the same status relationships may be found to obtain in quite different identity relationships. We have already observed that the same identity may be in different status relationships according to the different identity relationships into which it can enter. These observations demonstrate that the structure of a society's status relationships must be analyzed and described in different terms from those that describe the structure of its identity relationships. A culturally ordered system of *social relationships*, then, is composed (among other things) of identity relationships, status relationships, and the ways in which they are mutually distributed.

THE ANALYSIS OF STATUSES

How duties distribute in the identity relationships in which people participate is a function of at least several independent considerations. For any identity relationship in which we participate in our society, for example, we must ask ourselves how much (if any) deference we owe? How much (if any) cordiality, reverence, and display of affection? How much sexual distance must we maintain? How much emotional independence?

These are only some of the considerations that are relevant for the allocation of rights and duties among us. Each one of them presumably represents a single dimension of status difference in our culture's organization of status relationships. If this is so, then the several duties that in different combinations indicate socially significant differences along one such dimension will be mutually distributed in identity relationships according to the patterns of a 'Guttman scale' (Guttman, 1944, 1950; Goodenough, 1944).

For purposes of illustration here, I shall confine discussion to the simplest scale pattern. Suppose that the duties expressing lowest degree of deference are most widely distributed in identity relationships; suppose that the duties expressing the next higher degree of deference are next most widely distributed and only in relationships in which duties expressing the lowest degree are also owed; and suppose that duties expressing the highest degree of deference are distributed in the fewest relationships, and in all of them duties expressing lesser degrees of deference are also owed. With such successively inclusive distributions, both the social identities for every identity-relationship in which they occur and the duties expressive of deference can be ranked simultaneously against each other in a special type of matrix table known as a 'scalogram' (Guttman, 1950; Suchman, 1950). Our ability so to rank them is the empirical test that the duties in question are distributed in accordance with a scale pattern and that they are indeed functions of one consideration or status dimension.

We anticipate, therefore, that analysis of scales will provide a means whereby we can empirically determine what duties are functions of the same dimension and at the same time discover the minimum number of dimensions needed to account for the distribution of all culturally defined duties in a system of social relationships. As a result of such analysis, all the duties would be sorted into several distinct sets. The duties in each set would form a scale, but those in different sets would not.

Table 1 presents a hypothetical example of a scalogram such as one might obtain for one set of duties. Each distinctive combination of duties represents a different status on the status dimension represented. Identity relationships are grouped and ranked

9

according to the combinations of duties owed by the ego-identity to the alter-identity in each, so that every identity relationship appears twice in the scalogram according to which of the two social identities in it is the ego-identity and which the alter-identity. Duties that have identical distributions and that do not,

TABLE 1

Hypothetical Status Scale

Status (scale) type	Relationship Ego's identity	Alter's identity	Specific alter	Duties and duty clusters							
				I (1)	II (2)	III (3)	(4)	IV (5)	V (6)	(7)	VI (8)
1	A	X	a	Y	Y	Y	Y	Y	Y	Y	Y
	A	X	b	Y	Y	Y	Y	Y	Y	Y	Y
2	B	Y	c	Y	Y	Y	Y	Y	Y	Y	N
	B	Y	d	Y	Y	Y	Y	Y	Y	Y	N
	C	Z	e	Y	Y	Y	Y	Y	Y	Y	N
3	D	W	b	Y	Y	Y	Y	Y	N	N	N
	D	W	f	Y	Y	Y	Y	Y	N	N	N
4	D	Z	g	Y	Y	Y	Y	N	N	N	N
	E	G	h	Y	Y	Y	Y	N	N	N	N
	E	G	i	Y	Y	Y	Y	N	N	N	N
5	F	R	j	Y	Y	N	N	N	N	N	N
	R	F	k	Y	Y	N	N	N	N	N	N
	G	E	l	Y	Y	N	N	N	N	N	N
6	H	H	f	Y	N	N	N	N	N	N	N
	H	H	m	Y	N	N	N	N	N	N	N
	X	A	n	Y	N	N	N	N	N	N	N
	Y	B	o	Y	N	N	N	N	N	N	N
	I	N	p	Y	N	N	N	N	N	N	N
7	K	J	q	N	N	N	N	N	N	N	N
	J	K	r	N	N	N	N	N	N	N	N
	Z	C	s	N	N	N	N	N	N	N	N
	Z	D	t	N	N	N	N	N	N	N	N
	W	D	u	N	N	N	N	N	N	N	N
	M	I	v	N	N	N	N	N	N	N	N
	N	I	w	N	N	N	N	N	N	N	N
	I	M	m	N	N	N	N	N	N	N	N

Key: Under 'relationship' capital letters represent specific social identities. The small letters represent specific alters. In the duty columns, Y indicates that the duty is owed by ego's identity to alter's identity, and N indicates that it is not owed. Alters b, f, and m appear in more than one identity relationship with ego. The entire scale is from the point of view of a single informant as ego.

therefore, discriminate status differences on the scale are grouped into duty clusters.

The scale in *Table 1* shows the distribution of duties for one person as ego in all the identity relationships in which he participates. Indeed, the procedure for gathering data for this kind of analysis requires that the informant be held constant, since there is no guarantee that different individuals have exactly the same conceptual organizations of status relationships. Data gathering and analysis must be done over again, independently, for each informant. The degree to which the resulting organizations of status relationships coincide indicates the degree of consensus among informants as to their expectations in social relationships.

Because status scales are worked out separately for each informant, they tend to be 'perfect' scales, in which no item is distributed in a way that is inconsistent at any point with the distributions of other items in the pattern of a scale. This makes the use of Guttman-scaling techniques much less complicated in the analysis of status relationships than is the case in attitude and opinion surveys, where many informants are asked the same set of questions relating to a single object and their different responses are plotted so as to rank the informants and the specific answers to the questions against each other simultaneously. Since different informants do not share the same cognitive organization of the subject under study in all respects, perfect scales cannot be obtained. Here, however, we are looking at how identity relationships and duties are simultaneously ranked against one another in the mind of one informant as revealed by the distribution of his answers. Under such circumstances almost perfect scales may reasonably be expected.

AN EXAMPLE FROM TRUK

A scale from an informant on Truk (Goodenough, 1951, p. 113), reproduced in *Table 2*, provides a concrete example of a series of duties whose distributions are functions of a single status dimension.[13] The duties are:

(a) to use the greeting *fääjiro* when encountering alter;

(b) to avoid being physically higher than alter in alter's presence, and therefore to crouch or crawl if alter is seated;

11

(*c*) to avoid initiating direct interaction with alter, to interact with him only at his pleasure;

(*d*) to honor any request that alter can make of ego, if alter insists;

(*e*) to avoid speaking harshly to alter or taking him personally to task for his actions;

(*f*) to avoid using 'fight talk' to alter or directly assaulting him regardless of provocation.

Each scale type in *Table 2* corresponds to a status. Under scale type 7 are all those relationships in which none of these duties is owed (in which ego is in duty-status 7 to alter), and under scale type 1 are those relationships in which all the duties are owed (in which ego is in duty-status 1 to alter).

The reason ego owes the four duties that mark statuses 1-4 is because he is not supposed to 'be above' alter. The seven scale combinations of duty express the degree to which ego is or is not forbidden from being above alter. The dimension in question seems best characterized as one of deference.

This scale illustrates that knowledge of ego's duty-status and alter's corresponding right-status does not allow one to deduce ego's right-status and alter's duty-status in an identity relationship. In the relationships 'brother' – 'sister' (man to *feefinej* and woman to *mwääni*) and husband – wife (man to Wi and woman to Hu), both brother and husband are in duty-status 7 on the scale and sister and wife are in right-status 7. But brother is in right-status and sister in duty-status 2, whereas husband is in right-status and wife in duty-status 7.

COMPOSITE STATUSES

Another dimension on which status distinctions are made in Truk is that of sexual distance. The duty scale for this dimension is shown in *Table 3* as it pertains to male-female kin relationships (it has not been worked out exhaustively for all identity relationships). Obviously, whenever any Trukese man and woman interact, the identities in terms of which they compose their behavior call for mutual placement simultaneously on both the deference and sexual distance scales – in two different status systems at the same time. In any relationship, therefore, it

TABLE 2

Duty Scale of 'Setting Oneself Above Another' in Truk

(Adapted from Goodenough, 1951, p. 113)

Relationship in which duty owed	Must say *fääjiro*	Must crawl	Must avoid	Must obey	Must not scold	Must not fight
Non-kinsman to chief	Yes	Yes	Yes	Yes	Yes	Yes
Non-kinsman to *jitag*	Yes	Yes	Yes	Yes	Yes	Yes
Man to female *neji*	No	Yes	Yes	Yes	Yes	Yes
Man to Wi's *mwääni*	No	Yes	Yes	Yes	Yes	Yes
Woman to So of *mwääni*	No	Yes	No (?)	Yes	Yes	Yes
Woman to *mwääni*	No	Yes	Yes	Yes	Yes	Yes
Woman to So of Hu's older *pwiij*	No	Yes	Yes	Yes	Yes	Yes
Woman to Wi of *mwääni*	No	Yes	Yes	Yes	Yes	Yes
Man to older *pwiij*	No	No	Yes	Yes	Yes	Yes
Woman to older *pwiij*	No	No	Yes	Yes	Yes	Yes
Man to male *neji*	No	No	No	Yes	Yes	Yes
Man to Wi of older *pwiij*	No	No	No	Yes	Yes	Yes
Woman to Da of *mwääni*	No	No	No	Yes	Yes	Yes
Woman to Da of Hu's *pwiij*	No	No	No	Yes	Yes	Yes
Woman to So of Hu's younger *pwiij*	No	No	No	Yes	Yes	Yes
Woman to Da of Hu's *feefinej*	No	No	No	Yes	Yes	Yes
Woman to So of Hu's *feefinej*	No	No	No	Yes	Yes	Yes
Woman to Hu of older *pwiij*	No	No	No	Yes	Yes	Yes
Woman to Da's Hu	No	No	No	Yes	Yes	Yes
Woman to So's Wi	No	No	No	Yes	Yes	Yes
Man to younger *pwiij*	No	No	No	No	Yes	Yes
Man to Wi's older *pwiij*	No	No	No	No	Yes	Yes
Woman to younger *pwiij*	No	No	No	No	Yes	Yes
Woman to So of *pwiij*	No	No	No	No	Yes	Yes
Woman to Hu's older *pwiij*	No	No	No	No	Yes	Yes
Man to Wi of younger *pwiij*	No	No	No	No	No	Yes
Woman to own So	No	No	No	No	No	Yes
Woman to Hu's younger *pwiij*	No	No	No	No	No	Yes
Man to *semej*	No	No	No	No	No	No
Man to *jinej*	No	No	No	No	No	No
Man to *feefinej*	No	No	No	No	No	No
Man to Hu of *feefinej*	No	No	No	No	No	No
Man to Wi	No	No	No	No	No	No
Man to Wi's younger *pwiij*	No	No	No	No	No	No
Woman to *semej*	No	No	No	No	No	No
Woman to *jinej*	No	No	No	No	No	No
Woman to own Da	No	No	No	No	No	No
Woman to Da of *pwiij*	No	No	No	No	No	No
Woman to Hu	No	No	No	No	No	No
Woman to Hu of younger *pwiij*	No	No	No	No	No	No
Woman to Hu's *feefinej*	No	No	No	No	No	No

Abbreviations are: Da, daughter; Hu, husband; So, son; and Wi, wife. The Trukese terms nate categories of kin. English kin terms are used only to subdivide the Trukese kinship ories when behavioral distinctions are made within them.

appears that the duties owed are functions not of one but of several status dimensions at once. Indeed, in every identity relationship in which a person participates he has a duty-status and a right-status on every status dimension in his culture's system of social relationships. The particular combination of duty-statuses occupied by an identity on all these dimensions at once in a given identity relationship is its composite duty-status (its Duty-Status with a capital D and S) in that relationship.

TABLE 3

Status Scale of Sexual Distance in Truk

(Adapted from Goodenough, 1951, p. 117)

Status or scale type	Ego in relation to alter	Avoidance duties				
		Sleep in same house	Be seen in company	See breasts exposed	Have inter- course	Joke sexually in public
1	Man with *feefinej*	F	F	F	F	F
2	Man with female *neji* (except Da of Wi's *mwääni*)	A	A	F	F	F
3	Man with Da of Wi's *mwääni*	A	A	D	F	F
4	Man with consan- guineal *jinej*	A	A	A	F	F
5	Man with affinal *jinej*	A	A	A	D	D
6	Man with Wi	A	A	A	A	D
7	Man with *pwynywej* (other than Wi)	A	A	A	A	A

Key: Abbreviations used are: A, allowed; D, disapproved; F, forbidden; Da, daughter; Wi, wife. The Trukese terms designate categories of kin.

A complete analysis of a system of social relationships should permit us to construct a table in which every column (A, B, C, D ... N) represents a status dimension and each number in a given column represents a status (scale combination of duties) on that dimension, as shown in *Table 4*. From such a table we could write the formula for every possible composite duty-status (e.g. A3-B1-C6-D7 . . . N2). We could compile an inventory of all possible identity relationships and after each one give the formulae for the composite duty-statuses (or right-statuses) of each identity in the relationship. This would provide a corpus of

14

materials on which further analysis of cultural structure could then be undertaken.

For one thing, we could see how identity relationships group into classes according to similarities of their reciprocal composite duty-statuses. We could do the same thing for each dimension separately and see the extent to which the same identity relationships bunch in the same classes from dimension to dimension. Cross-cultural differences in the organization of such syntactic classes could then be systematically explored.

TABLE 4

Hypothetical Table of all Status Dimensions

Dimensions	A	B	C	D	.	.	N
	1	1	1	1	.	.	1
Numbered	2	2	2	2	.	.	2
statuses	3	3	3	3	.	.	3
for each	4		4	4	.	.	4
dimension	5		5	5	.	.	5
			6	6	.	.	6
			7	7			

For another thing, with the table in *Table 4* in mind, we are in a position to anticipate what I am certain research will show to be an interesting feature of the cultural organization of behavior, one that is responsible for a great deal of its apparent complexity. This has to do with the compatibility of the duties on different status dimensions for ready synthesis in a composite duty-status. Suppose, for example, that in terms of the possibilities in *Table 4*, the composite duty-status of identity X in relation to identity Y is A4-B2-C1-D1 ... N4, and that the nature of one of the duties defining status B2 is such that honoring it precludes the possibility of honoring one of the duties in status C1. Some accommodation will have to be made in one of three possible ways: (1) one of the duties will have to be dropped in favor of the other; (2) one or both duties will have to be capable of being honored in more than one way, with allowance for the selection of compatible alternative modes of behavior; (3) both duties may be replaced by a distinctive third one that is simultaneously an alternative for both.

15

For example, it is my duty on certain occasions to rise when a lady enters the room. It often happens that I am for one reason or another unable to do so, in which case I have the alternative duty to ask pardon for not rising. Here are two distinctive ways of honoring the same duty with a clear order of preference (it is wrong for me to ask pardon for not rising if I am clearly able to rise).

It is obvious that problems of this kind must arise frequently in composing actual behavior, especially when we consider that interactions often involve not a single identity relationship but several at once, for on many occasions the social personae of the participant actors are likely to consist of more than one relevant identity. Interactions involving more than two actors create even further possibilities of conflict among duties. In any social system, therefore, we can anticipate that there will be orderly procedures for handling conflicts of this kind, procedures that can be stated in the form of rules not unlike the rules of *sandhi* and vowel harmony in some languages.[14]

ROLES

From the combinations in *Table 4*, we can readily describe all the composite duty-statuses and right-statuses for a given identity in all the identity relationships that are grammatically possible for it. The aggregate of its composite statuses may be said to constitute the identity's *role* in a sense a little less comprehensive than but otherwise close to Nadel's (1957) use of the term. It would be equivalent to a comprehensive 'role-set' in Merton's (1957, p. 369) terms.

When we compare identities according to their respective roles, as thus defined, some identities will obviously be found to net more privileges (fewer duties) and/or more rights in all their identity relationships taken together than others. That is, the roles of some identities will have greater possibilities for gratification than the roles of others; some roles will allow more freedom of choice in action generally than others; and some will be more and some less cramping to particular personal styles of operation. Thus, different identities may be said to have different functions in the social system as a whole and to enjoy different

16

value accordingly. Just how they differ, and how these differences relate to informants' evaluations of them, can be precisely described in relation to the sets of formulae that characterize the several composite statuses possible for each.

To map out a social system in this way may be possible in theory, but is it not too time-consuming and tedious for investigator and informant alike? Certainly, collecting data of this kind is tedious. Nevertheless, Mahar (1959) was able to get a purity-pollution or ritual distance scale from eighteen different informants in Khalapur, India, with very satisfactory results, neatly solving the difficult problem of empirically determining local caste rankings and the degree of cross-caste agreement in these rankings.[15] Her experience, added to my own from Truk, is encouraging.

But, we may ask, in any society we study, are there not so many duties, so many status dimensions, and so many identity relationships as to render the possibility of ever doing a complete analysis impracticable, however successful we may be in ferreting out a few scales? I do not think so. We are dealing with things that people manage to learn in the normal course of their lives without the benefit of systematic data collection and analysis. They are not likely, therefore, to be so complicated as to defy analysis.

On this point, findings in the psychology of cognition are highly suggestive. George Miller (1956) has called attention to impressive evidence that the human capacity to make judgements about where to class stimuli on unidimensional scales is severely limited. The greatest number of discriminations that can be made consistently on one dimension seems to be about seven (plus or minus two). In every interaction, on the basis of what he can observe of alter's behavior, ego has to make a judgement about where alter is putting him on every status scale, a judgement, that is, about the composite right-status that alter is ascribing to him in the relationship as alter perceives it. Ego may make these judgements for each dimension separately, but for any one dimension, the number of statuses about which he can make accurate judgements presumably will not exceed about seven. We expect, therefore, that no matter how many duties may fit into the same scale,

D   17 the number of distinctive distribution combinations (scale types) they will show will be within this limit for any one status dimension. This means that when there are more than six duties in a set forming a scale, some will have identical distributions, producing duty clusters on the scale, as shown in *Table 1*. Seven is in fact the number of statuses I obtained for each of the two status scales from Truk (*Tables 2* and *3*). Mahar (1959), moreover, found that of the thirteen actions whose distributions were clearly a function of ritual distance, some had to be treated as equivalent, so that she could derive only seven scale types from them for the purpose of scoring status differences.

Proceeding from dimension to dimension, ego may make several successive judgements in assessing what composite status alter is ascribing to him. But even this procedure must become cognitively difficult and cumbersome if many status dimensions are involved.[16]

Finally, as complicatedly variable as human behavior seems to be, we must remember that the analysis outlined here is concerned only with duties (or rights). Many specific acts, I have suggested, are no more than different expressions of the same duty, like allomorphs of a morpheme in language. In this event their selection reflects syntactic rules of composition that are themselves ordered according to a limited number of principles. Much other variation in behavior reflects differences in behavioral styles, differences in the ways actors choose to elect their free options and exercise their privileges. Such variations need not concern us in deriving the formal properties of status systems.

These reasons lead me confidently to predict that the number of status dimensions in any system of social relationships will prove to be severely limited and that the number of statuses that are culturally discriminated on each dimension will prove to be in the neighbourhood of seven or less.

DUTY SCALES AS INSTRUMENTS OF SOCIAL ANALYSIS

So far I have presented a method for constructing models of how specific cultures have organized social relationships. I have also considered the feasibility of the method. But crucial questions remain: What can we do with the models once we have constructed them? Are they just an intellectual game? Or do they enable us to understand things about behavior that eluded us before? Answer to these questions is provided by the duty scales from Truk.

Scaling duties allows us to see the circumstances under which a breach of duty will be regarded as more or less serious. We would assume from *Table 2* that failure to honor a request would be least serious in Truk if alter were in right-status 4, the status in which this is the severest duty owed. It would be most serious if alter were in right-status 1, and there would be in-between degrees of seriousness if alter were in right-status 2 or 3. It is also possible that in those relationships in which a duty is the severest one owed, there is variation in the force of the obligation, its breach being forbidden in some instances and only disapproved in others. This is what we find in the second scale obtained from Truk (*Table 3*), one having to do with degrees of sexual distance (Goodenough, 1951, p. 117). If all four instances of 'disapproved' (D) in the scale were changed to 'forbidden' (F), eliminating this refinement, statuses 2 and 3 would merge, as would 4 and 5, and the total number of statuses discriminated on the dimension of sexual distance would be reduced from seven to five.

In every interaction, moreover, a Trukese ego has to decide to what extent he is forbidden from 'being above' alter and what is the appropriate cut-off point of his obligation on the duty scale shown in *Table 2*. If he wishes to flatter alter, he may act as if he were rendering one more duty than he feels is in fact required; and if he wishes to insult alter, he may render him one duty less. He must also decide what duties alter owes him and assess alter's behavior as proper, flattering, or insulting. The number of scale positions by which alter's behavior appears inappropriate measures the apparent degree of flattery or insult.

With this in mind, let us consider the occasion I encountered when an irate father struck his married daughter (right-status 2), to whom he owed all duties but the greeting *fääjiro*. Informants explained that he was angry, or he would not have done such a thing. Indeed, the fact that he was six points down the seven-point scale was a measure of how very angry he was. His daughter, it happened, was a self-centered and disagreeable young woman, whose petulant behavior had been getting on her kinsmen's nerves for some time. A good, hard jolt was just what she deserved. Being struck by her brother or husband, who were under no obligation not to strike her, would have had little dramatic impact. That her father struck her, however, the last man in the world who should, this was something she could not dismiss lightly. What provoked the incident was her indulgence in an early morning tirade against her husband whom she suspected of having just come from an amorous visit to her lineage sister next door. It is a Trukese man's privilege to sleep with his wife's lineage sisters (he is in duty-status 7 to them in *Table 3*), and men and women are not supposed to show any feelings of jealousy when this privilege is exercised. Her shrieking outburst against her husband, therefore, was another example of the 'spoiled child' behavior that made her unpleasant to live with. Witnesses seemed to relish her undoing as full of what we would call 'poetic justice'. I could not possibly have understood why they did so, if I had not already worked out the status scale of 'being above' another. Nor would I have been able to anticipate the feelings of shocked horror that people would have exhibited had the same act been performed in other circumstances. Indeed, relations between one informant and his older brother had been severely strained for about a year, because the former had violated his duties and told off his older brother (right-status 4) when the latter had exercised his privilege and struck their much older sister (right-status 7) in displeasure over some small thing she had done.

Methods that allow us objectively to measure such things as anger, insult, flattery, and the gravity of offenses, and that help us to appreciate the poetic justice of events in alien cultural contexts, such methods, I submit, are not exercises in sterile formalism. They promise to be powerful analytical tools. They encourage me to great optimism about the possibility of developing considerable precision in the science of social behavior.

NOTES

1. This is a revised and expanded version of a paper entitled 'Formal Properties of Status Relationships' read at the Annual Meeting of the American Anthropological Association, 16 November 1961.

2. For other contributions to this type of semantic analysis, see Conklin (1955, 1962a, 1962b), Frake (1961, 1962), Lounsbury (1956), Wallace & Atkins (1960).

3. This has been thoroughly documented by Atkins (1954).

4. The concepts have been useful for collecting and organizing data in studies of specific social positions or limited social settings (e.g. Gross, Mason & McEachern, 1958), but they have not proved helpful in the analysis of social systems as wholes, as Nadel (1957) has observed. See also the critique by Goffman (1961, pp. 91-95).

5. Rights and duties correspond in part to what Nadel (1957, p. 56) called the 'passive' and 'active' attributes of roles respectively. It should be noted that some writers have misunderstood the idea that each right has a duty counterpart by interpreting it as meaning that privilege also carries responsibility in the sense of *noblesse oblige*. This notion is peculiar to the former system of social 'estates' in Western Europe and is demonstrably without utility for social and juridical analysis.

6. This calls attention to an unfortunate tendency in the literature to treat statuses as properties of social identities and to talk about the status of a chief or employer without specifying the identity of the alter. Recognizing this problem, Nadel (1957) separated the concepts of status and role. By his definition, 'the role concept is basically a type or class concept' that 'labels and brings together numbers of individuals – human beings in our case – in virtue of certain properties they have in common' (1957, p. 22). As he goes on to discuss it, it is clear that for him a role encompasses what I am calling a social identity and all the things associated with it, as well. He uses the term 'status' more narrowly as referring to the 'particular sets of rights and obligations falling to persons' (1957, p. 29), but without specific regard to identity relationships, making his 'status' equivalent to Merton's (1957, p. 369) 'role set'. Although 'status' still lacks precision as he conceived it, by abandoning status and role as complementary concepts (one the dynamic aspect of the other) and by restoring to 'role' a meaning more like that of ordinary or dramatistic usage, Nadel brought into sharper focus a useful analytical entity. How it relates to status, as I treat it here, will be clarified below.

7. Whenever a group is conceived as a unit having a status apart from the statuses of the individuals comprising its membership – that is, as having rights and duties pertaining to it as a party to a relationship – the group is a *corporation* for the duration of the relationship in which it enjoys status.

8. The sum of all the identities that a person has in social fact and in which he may legitimately choose to operate correspond to what Merton has termed a person's 'status-set' (in my terminology his identity-set).

9. The qualifications for a social identity are the conditions for being referred to by the linguistic expression that names the identity (Goodenough, 1956).

10. Actually this example involves a further complication. Under the rules of my culture I can never approach a friend without acknowledging my recognition of our friendship. When consulting a physician for medical reasons, my dealings with him vary considerably depending on whether he is also a friend or not. This fusing of statuses attendant upon several different identity relationships that are in effect at the same time is an important matter to be considered below.

21

11. The display of such signs, along with those that serve as credentials implying or verifying our qualifications for assuming certain identities, corresponds to what Goffman (1959, p. 22) has termed the maintenance of 'front'. We try to assume ego-identities for which the culturally possible identity relationships accord us right-statuses and duty-statuses appropriate to the ends we wish to serve in the interaction (see the discussion of roles below).

12. I am here using the term 'persona' in much the same sense as Goffman (1959, p. 252) uses the term 'character' as distinct from 'performer'. Because of the many other connotations of Goffman's term in ordinary usage, it is unsuitable as a technical term.

13. The Trukese words in *Tables 2* and *3* refer mostly to categories of kinsmen (kinship identities), which need not be explicated for present purposes. The interested reader will find them discussed at length elsewhere (Goodenough, 1951, 1956).

14. For example, the phonology of Truk's language allows only for a limited number of consonant combinations in sequence without an intermediate pause. In composing phrases a speaker frequently puts together words such that one ends and the next begins with consonants that cannot occur in sequence. Either there must be a pause between them (as may happen in slow or deliberate speech), one of the consonants must undergo modification (e.g. *jesapw fejinnō* becomes *jesaf fejinnō*, *mejiwor nowumw* becomes *mejiwor rowumw*), or a vowel must be introduced according to rules of vowel harmony (e.g. *gaag cëk* becomes *gaagy cëk* whereas *jeen cëk* becomes *jeec cëk*). Thus for each word in Trukese there are several variant forms from among which selection is made according to the other words with which it is to be composed in an utterance.

15. I am grateful to Robert J. Smith for calling my attention to Mahar's paper.

16. Wallace (1961, p. 463) suggests 'the numerical value of 2^6 for maximum size of folk taxonomies', but whether or not this limit applies to systems of status relationships and, if so, how are matters that cannot be determined until we have a sample of these systems analyzed and described in the manner suggested here.

REFERENCES

ATKINS, JOHN RICHARD. 1954. Some Observations on the Concept of 'Role' in Social Science. Unpublished MA thesis, University of Pennsylvania.

CONKLIN, HAROLD C. 1955. Hanunóo Color Categories. *Southwestern Journal of Anthropology* 11: 339-344.

—— 1962a. Lexicographical Treatment of Folk Taxonomies. In Fred W. Householder & Sol Saporta (eds.), *Problems in Lexicography*. Supplement to *International Journal of American Linguistics* 28, No. 2. Indiana University Research Center in Anthropology, Folklore, and Linguistics, Publication 21. Bloomington.

—— 1962b. Comment (on Ethnographic Study of Cognitive Systems). In Thomas Gladwin & William C. Sturtevant (eds.), *Anthropology and Human Behavior*. Washington, D.C.: Anthropological Society of Washington.

FRAKE, CHARLES O. 1961. The Diagnosis of Disease among the Subanunun of Mindanao. *American Anthropologist* 63: 111-132.

—— 1962. The Ethnographic Study of Cognitive Systems. In Thomas Gladwin & William C. Sturtevant (eds.), *Anthropology and Human Behavior*. Washington, D.C.: Anthropological Society of Washington.

GOFFMAN, ERVING. 1959. *The Presentation of Self in Everyday Life*. New York: Doubleday Anchor Books.

—— 1961. *Encounters: Two Studies in the Sociology of Interaction*. Indianapolis: Bobbs-Merrill Co.

GOODENOUGH, WARD H. 1944. A Technique for Scale Analysis. *Educational and Psychological Measurement* 4: 179-190.

—— 1951. *Property, Kin, and Community on Truk*. Yale University Publications in Anthropology No. 46. New Haven.

—— 1956. Componential Analysis and the Study of Meaning. *Language* 32: 195-212.

—— 1957. Cultural Anthropology and Linguistics. *Georgetown University Series on Language and Linguistics*, No. 9, pp. 167-173.

GROSS, NEAL, MASON, WARD S. & MCEACHERN, ALEXANDER W. 1958. *Explorations in Role Analysis: Studies of the School Superintendency Role*. New York: Wiley.

GUTTMAN, LOUIS. 1944. A Basis for Scaling Qualitative Data. *American Sociological Review* 9: 139-150.

—— 1950. The Basis for Scalogram Analysis. *Studies in Social Psychology in World War II*, vol. 4: Measurement and Prediction, pp. 60-90. Princeton, N.J.: Princeton University Press.

HOEBEL, E. ADAMSON. 1954. *The Law of Primitive Man*. Cambridge, Mass.: Harvard University Press.

LINTON, RALPH. 1936. *The Study of Man*. New York: D. Appleton-Century Company.

LOUNSBURY, FLOYD G. 1956. A Semantic Analysis of the Pawnee Kinship Usage. *Language* 32: 158-194.

MAHAR, P. M. 1959. A Multiple Scaling Technique for Caste Ranking. *Man in India* 39: 127-147.

MERTON, ROBERT K. 1957. *Social Theory and Social Structure* (rev. and enlarged edn.). Glencoe, Ill.: The Free Press.

23

MILLER, GEORGE A. 1956. The Magical Number Seven, plus or minus Two: some Limits on our Capacity for processing Information. *Psychological Review* **63**: 81-97.

NADEL, S. F. 1957. *The Theory of Social Structure*. Glencoe, Ill.: The Free Press.

SUCHMAN, EDWARD A. 1950. The Scalogram Board Technique for Scale Analysis. *Studies in Social Psychology in World War II*, vol. 4: Measurement and Prediction, pp. 91-121. Princeton, N.J.: Princeton University Press.

WALLACE, ANTHONY F. C. 1961. On Being Just Complicated Enough. *Proceedings of the National Academy of Sciences* **47**: 458-464.

WALLACE, ANTHONY F. C. & ATKINS, JOHN. 1960. The Meaning of Kinship Terms. *American Anthropologist* **62**: 58-80.

David M. Schneider

Some Muddles in the Models:
Or, How the System really Works[1]

PART ONE. ALLIANCE

I. The phrase 'alliance theory' and its opposition to what has been called 'descent theory' was first suggested by Dumont (1961a).

Alliance theory, with roots clearly in Durkheim and Mauss, has specifically arisen out of Lévi-Strauss's *Structures élémentaires* ... (1949) and has been developed by Lévi-Strauss, Dumont, Leach, and Needham. Descent theory also has its roots in Durkheim and Mauss, but its development has been through Radcliffe-Brown to Fortes, Goody, Gough, Gluckman, and, in certain respects, Firth.

This is an oversimplified picture, of course, but one which provides a reasonable beginning. It would oversimplify matters, too, but also be useful to point out, that where Durkheim tried to bridge the gap between positivism and idealism and ended up as an idealist in the remnants of some positivist clothing, Needham's version of alliance theory is, if anything, squarely on the side of the idealists. Lévi-Strauss and Dumont, on the other hand, go with Hegel (Murphy, 1963). Descent theory has moved in the direction of positivism; some of its misunderstandings stem from its positivist premises; and the direction which the younger descent theory people (Goody, Gough) have taken seems to me to be consistent with this view.

The dilemma of positivism is exemplified by a statement of Lévi-Strauss. Replying to Maybury-Lewis's criticisms, Lévi-Strauss says:

'. . . Mr. M. L. remains, to some extent, the prisoner of the naturalistic misconceptions which have so long pervaded the British school . . . he is still a structuralist in Radcliffe-Brown's terms, namely, he believes the structure to lie at the level of empirical reality, and to be a part of it. Therefore, when he is presented a structural model which departs from empirical reality, he feels cheated in some devious way. To him, social

25

structure is like a kind of jigsaw puzzle, and everything is achieved when one has discovered how the pieces fit together. But, if the pieces have been arbitrarily cut, there is no structure at all. On the other hand, if, as is sometimes done, the pieces were automatically cut in different shapes by a mechanical saw, the movements of which are regularly modified by a cam-shaft, the structure of the puzzle exists, not at the empirical level (since there are many ways of recognizing the pieces which fit together); its key lies in the mathematical formula express-ing the shape of the cams and their speed of rotation; some-thing very remote from the puzzle as it appears to the player, although it "explains" the puzzle in the one and only intelli-gible way' (Lévi-Strauss, 1960, p. 52).

The contrast may be put more specifically. To a degree, both alliance and descent theory are concerned with social structure. But, for descent theory, social structure is considered one or another variant of the concept of (*a*) concrete relations or group-ings, socially defined, which (*b*) endure over time. To Radcliffe-Brown, social structure is the network of 'actual social relations'; for Evans-Pritchard in discussing the Nuer (Evans-Pritchard, 1940) it is the enduring social groups, the concrete lineages.[2]

For alliance theory, the problem is not what the concrete patterns of social relations actually are, although these are not neglected; it is not the actual organization of any specific group like a lineage. It is, instead, that construct or model which is fabricated by the anthropologist and which is presumed to have, as its concrete expression, the norms for social relations and the rules governing the constitution of social groups and their inter-relations (Lévi-Strauss, 1953).

Alliance theory grows out of (1) Durkheim's distinction between mechanical and organic solidarity; (2) his notion of collective representations and specifically his and Mauss's in-sistence that the fundamental socio-cultural categories of the culture itself must be understood in its own terms; and (3) out of Mauss's ideas that are expressed in his essay, *The Gift*. This is perhaps the minimal and most immediately relevant set of ideas. Others more derivative or tangential are involved, but need not detain us at this point.

26

First, organic solidarity is essentially a state of affairs in which functionally differentiated parts are each non-viable parts but, when joined together, become a single, coherent, and viable 'organism'. Functional differentiation is in turn based on two kinds of condition. One is that the parts have different roles which get those things done which need to be done if the whole is to survive. The other is that for the parts to work properly they must be oriented toward common goals. If the goals of one part are disparate from the goals of the other, then the parts will not make up a single, coherent, viable whole. This second feature may be considered to be most intimately related to 'coherence'. Each part by itself means nothing; the parts together make an integrated and viable unit. The simplest example is of two unilineal lineages, each being able to provide for its essential needs in all ways except one: the rule of exogamy requires that marriage partners come from outside the group. These two lineages, both having a common aim – to provide for wives – exchange wives. The two lineages together, then, make up one viable and coherent society. That they may also exchange differentiated economic products only elaborates and reinforces their differentiation and interdependence.

The simplest form of differentiation centers on the definition of opposed but interrelated parts. Again, exogamy is the pertinent example. From the point of view of either of the two lineages, one 'needs' wives, the other 'has wives to give'. The definitions are plus and minus, have and have not, and so on. These are essentially opposed elements, defined in terms of their polar qualities. Just what particular form this differentiation will take in any society is an empirical question. Yet it is implied, I think, that all societies operate in fundamentally this way: at every point of differentiation, there is at rock-bottom a polar, opposite kind of differentiating definition which in any particular case may be elaborated into gradients, subdivided into qualities, but basically, and in some sense 'originally', the elements are oppositional, unitary, and polar. (Lévi-Strauss, 1945, 1949, 1955, 1962, 1963; Needham 1958a, 1960d.)

There remains always the substantive problem: how is *this particular* social structure differentiated? What are *its* constituent parts? How are they interrelated? Here the idealistic

27

foundation of the theory becomes apparent. On the one hand, as a fundamental category of human mentality, dualism is expressed in a wide variety of particular social forms; on the other hand, it is the particular ideational categories, as these are consciously or unconsciously conceived by the members of the society itself, which play a role in regulating their action.

For example, in a matrilateral cross-cousin marriage system, where a 'positive marriage rule' (Dumont's phrase (Dumont, 1961); a prescriptive system in Needham's terms) obtains, the system is conceived of, from the point of view of any given lineage in that system, as one which is made up of dual relations – 'we' versus 'they' as wife-givers to wife-takers; 'they' versus 'we' as wife-takers to wife-givers. The system *as a system* is triadic; yet the conceptualization of the system from the point of view of the given lineage is dyadic (Lévi-Strauss, 1949, 1956; Needham 1958a, 1960d, 1962a).

But one must go further; in any society having a positive marriage rule, that class of persons who are potential wives is categorized in some particular way. To call this, for instance, MoBrDa is to commit the error of imposing *our* way of thinking on *their* system when these may (though they may not) be radically different. It is thus necessary to find out how *they* conceptualize their system, what *their* categories of social objects and actors are, how they are constituted and how they are conceived to behave.

This raises a core problem: symbolism. In alliance theory, it is held that a given structural relationship in a very important sense cannot be seen or observed as such. It is, instead, 'expressed' in a wide variety of different ways, and the 'expressions' of the relationship tend to be reiterative, though seldom identical from one form of expression to another. The problem in analyzing social structure is thus to search out the various forms of expression in order to comprehend the basic relationship which is structurally operative, but no particular form of it, no particular expression of it, can be taken as 'it' (Lévi-Strauss, 1960).

The contrast here with Radcliffe-Brown's, Murdock's, and similar conceptions is very clear. For Murdock, it is the concrete fact of where specific people actually reside which, bringing them in proximity with one another, creates unilineal descent groups (Murdock, 1949). For the intellectualist, where they live, how they are brought into proximity with one another, and how the unilineal descent group is organized are all equally symbols of, or expressions of, the *same* inherent structural principle. Where residence rules cause or determine descent groups for Murdock, it is structural principles which account for *both* residence rules and descent groups for alliance theorists (Lévi-Strauss,1960, p. 54; see Murphy, 1963, in this connection).

II. Lévi-Strauss, Needham, and George Homans are all psychological reductionists – each in his own way, of course.

Lévi-Strauss is quite emphatic that 'sentiments' and 'emotion' explain very little, if anything. His discussion of 'anxiety' as an explanation (either in Malinowski's or Freud's terms) is, however, the only discussion provided in any detail in his book *Totemism*. Here he rests his case on Radcliffe-Brown's 'turn-about' argument, namely, that it is not because people feel anxiety that they make magic, but that they feel anxiety because they make magic. Further, he adds an apparent empirical exception to Malinowski's supposed 'rule', saying, 'The empirical relationship postulated by Malinowski is thus not verified' (Lévi-Strauss, 1963, p. 67). He bases this on the case of the Ngindo bee-keepers, but he does not cite Kroeber's earlier example of the Eskimo (Kroeber, 1948, pp. 603-604).

But for the rest, his position against sentiment, emotion, or anxiety remains an assertion.

'Contrary to what Freud maintained, social constraints, whether positive or negative, cannot be explained, either in their origin or in their persistence, as the effects of impulses or emotions which appear again and again, with the same characteristics and during the course of centuries and mill-ennia, in different individuals. For if the recurrence of the sentiments explained the persistence of customs, the origin of the customs ought to coincide with the origin of the appearance of the sentiments, and Freud's thesis would be unchanged even if the parricidal impulse corresponded to a typical situation instead of to a historical event.

29

David M. Schneider

'We do not know, and never shall know, anything about the first origin of beliefs and customs the roots of which plunge into a distant past but, as far as the present is concerned, it is certain that social behavior is not produced spontaneously by each individual, under the influence of emotions of the moment. Men do not act, as members of a group, in accordance with what each feels as an individual; each man feels as a function of the way in which he is permitted or obliged to act.' (Lévi-Strauss, 1963, pp. 69-70).

Lévi-Strauss sharply dissociates himself from Durkheim's position.

'. . . in the last analysis Durkheim derives social phenomena as well from affectivity. His theory of totemism starts with an urge, and ends with recourse to sentiment' (ibid., pp. 70-71). 'Actually, impulses and emotions explain nothing: they are always *results*, either of the power of the body or of the impotence of the mind. In both cases they are consequences, never causes. The latter can be sought only in the organism, which is the exclusive concern of biology, or in the intellect, which is the sole way offered to psychology, and to anthropology as well' (ibid., p. 71).

And so the intellect, cognition, how people think and not their emotions are the explanatory conditions for social phenomena. But notice how close is the pattern to that which is explicitly repudiated when phrased in terms of sentiment.

'The advent of culture thus coincides with the birth of the intellect. Furthermore, the opposition between the continuous and the discontinuous, which seems irreducible on the biological plane because it is expressed by the seriality of individuals within the species, and in the heterogeniety of the species among each other, is surmounted in culture, which is based on the aptitude of man to perfect himself . . .' (ibid., p. 100).

Origins, in other words, are not recoverable if we try to locate their emotional beginnings, but they are recoverable if we consider them to be in the intellect. This, it would seem, is because the intellect is the source, the beginning and the continuing source.

'... Bergson and Rousseau ... have succeeded in getting right to the psychological foundations of exotic institutions ... by a process of internalization, i.e., by trying on themselves modes of thought taken from elsewhere or simply imagined. They thus demonstrate that every human mind is a locus of virtual experience where what goes on in the minds of men, however remote they may be, can be investigated' (ibid., p. 103).

The mathematical formula expressing the shape of the cams and their speed of rotation now assumes the form of the human intellect. It is the inventiveness of the human intellect, the rules of operation of the human mind, the fundamental qualities of mind which are the explanations.

'It is certainly the case that one consequence of modern structuralism (not, however, clearly enunciated) ought to be to rescue associational psychology from the discredit into which it has fallen. Associationism had the great merit of sketching the contours of this elementary logic, which is like the least common denominator of all thought, and its only failure was not to recognize that it was an original logic, a direct expression of the structure of the mind (and behind the mind, probably, of the brain), and not an inert product of the action of the environment on an amorphous consciousness.' (ibid., p. 90).

Except for minor embellishments, Lévi-Strauss has returned to the position at the turn of this century which Durkheim, Lévy-Bruhl, Boas, and Kroeber held. This is simply the position that culture, custom, belief, or social constraints are products of the human mind, understandable only when the laws of the human mind are known.

It is disconcerting, therefore, to follow the discussion of *Totemism* (Lévi-Strauss, 1963), which seems to review the history of our understanding of that phenomenon. It moves with care from the illusion of an entity shattered by Boas and Goldenweiser's cold analysis, on to Elkin's fumbling with too many broken pieces, and then on through to functionalism's confusions until it reaches the climax in Chapter 4, 'Toward the Intellect'.

31

Toward the intellect, away from emotion and sentiment, using structural linguistics as the vehicle to ride to the rescue of associational psychology! But one suddenly notices that the intellect toward which one is headed is in one case fresh from the eighteenth century, and in the other from the earliest part of the twentieth; that the confusions of functionalism are all historically later developments; that the devastation of the entity called totemism by Goldenweiser, following directions clearly stated by Boas, comes after the very time and the very position to which Lévi-Strauss has returned by such a circuitous route. It was Boas, of course, who first wrote *The Mind of Primitive Man* in 1911, and Kroeber who insisted that kinship terms could be understood only as linguistic and psychological phenomena in 1917, just as it is Lévi-Strauss in 1962 who says that totemism is understandable as a product of the human mind.

One can only suppose that the separation of mind into 'intellect' and 'emotion' is the end-product of the same series of events which have led Homans up the Skinnerian path. Skinnerian psychology is not really too far from structural linguistics and Lévi-Strauss's 'intellect' (Homans, 1962).

Homans and Lévi-Strauss have converged on the same intellectual position, each from his own very different starting-point, each backing away from the other with more than passing vigor, each denying any validity to the other's position. Homans along a path of positivism, Lévi-Strauss following the course of intellectualism, both as psychological reductionists.

III. In certain respects three very old ideas form the core of all cross-cousin marriage theories: the first is the idea that cross-cousin marriage is somehow an integrative device. The second, that different cross-cousin marriage rules with different rules of descent form different kinds of units, so that, for instance, bilateral cross-cousin marriage yields a very different kind of arrangement from unilateral forms. The implications of the different forms of unilateral rule for the kind of integration which ensues is the third old idea, and this one dates at least back to Fortune (1933).

Cross-cousin marriage theories differ in significant details, on the 'meaning' of these details, and on 'how the system really works' (Needham, 1957, p. 168). The derivation of much of the analysis from Rivers (Rivers, 1914a and b), and particularly the terminological correlates of the different forms of cross-cousin marriage, should be noted.

What Lévi-Strauss, Dumont, Leach, and Needham have done is to set these fairly well-established points in the context of a general theory of society, and to develop from that combination certain specific and specifically useful (as well as debatable) ideas which were not generally available before.

The first such specific outcome to be taken up here is that the relationship between intermarrying units in a society practicing cross-cousin marriage is one of 'alliance'. And the problematic aspect of this is the question of just what is meant by 'alliance'.

There is a series of closely interrelated ideas at work here. First, of course, there is the notion of organic solidarity, that is, the interrelation of differentiated parts no one of which can by itself be autonomous. Second, there is the notion that every social definition must in the nature of human mentality and in the nature of society be stipulated in terms of opposition, complementary dualism, and so forth. Third, there is the notion that structure inheres not in the concrete constitution of any particular society, but rather in the 'model' or the construct which must be developed by the anthropologist in order to understand that society; yet the structural principles which are 'at work', so to speak (my phrase, my phrasing), are somehow 'real', 'existent', 'substantive' and are expressed in the social definitions, the social conventions, the social rules of a particular society (Lévi-Strauss, 1953, 1960).

Briefly, there are two enduring structural features of any society practicing cross-cousin marriage, or having any 'positive marriage rule' (sister exchange, asymmetrical marriage rules, etc.). First, the rule of descent which aligns (not allies) a group into one unit; second, that of 'alliance', the relationship between two or more such units of which marriage is an expression.

Alliance theory insists that in the nature of social definitions, arising as they do from the inherent features of human mentality, 'consanguinity' can be defined only in opposition to 'affinity', and 'affinity' in opposition to 'consanguinity'. Hence it is incon-

33

ceivable that a society with a positive marriage rule could consist in *one* consanguineally related group of social persons. Radcliffe-Brown (1953, p. 169), in criticizing Dumont's treatment of Dravidian kinship terms, brings this issue out clearly. Radcliffe-Brown asserts that for the Kariera, 'the terms "nuba", "kaga" and "toa", which are applied to large numbers of persons, are not terms for relatives by marriage'. In short, he denies that affinity, as a principle, is applicable to this society, and by implication that a society can consist only in statuses socially defined by consanguinity.

So far as cross-cousin marriage systems are concerned, this problem of the necessary existence of a principle of alliance opposed to one of descent brings into question both the interpretation of the terminological system and the nature of the integration of such systems.

The problem of integration focuses on the implications of the idea of general exchange as proposed by Mauss (1954). Specifically, Lévi-Strauss follows Mauss in suggesting that if marriage is one mode of exchange, and if exchange between differentiated parts is seen as the basic mode of integration, not one exchange, nor one kind of exchange, but rather a series of exchanges of various kinds will all occur, and will all reinforce and reiterate the integration between exchanging groups. Hence the exchange of bridewealth, of goods and services, and so on are all understandable as part of the total exchange system and are all equally fundamental expressions of the structural principle of alliance. All expressions of alliance, be they pigs, gongs, food and services, or women, are equally expressions of this structural principle. In this sense, each expresses the principle.

Yet it is difficult to distinguish in the writings of alliance theorists between marriage as an *expression of* alliance, and marriage as *creating* alliance. It is one thing to say that marriage is one among many expressions of the structural principle of alliance; it is quite another to say that marriage creates alliance. To go a step further and say that both statements are true is to move into yet a third and not at all compatible position.

IV. In an asymmetrical marriage system, a prescriptive system with a positive marriage rule, the system is essentially triadic.

Nevertheless, the symbolic system is dyadic. This is shown by both Lévi-Strauss and Needham, and Leach seems to concur (Leach, 1961). The reason for this is that from the point of view of any given lineage or ego there are only two relations: wife-giver or wife-taker.

Needham may help to explicate matters. Near the conclusion of his reiterated exposition of Purum he says:

'We see here, as elsewhere with prescriptive alliance, a mode of classification by which things, individuals, groups, qualities, values, spatial notions, and other ideas of the most disparate kinds are identically ordered within one system of relations. In particular, *I would draw attention to the remarkable concordance and interconnection of social and symbolic structure* [emphasis supplied]. In spite of the fact that structurally there must be three cyclically-related lines in the alliance system, the basic scheme of Purum society is not triadic but dyadic. Any given alliance group is wife-taker and therefore inferior to another, but it is also wife-giver and therefore superior to another group in a different context. That is, alliance status is not absolute but relative. The distinction to be appreciated is that between the triadic *system* and its component dyadic *relation*. It is through this mode of relation that the social order concords with the symbolic order' (Needham, 1962a, pp. 95-96).

But a closer inspection reveals that both triadic systems and dyadic systems concord with dyadic *symbolic* systems. Needham says,

'. . . the Aimol scheme of symbolic classification, which accompanies a two-section (symmetric) system, exhibits the same principles and even embodies some of the same pairs of terms as the Purum scheme, which accompanies an asymmetric system . . . our task is to see how a common mode of symbolic classification can cohere with these different social forms.

'The key to this question is that in spite of the necessarily triadic structure of an asymmetric system its fundamental relation is dyadic . . ., and that the fundamental relation of Aimol society, though differently defined, is also dyadic. Here lies the basic similarity between the two social systems, and the structural feature with which the dualistic symbolic

35

classification is in both cases concordant. We may now regard these two systems as different but related means of ordering social relations as well as other phenomena by the same (dualistic) mode of thought. If this is the case, it is this mode of thought itself which demands our attention if we are to understand them in any radical fashion' (Needham, 1960d, pp. 100-101).

One must distinguish, then, between dyadic and triadic *systems*: the first a two-section system, and one of symmetrical cross-cousin marriage, and the other an asymmetric, perhaps matrilateral, cross-cousin marriage *system*. These, in turn, are distinct from the *symbolic* system, that is, '... a mode of classification by which things, individuals, groups, qualities, values, spatial notions, and other ideas of the most disperate kinds are identically ordered within one system of relations' (Needham, 1962, p. 95). The *symbolic* system '... concords with ...' the *social* system.

But just what does this concordance mean? Needham explains it in this way: '... what one is really dealing with in such a society as this is a classification, a system of categories, which orders both social life and the cosmos. That is, Purum social organization is ideologically a part of a cosmological conceptual order and is governed identically by its ruling ideas' (Needham, 1962, p. 96).

In other words, 'the social order' is itself a symbolic order and is on no account to be confused with actual living persons, concrete groups, actual numbers, or actual relations between actual persons or groups.

V. The descent theory which follows from Radcliffe-Brown deals with actual living persons, concrete groups, actual relations between actual persons or groups. Consistent with such a view, Livingstone (1959) attacked Needham's Purum analysis precisely on the ground that the system, if it worked at all, could not work very well, since some of the units in the exchange system have too many women to dispose of, and some not enough. Livingstone's point is that, at best, the rules are difficult for people to follow; at worst, the rules are unworkable in real life.

Needham's reply stresses, as one might well expect, that the structure of the system does not lie in the concrete constitution of any particular exchanging group, nor in any particular cycle of exchanges. 'Particular alliances and alliance groups may be expected to change, but the essential point is that the rules (matrilateral prescription, patrilateral prohibition) have not changed' (Needham, 1960h, p. 499). Needham continues:

'A social system is an abstraction relating (in this context) to lineal descent groups which are also abstractions. There is no place in an abstraction for substantive "specific groups". It would be an odd and profitless use of the notion of social system to so identify it with substantive reality that every change ... would be said to constitute a "breakdown" ' (p. 499). 'I do not claim, though, that it is utterly unknown for a marriage to take place within the clan in an asymmetric system ...' (p. 499-500). 'That the definition of alliance groups can be changed, and that alliances can be reversed, are well known facts in the literature on such systems as the Purum' (p. 501). 'When I used the word "stable", on the other hand, I meant precisely (as I wrote) that in spite of demographic changes and fission of segments the rules of the alliance system continue to maintain the same type of social order between whatever groups are pragmatically distinguished' (p. 502).

Needham's reply to Livingstone clarifies this matter. But to my knowledge, no one has published a reply to Leach's paper, 'Structural Implications ...' (Leach, 1962). One of the points which Leach makes in this paper is that it is not 'social segments' conceived of as diagram lines which actually undertake marriage-in-a-circle; it is the social segment which Leach calls 'local descent lines', concrete units 'on the ground', which undertakes such marriages. For Needham's version of alliance theory, Leach's distinction, however true, is quite irrelevant. It is the social order as a conceptual order, the social system as a system of relational rules, which is the concern of alliance theory. Alliance theory is precisely and explicitly *diagram lines as models of a social order* for Needham.

Not so for Lévi-Strauss (or Dumont), however. Maybury-Lewis (1960) takes Lévi-Strauss sternly to task for this same error. Indeed, one may say that the criticism is the Leach Criticism, and consists in accusing Lévi-Strauss of confusing models with

37

reality, of mixing phenomena from disparate levels of abstraction in the same analytic image. And Lévi-Strauss's reply to Maybury-Lewis (1960) should apply to Leach's paper as well: '. . . I cannot be reproached for confusing dual organization, dualist system and dualism. As a matter of fact, I was avowedly trying to override these classical distinctions, with the aim of finding out if they could be dealt with as open – and to some extent conflicting – *expressions of a reality, to be looked for at a deeper level*' (Lévi-Strauss, 1960, p. 46. Emphasis supplied). Or again, in the same vein, later in the same paper: 'Hence the conclusion that "actual social segments" and "symbolic representations" may not be as heterogeneous as it seems, but that, to some extent, they may correspond to permutable codes. Here lies one's right to deal with social segments and symbolic representations as parts of an underlying system endowed with a better explanatory value, although – or rather, because – empirical observation will never apprehend it as such' (Lévi-Strauss, 1960, p. 54).

This should also help to clarify Lévi-Strauss's view of the nature of 'reductionism'. Where, for some, the reduction of one order of phenomenon to another constitutes a breach of analytic rules, it constitutes a proper form of explanation for Lévi-Strauss, Needham, and Dumont at least.

VI. Alliance theory continues a phrase closely associated with Durkheim, but alters its meaning in some respects. Durkheim saw and described 'the social order' as a system of norms and rules and regulations, values and ethical elements, and so he described it as a *moral system*, because it constrained people's action. The phrase 'moral system' and the notion of morality are notably missing from Lévi-Strauss, Dumont, Needham, and Leach.

In Durkheim's treatment of the problem of suicide the intimate, close connection between norms, values, constructs, and actual behavior is the very essence of the analysis. Perhaps it had to be, since he had forced himself by the skill of his intellect to deal with a problem of *rate*, which he was among the very first to distinguish clearly from that of incidence. The actor's *commitment* to the norms and not the constitution of the norm itself, decided his fate.

The problem of social order for Durkheim was the question of explaining how constraints actually operated to define, guide, and channel the behavior – the actual behavior – of people: real, living people. Social order is the order that is imposed on a person's action (Parsons, 1949).

But 'social order' for Needham is the congruence of symbolic systems seen in logical terms; it has almost nothing to do with 'groups *pragmatically* distinguished'. The word pragmatic can only make sense if it is taken to mean 'conceptually', and this in turn can mean that some native will talk about it. A figment of a figment of a figment of a native's imagination will do – and indeed this is precisely the susbstantive element in the social order. Needham does not ever raise or deal with the problem of social order in this Durkheimian sense, which is the problem which Livingstone put to him: the symbolic system cannot order the actual marriages of the Purum very well. Needham replied that the social order that he is discussing is not to be located in the 'rate', but instead occurs at the level of the symbols, constructs, ideas, categories, rules for relating these, and so on (Needham, 1960, p. 499).

VII. Is it at this point that Lévi-Strauss's separation of mind into intellect, on the one hand, and emotions and sentiments, on the other, becomes a less arbitrary action than it first seemed? It is not at all clear from his assertions just why this separation is necessary. It is conceivable that if Lévi-Strauss is concerned with the social order as a symbolic order, with the organization and configuration of that symbolic order, with the relationships between sub-systems of symbols, that the enormous weight, and almost indisputable weight, of Freud's work on symbolism would serve him well. But instead Lévi-Strauss tells us that, unlike Kroeber's, his own attitude toward *Totem and Taboo* has hardened over the years (Lévi-Strauss, 1963, p. 70).

It is odd, too, that the non-logical and irrational character of the logic of the unconscious as Freud describes it should fail to appeal to Lévi-Strauss.

But the other side remains clear. Durkheim was concerned with the actor's commitment; Lévi-Strauss is concerned with what the actor may be committed to. Durkheim was concerned with the integration of the objects of the actor's commitment in the actor, as the actor saw it and was impelled to act on it; Lévi-Strauss is concerned with the integration of the system of objects of commitment, and how they integrate one with another. Durkheim needed something like an 'urge' and a 'sentiment' to explain how actors got and remained committed to objects; Lévi-Strauss needs something like intellect to explain the logic of the order among symbols. And, of course, how can there be, either in nature or in theory, intellect without emotion or emotion without intellect? Perhaps this explains why Freud haunts the pages of Lévi-Strauss, from the *Structures élémentaires* through the recent *Totemisme*.

The social order is a symbolic order, an order of ideas and categories, concepts and rules all 'ordered' by their logical relation. What imposes this order? How are the different levels of order related? Needham brings it all together in a single, felicitous paragraph which may well be the brief outline for a series of detailed volumes:

'The present analysis [Aimol], together with that of Purum society, permits the proposition that both of the major types of prescriptive alliance feature basically a dyadic social relationship, and that with this there concords in these cases a dualistic scheme of symbolic classification [footnote omitted]. Furthermore, wherever the ethnography is adequate to the purposes of this type of investigation, it can be seen that in societies practising prescriptive alliance it is a dualistic symbolic classification which orders both the social and the symbolic system, characterizing both by the same mode of thought. This type of classification is the analogical elaboration, in all spheres of social concern, of a *structural principle* of complementary dualism; and this itself is one manifestation of the logical principle of opposition. It is in this sense that societies founded on prescriptive alliance may be interpreted as the most direct forms known of the social expression of a fundamental feature of the human mind' (Needham, 1960d, p. 106).

In the same place, Needham stipulates some of his differences with Lévi-Strauss:

'In trying to pin down Lévi-Strauss' idea of what is fundamentally important in the analysis of the sort of system we are examining two conclusions seem me [sic] to emerge: (1) in the matter of features of the human mind he proposes a number of formulations, each rather different from the others, which he declines to analyse further on the ground that they are psychological data; (2) for him the radically and essentially important idea is that of reciprocity. Admittedly, he is concerned with marriage regulation as means of exchanging women, a context in which reciprocity has an especially important place, but even here I think he over-rates its importance; for he disregards the conceptual systems of the societies within which women are exchanged, systems which are solidary with the exchange systems and which cannot be explained by the notion of reciprocity. Durkheim and Mauss indeed tried to derive 'concepts from social organization ... but Lévi-Strauss would surely not do so in this case, since the notions he isolates are far more general than the forms of affinal alliance he examines' (Needham, 1960d, p. 102).

VIII. A rule is certainly not the same thing as its observance. The rule that good little children go to heaven while those who are naughty go elsewhere must certainly be distinguished from an actual census conducted in Heaven, although the latter might possibly provide a statistical model (Lévi-Strauss, 1953). And even if it could be shown that not a single good child actually got to heaven, it would hardly alter the fact that this remains a rule, at least in some circles.

How can such a rule be 'expressed by' or 'contained in' some terminological pattern about children, goodness, naughtiness, heaven, or hell? This is perhaps difficult. But the matter is quite different with kinship terms. Here are symbols which, in some aspect of their character, can 'embody' or 'express' marriage rules. So Dumont (1953, 1957) and Yalman (1962) affirm for Dravidian kin terms, though Epling (1961) denies this. (We will come to Radcliffe-Brown's objections shortly.)

This brings us around again to the question raised earlier, is marriage an expression of alliance, or does it create alliance as well as express it?

David M. Schneider

This problem can be seen best in the matter of the radical distinction between prescriptive and preferential systems which Needham has drawn.

It seems doubtful that Lévi-Strauss and Dumont follow this distinction, but we have Leach's statement which implies that he does (Leach, 1961).

If a marriage rule is to be treated as an expression of a structural principle, and if a marriage rule such as MoBrDa is taken as one expression of that principle, then it would seem to follow that a preferential rule (as distinct from the prescriptive rule) is equally clearly an expression of that same structural principle.

One might say that the preferential rule is modified, as an expression of the principle (as in Lévi-Strauss, 1960) but that in effect the 'type of social-order' (Needham, 1960h, p. 502) is unmodified. If the marriage rule is an expression of the principle of alliance, is it any less so if the rule is not, for some set of good reasons, required? The principle is still there. It is still expressed in the marriage rule. Just as the concrete number of actual marriages which follow the rule has no bearing on the structural analysis, so too it might seem that the rule expressed as an *obligation* or the rule expressed as a *preference* is equally clearly an expression of one and the same structural principle.

The marriage rule, like the terminological pattern and the goods which are exchanged, all reflect the principle of alliance. Hence it does not seem clear why Needham should insist that for any given society there must simultaneously be certain forms of expression, and that each should be perfectly internally consistent as a form of expression of the structural principle. Needham insists that the terminological pattern must be consistent, or that the ethnographer has made a mistake (Purum); that the marriage rule *must be* prescriptive; he further finds it very hard to accept the fact that certain marriages which are wrong marriages (according to the rule) occur, though he contents himself that they are very few in number. (Dumont seems to differ on this point, if his genealogical examples in *Hierarchy and Marriage Alliance* are to be taken as an expression of his own views in this matter.)

Let me restate this in another way. Needham makes the radical distinction between prescriptive systems and preferential

42

systems. He goes to considerable trouble to assert which of thirty-three societies are prescriptive and which preferential (i.e. Needham, 1962). He then proceeds to deal with the prescriptive systems alone. He has not dealt with preferential systems, neither has he stated in understandable terms why preferential systems *cannot* be treated as having the same structure as prescriptive systems. It is by no means self-evident that they are different from the point of view of alliance theory. Indeed, I suggest that it is an induction from alliance theory that they are *not* different at all and that Needham fails to understand his own theory when he says that they are.

PART TWO. SEGMENTS

IX. The suggestion that Needham does not understand the implications of the theory he is following is perhaps premature at this point. It is true that Needham does not discuss at length the distinction between prescriptive and preferential systems. Neither does he explain why he insists on the radical distinction which he makes. It is certainly true that he might have analyzed a society like the Yaroro of Venezuela to show '. . . how such a system really works' (Needham, 1957, 1958c, p. 323), for he obviously considers the material on that society valid and reliable, although he describes the source as being 'unimpressive', a word he does not clarify (Needham, 1962, p. 62). It is easy to see that the analysis of Purum as a *prescriptive* matrilateral system would be immeasurably strengthened by the analysis of a *preferential* matrilateral system to show, by contrast and example, precisely where the differences between such systems do lie and just what is at issue here.

What is at issue here is the idea that is best expressed by the oft-repeated phrase '. . . the same type of social order . . .' (Needham, 1960, p. 502), or 'a certain type of society' (Dumont, 1961, for instance, where the phrase is also found as '. . . different types of societies'). In its simplest form, this means that one type of society has 'a positive marriage rule' and the other has not (Dumont, like Lévi-Strauss, sometimes says '. . . a "marriage preference"' Dumont, 1961). The type without a positive marriage rule is one in which individual choice is exercised *not* with respect to aesthetic or purely personal considerations, but

43

one in which there is no limitation in principle on the social category (kinship category is a particular social category) from which the spouse is drawn, provided that the incest prohibition is observed (Lévi-Strauss, 1949).

This basic distinction, developed in this particular form by Lévi-Strauss in 1949, has a long history and a wide group of supporters of one or another of its forms, including Leach (1962), Goody (1959, 1961), Fortes (1959), and Freeman (1961).

The distinction follows from Durkheim's notion of a 'segmental society'. The image is that of a concrete society formed of homogeneous, repetitive parts. The parts are clans, and clans grow out of territorially based hordes (Durkheim, 1947, pp. 175 ff). The link between the homogeneous parts, in the limiting case which Durkheim posed, is nothing more than similarity, a kind of 'birds-of-a-feather-flock-together' principle. Only when the parts become functionally differentiated does a society begin to move away from, and fall on a point of the scale away from, that of mechanical solidarity and segmental organization (Durkheim's evolutionary view is retained here).

But the problem which Durkheim did not solve satisfactorily remains. How are the segments defined and in what do they consist? How are they formed or maintained? Durkheim swung back and forth between a physically discrete aggregate or group of real persons, and the ideas ('collective representations') in terms of which such a physically discrete category might be formed. As I have already suggested, Radcliffe-Brown wrote as if he had the physical segment in mind ('actual social relations'), Lévi-Strauss, Dumont, and Needham confine themselves to the rules which flow from the structural principles.

But in either case, some kind of 'rules' yields this particular 'kind' of society. Any other kind of 'rules' should not produce such a society.

The contrast between unilineal descent and bilateral systems seems to have been one of the most enduring models for this problem. (See Leach, 1962b, p. 132, quoted in Section XVII below, for a clear statement of this position.) With any of the unilineal descent rules (matrilineal, patrilineal, double unilineal), discrete, exclusive, multifunctional units can be formed within a single society when the unilineal units are exogamic. Where there

44

s no unilineal rule, such units cannot form within the endogamic boundary. Any *endogamic* unit can be discrete, exclusive, multi-functional as well and, given that it has certain other minimal characteristics, can form a self-sufficient entity within a society. Thus a caste within a society can be discrete, exclusive, multi-functional. The endogamic-exogamic boundaries must be stated n this problem.

It is, therefore, the exclusive, discrete unit which can be multi-functional. A unit which is discrete and exclusive and multi-functional, which is a self-contained, self-consistent, and self-perpetuating unit is, of course, a society. If it lacks one function necessary to maintain itself as such a unit it can nevertheless be a major social segment in a 'segmental' system, and, of course, one could conceivably scale societies according to the degree to which they are segmental.

We can now return to the problem of the conditions which can yield such segments, and of how within-segment and between-segment relations are defined. And this is the problem about which ideas and phrases such as 'a certain type of society' center; it is the problem between Fortes and Goody on the one hand, and Lévi-Strauss, Leach, and Dumont on the other.

For alliance theory, and for Lévi-Strauss who developed this variant of the notion, '... a certain type of society' means a society which is very close to or approaches the model of the segmental society first stated by Durkheim. The limiting case of mechanical solidarity occurring entirely in terms of similarity is dropped as a model. Instead the next simplest form of organic solidarity – exogamy with a marriage rule – is used. Hence '... a certain type of society' has a positive marriage rule, not a state of free choice, which is its opposite.

But this is the crux of the difference with Fortes and Goody. They do not concern themselves with the problem of whether the simplest form of organic solidarity is formed by a marriage rule and exogamy. They are concerned with segmental societies because they have a special theory of their own about how segments are formed and in what they consist, and how within-segment relations are ordered and how between-segment relations are structured. Marriage enters into this theory, but in a very different way.

45

X. On one point both alliance theory and descent theory are in agreement. If a segment is to remain discrete, conceptually or concretely, it cannot have overlapping membership with any other segment. It can have relationships, but not overlapping membership.

Freeman (1961, pp. 200, 202) and Goodenough (1955), to cite but two writers on this point, maintain that the kindred cannot form a 'group', or corporate group, but must remain a category. Freeman makes the very useful distinction between the kindred and a kindred-based group, for portions of a kindred can come together for some specific purpose, for some limited time and thus form an *ad hoc* group.

The point remains the same. The kindred itself cannot be a group because it is defined by reference to a specific ego, because the category has overlapping interlocking membership, because at best it can become a discrete physical unit and remain so only for a limited time, by permitting some members to drop out (the 'optive' condition in Freeman, 1961, pp. 209-211) and rallying the rest for a stipulated short-run goal.

The whole man has to be in one and only one group, so that the group can be a physical as well as a conceptual group. But why is it necessary to be able to separate physically all of the groups?

I think that the reason for this, one to which both alliance theory and descent theory subscribe, is not that segments have to be spatially and physically separate and identifiable as such, but that the whole person as an aggregate of different commitments must be able to provide unqualified solidarity with the unit to which he belongs. It is this which permits the segment under certain conditions to be physically identifiable as such. But if a single person's solidarity is qualified by membership in two or more different units *of like order*, then his commitment to, his solidarity with, one of them is qualified by the claims of the other upon him. Conflicting claims on two different persons are easily soluble; one goes one way, the other his own way. But conflicting claims on one person have to be adjudicated; one wins, the other wins, or both are qualified and compromised in some way.

If a system of intersecting claims on persons requires the adjudication of those claims, then this in itself becomes a mode of integration in such situations and also in such societies. This

46

has been repeatedly shown for feuds and so forth. It should not require explicit demonstration for the social system as a whole.

The whole person is thus of significance to both descent and alliance theory, and this notion constitutes, I suggest, an unanalyzed and unspecified condition of the model which alliance theory has produced. It is the condition of unqualified commitment which is requisite to the constitution of the segment-conceptually for alliance theory, concretely for descent theory – and it is this condition which radically reduces the kinds of segmental system to the few which have been pointed out. These are always based on kinship, because it is only descent rules – more precisely, unilineal descent rules or rigid endogamy – which dispose the whole man to one or another segment of society.

(At this point the argument could proceed along one of two different lines. One line would be to turn to the problem of choice, for Rivers, Fortes, Leach, Lévi-Strauss, and Needham are all quite explicit that it is only under conditions of unilineal descent, where choice is excluded, that the kinds of segment with which they are concerned can be formed. Rather than continue with that problem here, I have delayed its consideration to Section XVII and proceeded to discuss the descent theory views of the nature and constitution of segments.)

XI. A segment is a discrete conceptual or concrete entity in a segmental society. It is the descent rule which allocates whole persons to one or another segment. It is the descent rule which is the mode of recruitment that replaces the dead by the living. Because a discrete, exclusive unit is formed, this unit can be a perpetual unit (conceptually though not concretely; its members die and are replaced by new members).

A unit is one thing; a corporate group quite another. A descent rule, rigidly followed, only creates a conceptually distinct category. Its organization as a corporate unit depends upon other factors.

As a minimal definition, a corporate unit is one which is treated as internally undifferentiated by the other unit or units with which it has a specific relationship. Such units may be a person in a particular role, a group acting as a whole, a group represented by a person, and so forth.[3]

47

A corporate unit has a relationship with some other unit. The other's treatment of it is consistent with its conception of that unit. If the unit is conceived of by the other as having an un-differentiated, unitary identity, then for that purpose, or for that particular relationship, it is corporate.

But it may be argued that to *be* corporate for some purpose or other equally means that the unit must also be able to *act* in a corporate fashion. Not only must it be conceived of as corporate but it must be able to act as a corporate unit.

Both of these conditions are met when the members of the unit see their relationship to each other as being 'the same', and when that same relationship is seen as 'the same' for all outsiders. Thus a unit may be treated as consisting entirely of agnates, and the members may define their relationship to each other not as father-son, brother-brother, etc, but rather as one of agnates.

The degree to which members have solidary bonds with each other, then, may be held as a condition or at least as a related condition, to the unit's capacity to act as a unit and be treated as a unit.

Following Durkheim, it is presumed that solidarity is increased when different kinds of bond replicate each other. Hence the group which raises its food together, processes it, distributes it, consumes it; the group that is interdependent for its labor; the group which worships its own ancestors and thus is the same 'church'; the group which owns its property as a unit – such a group, with repetitive bonds, each reinforcing the other, is more strongly solidary than is the group which merely shares a single function – say, its name or its emblem. And the degree to which it is solidary is directly proportional to the number of different solidary bonds among its members, and this is inversely proportional to the strength of any particular member's bonds outside that unit. So that if the agnates within a descent unit all are tied with repetitive bonds, and none of them has any very strong bonds with persons outside the group, a strongly corporate unit results.

The multifunctional character of a social segment, then, is one of the conditions which helps to maintain a segment's segmental character. A unifunctional unit can hardly constitute a social segment.

48

The segmental character of a society, therefore, depends on the corporate character of its segments, and the corporate character of its segments depends on the strength of the bonds among the members of the segment. The strength of the bonds among the members is in turn dependent in part upon having no compromising allegiance for some members of a group outside the group, but is in part also dependent on the kind of functions which the members undertake in common, and it is from this that the intensity of their commitment, the strength of the bonds among them, the degree of the corporateness of the group derives.

What kind of function so unites a group? If a unilineal descent group holds property rights in love magic, does this so unite a group? If it controls a dance or a form of poetry? If it has the right to recite certain prayers? Hardly. If a unilineal descent unit owns and controls property, productive property, real estate or cattle, then and only then does its status as a true segment emerge.

It is property, productive property, an estate, which makes a segment a segment for Goody (1961), and it is at least the jural and political functions for Fortes, if I read him correctly (1959, 1962).

And so one sees the descent group defined by certain of its functions for Goody and Fortes. A descent group is a property-holding group where the property is productive property; it is (along with its descent rule) *thereby* corporate, a jural and political unit.

XII. Fortes and Leach agree that the term 'descent' should be confined to *unilineal* descent and continually invoke Rivers's name in ways that suggest that in this context, at least, it is sacred (Fortes, 1959; Leach, 1962). Freeman (1961) performs feats of eloquence with the ethnography of All Souls and Wales to help maintain Rivers's division between descent as unilineal and a personal kindred as purely ego-centered. This unexpected concurrence arises, I suggest, from the fact that all three are committed to a particular model for a type of society, a segmental type of society. Note that this is not merely a descent rule, nor a combination of types of descent rules, nor a classification of descent systems. It is a type of society as a whole that is at stake.

Both descent theory and alliance theory have a vested interest,

E

49

so to speak, in particular definitions of segments which go to make up somewhat different theoretical models of segmental societies. Where alliance theory defines its model of a segment strictly in terms of a unilineal descent rule and exogamy, descent theory defines its segment in terms of corporate character. The corporate character of the segment is seen as a consequence of a unilineal descent rule, exogamy, *and* a high degree of solidarity related to the fact that it is the holder of productive property and so also is a jural and political unit. If alliance theory depends on the image of a descent rule plus marriage rule, descent theory depends on the image of a descent rule plus the jural and political functions which are connected with property ownership.

The last piece in the model of the segmental society, then, is the relationship between segments. And here is where so much of the smoke seems to come from. For alliance theory, the segments are related to each other by alliance, and alliance is either created by or expressed by (or both) marriage. For descent theory, the segments can be related to each other in a variety of different ways, among them, the bonds of complementary filiation and levels of segmentation. Some alliance theorists have complained that complementary filiation is just another name for descent and that descent theorists do not recognize marriage as a structural principle.

XIII. 'It is the whole nature of the concept of "descent" which is at issue' (Leach, 1961, p. 121).

Fortes, Freeman, and Goody have all gone to great pains to confine the concept of 'descent' to unilineal rules, forming *corporate groups* which have jural, political, and/or property-holding functions. Fortes (1959, pp. 207-208; 1962) also suggests that descent is, in the first instance, a matter of title to membership, citizenship, and that group membership, although of major importance, is not the only defining criterion.

Fortes agrees that affinity is important in any society but, according to Leach, he seems to deny that alliance constitutes a structural principle for certain of them. Fortes seems to say that for the Tallensi, the fundamental structural principle is that of descent, as well as the lineage principle which is so closely inter-woven with descent; that alliance is not a structural principle for ertain of the African lineage systems. (*NB:* Fortes *seems to say.* He does not say it in so many words.) Leach is on the offensive, yet cautious. Leach has not to my knowledge boldly asserted that, for Tallensi, alliance is just as fundamental a structural principle as the lineage principle. Instead, he has picked away from sheltered ground; he asserts that 'Fortes . . . disguises [affinity] under his expression "complementary filiation". . . . For Fortes, marriage ties, as such, do not form part of the structural system' (Leach, 1957a, p. 54).

But Leach makes a more positive point, in criticizing Fortes's notion of 'filiation'. His criticism, if I take it correctly, focuses on the fact that 'filiation' consists in a kind of descent rule, a relationship of consanguinity, when in fact it would seem that that relationship is precisely affinal. Hence his statement that 'It is the whole nature of the concept of "descent" which is at issue' (Leach, 1962, p. 121).

One confusion arises because of the somewhat different ways in which alliance theory and descent theory treat kinship terms. For alliance theory, kinship terms can be analyzed and understood without *direct* reference to the constitution of descent groups. For descent theory, this is not possible.

This can be seen from Dumont's treatment of Dravidian kinship terms. (That this is also part of the MoBr-SiSo problem will become evident.)

Dumont (1953) says that in Dravidian kinship terminology the MoBr is defined in opposition to the father as father's brother-in-law, the FaSi as the Mo's Si-in-Law, and the Mo as a consanguine.

Now, this looks like sheer nonsense in descent theory terms. If one takes mother alone for a moment, descent theorists treat her as father's wife; given a patrilineal lineage, she cannot ever be completely incorporated into ego's lineage since her lineage membership is gained through her father; hence her relationship to her husband, her children, and to the men of her husband's lineage is simply as an affinal, an in-marrying woman. The whole understanding of the levirate, the sororate, marital stability, and bridewealth turn on this. Thus marriage is brittle for the Hopi precisely because a woman is never released by her natal matrilineal lineage, her ties to her lineage remain strong, and so too the man's ties to his own natal matrilineal lineage are strong; hence the

51

strain which is put on the marital tie. Descent group strength, that is, the various kinds of descent group solidarity, are seen as inversely related to conjugal ties and as proportional to parent-child and sibling ties (see in this connection, Schneider, 1961).

Mother is a consanguine to ego for descent group theory, but her relationship is not the same as the relationship of co-members of the same descent group. The consanguineal tie of father to son in patriliny is not the same as mother to son, yet both are consanguineal ties. The father-son tie consists both in a tie of consanguinity and in common descent group membership where the tie of mother to son is that of consanguinity, is opposed to the common descent group membership tie of father-son, and is as an affinal to the son in his capacity as father's descent group member.

Mother, therefore, has a kind of composite status; this status turns on two kinds of relationship, one of affinity with respect to ego's descent group, if it is patrilineal, and one of consanguinity to ego. Hence she is terminologically 'wife' to her husband, 'mother' to her son.

As mother is affinal to ego's descent group, father's sister is a consanguineal and cannot ordinarily lose her descent group membership. Hence, under no conditions could she possibly be seen as an affinal to ego.

Conversely, as mother is a consanguineal relative for her son, and as her brother is a consanguineal relative to her, mother's brother is, through that series of links, a consanguineal of ego's. And this consanguineal line, since it is 'complementary' to the descent line, is the line of 'complementary filiation'.

Let me clear out immediately the misunderstanding based on Dumont's treatment of kinship terms apart from group structure or behavior.

Dumont's position is not so startling as it may look. Dumont is emphatically concerned with *kinship terminology*, he is not dealing with descent groups as such. Further, kinship terminology has to do with social *categories*. In his reply to Radcliffe-Brown, Dumont (1953b) is explicit; he is not dealing with *behavior*, but with the social definition of categories. There is a difference between kinship terminology and the structure of descent groups or the relation between the prescribed forms of behavior to ways in which kin are categorized. Kinship terminology '. . . is a contellation revolving around the Ego . . . what is here called kin 1as, of course, nothing to do with actual groups, being only an ıbstraction arising from the oppositions; this again centres in Ego. . . . The whole could be called "terminological kin" to avoid ‹onfusion, and opposed to "terminological affines". This is only ι framework which is used and shaped by each group according ‹o its particular institutions' (Dumont, 1953a, p. 37. See also Dumont's (1961a) attack on Gough, where the same position is ‹eiterated).

But this begs the issue. If, for Dumont, kinship terminology is ıot kinship behavior, and if it 'has . . . nothing to do with actual ;roups', and if it yields conclusions which seem contrary to those ιvhich follow if behavior and actual groups are to be considered, ıow are these differences to be explained or reconciled? Dumont ioes not face this issue. The problem is whether or not MoBr can ›e considered an affinal or a consanguineal relative, or both. The ›roblem is whether FaSi is to be considered an affinal or con-ιanguineal relative, or both. The problem is to explain the MoBr-SiSo relationship. The problem is whether these are ‹erminologically affinal or consanguineal relatives. To insist, as Dumont does, that terminology is and must be an ego-centered ιystem is only to raise the question of how the ego-centered ιystem articulates with the system as a total system. One cannot ake shelter behind the assertion that these are different. The ‹ery difference itself is problematic.

Leach in his essay *Rethinking Anthropology* (1962a) seems to ›e showing that the Trobriand father is symbolized as an affine ınd this may contradict what Dumont's Dravidian analysis ‹eems to show with reference to mother. Dumont may be able ‹o show that the Trobriand father is *terminologically* con-ιanguineal if taken from the point of view of his child as ego and ‹hat Leach's symbolic designation of the father as ari affine is ‹tated from the point of view of the wife and her matrilineal ıineage *vis-à-vis* the husband and his influence on the child. Dumont could have considered such a problem in replying to Radcliffe-Brown, but he chose instead to say that he was dealing ıeither with behavior nor with Australian aborigines, a reply ιvhich I find almost totally irrelevant to any significant issue ιvhatever.

53

XIV. What, then, is the relationship of MoBr-SiSo? Is this to be seen as one of affinity, expressing alliance, or as one of complementary filiation?

For Goody (1959), the problem is quite simple. He is able to dispose of Lévi-Strauss in a little over two pages, reduce Dumont to a pale imitation of Lévi-Strauss, dismiss Leach in a phrase or two, and proceed to deal with the MoBr-SiSo relationship '... in West Africa' in terms of the holder-heir conflict. The snatching and ritual stealing of objects by the SiSo is seen as a *residual claim* which he gets from his mother's membership in her natal patrilineal property-holding group. As a member of the group, she has rights in property. But as a woman she can exercise only a few of these rights, and her rights in inheritance are 'residual claims' '... the legitimate sister's son has nevertheless a shadowy claim upon the group by virtue of his mother's position' (p. 82). Leach's disquiet over such terms as 'shadowy claim', 'submerged rights' and 'residual sibling' is not entirely misplaced, in my view. His criticism that descent, in the hands of Fortes, Goody, Gluckman, Gough, becomes a sliding scale, the boundaries of which can never be clearly stipulated, is not without merit. The point is that if the rights of the sister's son over bits of property held by the mother's brother, including perhaps the mother's brother's wife whom sister's son may 'inherit', are rights which are based on the consanguineal tie through his mother, and rights which depend on descent group membership of his mother, then these rights are transmitted exactly as is descent group membership. These are rights, that is, that are based on descent. If this is so, the problem is whether matrilateral filiation is not in this sense a 'descent rule' and so all patrilineal descent systems with matrilateral filiation are by definition double unilineal descent systems. Goody (1961) takes up this problem specifically and tries to break the impasse by saying that true double descent should be defined as a situation in which both matrilineal and patrilineal groups have property-holding functions. That when one group is a property-holding group and the other is not, this should be regarded as a 'unilineal system with complementary descent group' (Goody, 1961).

The outcome is clear for Goody and for Fortes. Descent has to do with group membership. When membership in a corporate group is defined by one or other parent's affiliation, then we can speak of 'unilineal' descent (Fortes, 1959). Goody insists that the group must be a property-holding group, and that the property, to qualify as proper or true double descent, must be real property. Goody's position seems to depend on the assumption that in the long run it is things like food and wealth and power which really count, and if he criticizes Malinowski for reducing extra-familial kinship to intra-familial usages, and Lévi-Strauss for reducing kinship to marriage, it might be said with some grain of truth that property and power are what Goody prefers to reduce things to. (Goody's position seems to have been modified somewhat in his 1962 book.) But the issue is clear. For Fortes, descent means unilineal descent groups. All other systems are systems of filiation, and filiation is universally bilateral. Fortes returns to Rivers's definition of descent as meaning unilineal rules and group membership.

Briefly, then, Goody, following Fortes and Radcliffe-Brown, sees the MoBr-SiSo relationship as one in which residual sibling's rights are transmitted in attenuated form and, therefore, the right of the SiSo to snatch or steal property as a right based on filiation – '. . . a shadowy claim upon the group by virtue of his mother's position'. Leach criticizes the notions of shadowy claim, residual siblings, variable group strength, as basically making the notion of descent meaningless. He, following Lévi-Strauss, sees the claim of the mother's brother on the bridewealth of the sister's daughter as part of a continuing series of affinal exchanges of which the first bridewealth payment for the sister was but an initial act in the exchange. He would see the SiSo rights in the bits and pieces of the MoBr property as the other side of that exchange between allied, affinal groups. This view certainly avoids the involved and uncertain judgements of how shadowy a shadowy claim can be, or how residual a residual sibling may be, or how submerged a submerged right may be. Hence, for him, MoBr-SiSo is an affinal relationship, not a consanguineal one at all. But if it is an affinal relationship one must pose the question, can there be an affinal relationship without alliance? Can there be an affinal relationship between SiSo and MoBr without the structural principle of alliance being 'there' as one equal, if not more significant, structural feature of the system?

55

The problem with respect to bridewealth and marital stability is very much the same. There is no room here to spell it out in particular detail. Briefly, if marital stability depends, in Gluckman's formulation, on variable descent group strength, then the principle of descent is so elastic and so difficult to stipulate as to be virtually useless – in Leach's view. The distinction between consanguinity and descent which Fortes draws, reserving descent for 'group membership' and confining it only to unilineal groups, is such as to make much Oceanic and Southeast Asian material impossible to deal with in the framework of that theory. Leach's position seems to be the orthodox one we have encountered thus far. Bridewealth and marital stability depend on the particular expression of alliance which obtains in the particular society.

XV. We have come a long way from whether Needham does or does not understand the implications of the theory he is following. There is some reason to believe that he does not, but we are not yet in a position to decide. First we must ask what is the role which marriage plays in that theory. Does it merely symbolize alliance, as the exchange of pigs or gongs may do?

For both alliance and descent theory, it is a type of society which is at issue. The segments are constituted by a unilineal descent rule for descent theory as well as for alliance theory. For both alliance and descent theory, the segments are internally differentiated in terms of kinship relations. For alliance theory, the segment is maintained (given its definition in terms of a unilineal descent rule) by its systematic relationship in opposition to other like units and its systematic relationship of marriage with a particular category of kinsmen in the segment to which it is related. This is a scheme, it is a conceptual system which relies on the logical development of a series of dichotomous elements. It is the conceptual definition of the segments and the conceptual stipulation of how they are related which are the nub, the core, of alliance theory.

There are, then, two closely connected issues which create more unnecessary confusion than there need be. One is the issue of how the segments are conceptually defined, and of their 'formal' relationship to each other. The conceptual definition has a 'function', but it is not the function of a 'degree of corporateness' as a concrete state of affairs. Its function consists in its logical implications at a conceptual level. The second issue is the issue of how marriage relates two segments. It 'relates' two segments in that it is a kind of relationship, not an act undertaken by two passionate persons. As a relationship, it is defined in terms precisely opposite to those of descent, the principle in terms of which the solidarity of the descent unit is expressed. And it is one more thing: it is that kind of relationship which explicitly and systematically entails particular categories within each segment and at the same time the entire segment. The relationship between segments is one of exchange; the categories within the segments which represent the systematic nexuses of the linkages are MoBrDa-FaSiSo or perhaps simply cross-cousin. But it is this linkage between categories which are at once categories *within* the descent unit and anchors *between* descent units which constitutes 'marriage'.

Marriage, in this type of segmental system, is not the same thing as it is in a system constituted by unilineal descent units where the same kinship category is not the 'anchor point' *between* descent units. Where a man marries a woman who is until then in no sense a kinswoman, one may perhaps by stretching the term, speak of marriage *creating* an alliance. If the man represents one descent unit, and the woman represents another, and these two units are not already in a set or formal relationship to each other, then that particular marriage may create a bond and reiterate it in another way by the offspring of that union. But the classification of kinsmen within and between the descent units is not such that any particular union merely gives particular value to a relationship which existed beforehand in the classification of the kinship categories and their relationship.

In such a system, the definition of marriage is one which exists only with reference to and depends logically on the definition of the descent units, which in turn is dependent on the classification of kinship categories and aggregations of categories (units). These elements all depend on each other for their logical definition. To take marriage apart from the classification of kinsmen, or the mode of descent apart from the relationship between the segments, or the 'corporateness' of the segments apart from the way in which they are related to each other is simply to distort

57

and to deny their meaning. Marriage in such a system is not exactly the same thing as marriage in another system.

It is this, of course, that Dumont means when he says that Dravidian kinship terminology is an 'expression of marriage', and 'embodies a marriage rule' and so on. The terminology, as a system of classification, is so closely and inextricably articulated with the particular rule, that together they make a kind of unit to which each, apart, simply fails to add up.

What is marriage for a system without 'a positive marriage rule'? This is the innovative, inaugurative relationship which 'creates'. It does, as Fortes has so repeatedly stressed, constitute the core of a system of individuation, relating the child of the marriage to the class of mother's brothers to and through those who are brother to his mother. The exchange between the descent units and the relationship between the descent units is a very different thing. In one system, descent units are already related; in the other, they become related. In one system they are necessarily related in a particular way, in the other they are not necessarily related until they become so.

In one kind of system, therefore, marriage plays one kind of role in the maintenance of the segment, in its definition, and in the definition of within-unit and between-unit relations. In the other kind of system – and this is the crux of one of the matters – it is not marriage so much as exogamy which maintains the definition of the segment, and of its within-unit and between-unit relations. For such a segment it is only exogamy which is necessary; for segments where a marriage rule obtains, it is both exogamy *and* marriage which are crucial elements in the system.

XVI. Two different kinds of system, each made up of identically structured segments, are really at issue. In one system, the segments are articulated into a logically interrelated system by the descent rule, the mode of classification of kinsmen, and the relationship of perpetual alliance between segments. In the other, the segments are defined by the descent rule, exogamy, and the variable bounding of the segments in terms of specific functions (domestic, jural, political, residential, territorial, and so on). This second kind of system consists in the proliferation of segments along genealogical lines.

The first type of system can be called 'segmental', the second 'segmentary'. Marriage, as we have seen, plays a very different structural role in each. But it is not marriage alone which decisively separates the two types.

The segmental and the segmentary are two *types* of a whole society or a whole system. Fortes has defended the segmentary type with skill and intellectual force, but he is defending a *type*. He may sometimes use different names, but he clearly distinguishes this *type* from all others. In his most recent paper, he uses the term 'tribal society', and he remains concerned with 'residual rights'. 'A man has unrestricted rights over his wife's reproductive capacity in virtue of the bride-price he has paid to her father. But she never wholly forfeits her status as her father's daughter. This gives her residual claims on her father's protection and him a lien on her' (Fortes, 1962, p. 63). And Gluckman, in defending his sliding scale of corporateness, protests that he is only talking about a particular type of society.

Needham, in his turn, is defending a *type*; a whole closely articulated construct, but a type as a whole. He calls this 'prescriptive' and names the residual category, non-prescriptive types, 'preferential' and declines to discuss preferential systems. If one compares, as we have, for instance, what has been called 'marriage' in the two different types of society, it is evident that these are hardly the same phenomena, and perhaps should not be called by the same name and certainly should not be the bone of contention which Leach, Gough, and the others make of it. In a segmental system, a condition of perpetual alliance obtains conceptually; in a segmentary system, marriage is but the residuum of exogamy, the mark of the legitimate application of a descent rule, the condition providing for complementary filiation. To call these two things 'marriage' is to say that apples and eggs are both fruit because one is the fruit of a tree, the other of a hen.

In sum, the point of the discussion of this section is to show that the 'segmental type' and the 'segmentary type' do not refer to societies but to models. Any resemblance between these models (the models of Fortes, Leach, Lévi-Strauss, and Needham) and actual societies is wholly irrelevant to the point of this discussion, which is to show that Fortes's model of a 'segmentary' society is a type which is but one part of a typology; that Lévi-Strauss's model of a 'segmental' society is also one type of a typology; that Needham's 'prescriptive' and 'preferential' types are but two types of a typology; and that most of the heat of the discussion among these gentlemen is generated by the lively defense of a particular typology. Only occasionally (Livingstone is an example, Maybury-Lewis is another) has anyone said that the *applicability* of the model to a real society was gravely at fault. In the main, one author has argued that the other's model has features which are inconsistent with the model of the first. Or they have argued that the names for the parts of the model are not used correctly. ('Fortes . . . disguises [affinity] under his expression "complementary filiation". . . .' Leach, 1957a, p. 54).

My distinction between 'segmental' and 'segmentary' thus applies to models, not to societies. But it should not be concluded from this that the models under no circumstances relate or are applicable to real societies. This is perhaps, for some of us, the ultimate concern and the ultimate test.

PART THREE. CHOICE AND NEEDHAM'S TYPOLOGY

XVII. Following Lévi-Strauss, Needham formulates the basic difference between his prescriptive and preferential types in terms of whether ego has any *choice* in marriage. In a prescriptive system, '. . . the emphasis is on the very lack of choice; the category or type of person to be married is precisely determined, and this marriage is obligatory' (Needham, 1962b, p. 9). Leach takes substantially the same position, even to the point of apparently accepting Needham's typology of prescriptive and preferential where it might pay a few short-run polemic dividends (Leach, 1961). Later he elaborates at some length on the significance of choice (Leach, 1962b) and this elaboration is worth considering in detail to see just how the idea of choice operates in these different models.

Leach starts the discussion of double descent with the explicit declaration that he will follow Rivers's definition so that 'descent' means unilineal descent units which are not such that '. . . membership itself is at all times ambiguous' (Leach, 1962b, p. 132). The latter condition he exemplifies in terms of his ownership of shares in the British-American Tobacco Company and the Samoan kin groups called *aiga sa* and *fatelama*.

'. . . in such groups, not only is it the case that membership derives from choice rather than from descent, but the membership itself is at all times ambiguous. In a structure of this kind the potential groupings overlap, so that constantly each individual must ask himself: "Is it more to my advantage to fulfil my obligations towards group *A* or my very similar obligations towards group B?" It is because this ambiguity and choice does not automatically arise in true (that is, in unilineal) descent systems that Fortes and others have found it satisfactory to analyse unilineal descent systems as structures of jural obligation. In contrast, the analysis of any kind of cognatic kinship structure invariably ends by throwing the emphasis upon mechanisms of individual choice . . .' (Leach, 1962b, p. 132b).

Leach then proceeds to argue that

'. . . with a simple unilineal descent . . . each individual is a member by birth of one exclusive segment of the total society and is linked by ties of filiation or of affinity (or perhaps both) with various other analogous segments. While Ego's freedom of action with respect to membership of his own descent group is very severely restricted, his freedom of action with regard to his affinal and filiatory links with other descent groups is ordinarily wide' (Leach, 1962b, p. 132).

Let us begin with Leach's assertion that if ego is permitted to choose between being a member of one group or another, then by virtue of that mode of recruitment – actor's choice as against ascription – the membership of those groups will overlap and be ambiguous.

There is a series of different elements involved which should each be distinguished. First, there is the question of the rules governing membership. Can one belong to one and only one such group, or can membership be multiple?

Second, if multiple membership is possible, can these memberships be simultaneous or must they be successive?

Third, if multiple membership is possible, are the units com-

61

plementary or competitive? That is, from the dialogue of soul-searching which Leach describes for his ego, it would seem that groups A and B both compete for ego's commitment, and each requires the same token of commitment from ego. Ego is trying to resolve this conflict of competing claims by calling on his enlightened self-interest to guide him.

Fourth, if multiple membership is possible, and the units are competitive, do they call for the same or different tokens of commitment? Thus in two groups of like order, each claiming ego's commitment against the claims of the other, one claims ego's strength as a warrior, the other his skill as a farmer. Or the two groups could both call upon ego to contribute his labor.

Finally, there is the time dimension. For what period is membership required; is it single or multiple; for a year, for life, or for no stipulated period?

If the groups are single membership groups, and if, once choice is exercised, it cannot be changed but endures for life, then it is hard to see how the condition of *choice* makes membership in any sense 'ambiguous'. Choice and ascription yield equally unambiguous groups under this set of conditions, so far as I can see.

If the groups are multiple membership groups, and if these are sequential rather than simultaneous (ego belongs in series, first to group A, then B, then C, etc.), again I find it difficult to understand how Leach can claim that the membership of such groups is *by virtue of the matter of choice*, overlapping and ambiguous. It may be that ego's membership in a group is kept secret and so an outsider may not know who belongs and who does not, and an insider may be equally uncertain. Such a condition would surely make the membership of such a set of groups ambiguous. This is not a consequence of *choice*, but of *secrecy*.

If membership is multiple, and by choice, and the units are complementary, as in the case of double descent which Leach describes, then again there need be no ambiguity about membership as a consequence of *choice*, for it is quite clear from the case of double descent (in the pure sense in which Rivers defines descent) that if membership is by choice, or if it is by ascription, the consequences are precisely the same so far as ambiguity of membership is concerned. Within the units of like order – the patrilineal units, for instance – there is no overlapping, of course.

But those who are related to each other patrilineally, may not be related to each other matrilineally, and there is thus considerable overlapping, though there need be no ambiguity, in double descent systems. But if we once start considering double descent we must consider the problem of overlapping from the point of view of every kind of group and classificatory category within the society. It is obvious that there is always overlapping, there are always intersecting categories, and that some system of role segregation is required to integrate and articulate every social system.

It should be quite clear by now that what makes for ambiguous and overlapping membership is not necessarily the mode of recruitment at all. Even if recruitment is prescriptive and without choice, membership can be ambiguous if the criteria in terms of which membership is ascribed are ambiguous. Thus if recruitment is prescriptive on the basis of patrilineal descent and the criteria for establishing paternity are ambiguous, then multiple claims might well obfuscate membership lines.

In the particular form in which he presents it, Leach's argument that the mode of recruitment is closely related to the ambiguity of the membership unit does not stand up. Nevertheless, it seems obvious that in general the mode of recruitment must relate to certain aspects of the structure of the unit and the system within which it occurs.

But here we return to our major theme. The model which Leach uses implicitly here is the model of the segmentary system, and the muddled part of that model is the notion that somehow the segment is not only a conceptual segment, but also in some way a physically distinct and concrete segment. For it is only with a segment so conceived that choice of membership, and frequent changes of membership, and multiple membership may create the kind of ambiguity which Leach describes.

If we turn now to Needham's typology of prescriptive versus preferential, it seems clear why he uses choice as the essential discriminating element between these two types. The problem is that the segmental model requires that units be in an asymmetrical exchange relationship so that if A gives to B, A cannot receive that same kind of item from B, but must receive that kind of item from another unit. Thus, if A is a wife-giving unit, and B a wife-taking unit, then A must take wives from a unit other than B – perhaps unit C. Since the act of 'giving' is constituted by a woman who marries, and the act of 'taking' consists in a man's marriage, then the specification of obligation on the act of the man and the woman is simply another statement of the kind of relationship which obtains between the two units. If a man is *required* to take his wife from a wife-giving unit, there can be no mistake about the kind of relationship which obtains between those two units.

This seems perfectly straightforward and simple. It is true in yet another sense. If units A and B are in a wife-giving to wife-taking relationship, then the rule that a man of B must take his wife from unit A is really nothing more than an injunction that he obey the rules of the relationship between the two units. For him to go elsewhere for a wife would be to repudiate that alliance.

And this too, seems perfectly straightforward and simple. The relationship of alliance between units is the essence of the prescriptive type; it is the fact that the exchange between the units is asymmetric, that what one receives, it cannot return directly.

Indeed, if one can argue that the obligation to marry a particular category is not the precise correlate, at the level of individual action, of the structural relationship of the exchanging units, one may easily argue that the essence of the alliance model is corrupted by using the element of choice as the differentiating characteristic of the two major types. But such an argument seems unwarranted. It seems unwarranted because the guide to action, the imperative by which the men of such a system live, is only the necessary translation into action of the structural relationship of exchange. The requirement to marry MoBrDa is the statement at the level of action of the relationship of asymmetrical alliance between exchanging units.

Or so it would seem, except for two things. The first is that we are comparing the wrong things and so come to the wrong conclusion.

When we say that the system is prescriptive and mean by this '. . . the emphasis is on the very lack of choice; the category or type of person to be married is precisely determined, and this marriage is obligatory' (Needham, 1962, p. 9), we can understand such a statement in contrast to and in contradistinction to some

64

category to which it is opposed. Here prescription is contrasted to choice. We know what a prescription is. It is the obligation to marry MoBrDa in an asymmetrical alliance system. What is 'choice' then? Choice obviously is where ego can marry MoBrDa *or* FaSiDa; or MoMoBrDaDa, or anyone else who pleases him. Look at the array of categories! One against an almost unlimited number.

But is this the proper contrast? Are these indeed the correctly opposed categories? Is MoBrDa in one system in any sense the comparable contrast with MoBrDa, FaSiDa, MoMoBrDaDa and so on in the other system? By some stretch of the imagination it might be, if one had not learned by now the pitfalls of genealogy as against category (Needham, 1962b).

We early learned that in cross-cousin marriage systems the own real daughter of the own real brother of the own real mother in fact was not often married. We then learned that anyone who was 'classified' as mother's brother's daughter was an acceptable bride according to the rules in such cases, and this often included kin types such as mother's mother's brother's daughter's daughter, *and so on.* 'And so on' turned out, on analysis, to include women from certain lines, many of whom could not even trace a genealogical connection to ego, nor bothered to try. Moreover, if their actual genealogical connections prohibited them from being married, a rite could re-classify them into the marriageable category, as for instance is done in some societies like Purum. We learned too from Lévi-Strauss and Needham that although diagrams showed three lines in a circle, actually any given line might take wives from two, three, or four lines and might in turn give wives to two, three, or four lines, so that the chances of actually getting a genealogical category to coincide with marriage or alliance category were fairly slim indeed. And Lévi-Strauss showed how the essence of such a system was that of indirect exchange as opposed to direct exchange. A wife came from a wife-giving unit; a wife was given to a wife-taking unit; the unit which gave must take from elsewhere. Hence the better gloss for this category was 'marriageable woman, i.e. a woman from a wife-giving unit'.

Two very important points now follow. First, for us to think of such a system as a MoBrDa system is wrong, for the category is much more properly translated not by an irrelevant genealogical specification, but rather by such phrases as 'marriageable woman'. Second, the essential element in the system is the asymmetrical alliance.

Having found the correct translations and discarded the inappropriate and inaccurate ones, we may now return to the formula and do some simple substitution. A prescriptive system is one in which ego has no choice, but must marry a 'marriageable woman'. A 'marriageable woman' is a woman from a wife-giving unit. If this is a prescriptive system, what then is the opposite type? What is the contrast?

Is it a system in which ego has a 'choice'? If so, what can that choice consist in? The opposite of a marriageable woman is an unmarriageable woman, or a prohibited woman. Is this the proper opposition? Can we say that a prescriptive system is one in which ego is obliged to marry a woman whom he is permitted to marry and a preferential system one in which ego is permitted to marry a woman who is prohibited? This seems sheer nonsense, but it is to such sheer nonsense that one is led if one starts with a structural problem and tries to define it in terms of individual action (Needham, 1962) on a choice versus no-choice basis.

In all models that we have heard anything about, a man is obliged to marry a marriageable woman and prohibited from marrying a woman of prohibited category. This applies to segmental and segmentary models alike. A woman who is not marriageable is one to whom the incest taboo applies. This too applies in segmentary as well as segmental models.

In alliance theory as well as in descent theory, then, ego must marry a permitted and not a prohibited woman. In alliance theory a permitted woman is defined as one who comes from or who is a member of a wife-giving unit; in descent theory she is one who is from any unit other than ego's, since in that model units are not in an alliance relationship with each other.

To specify that in one system choice is permitted and in the other system it is precluded is to confound two different levels of analysis and to fail to deal with the categories in terms of their proper conceptual definition. But it is one more thing, and this perhaps is its gravest error: it is essentially to nullify and confound most of the clarification which Lévi-Strauss, Needham, and Leach have all contributed to this question.

It is fair to say that what started out as the study of cross-cousin marriage has made sense in proportion to the degree to which we have gotten away from genealogical cross-cousins. The more our terminology has clung to the traditional names, like MoBrDa and FaSiDa, the more confused the problem has become.

This brings me to the final point in this connection. When the definition of the system as a system is stated in terms of the conditions under which an individual may act, it does so within the context of a given structure. The word 'choice' in English takes as its focus the problem of the individual's action within the framework of a particular structure of the situation, and this structure is treated as given. Hence, it is a misplaced definition so far as the analysis of structure is concerned to discriminate two structures in terms of individual choice. The models are *systemic* models, they are not usable as models of situations within which actors choose among alternate courses. We are concerned with the question 'How is this system structured?' not with the question 'Given this structure, how can a man pick his way through it?' We are concerned with the question 'What is the structure of the relationship between segments?' not with the question 'Is a man allowed to marry his cousin?'

Needham's distinction between his prescriptive and preferential types is thus, from the point of view of alliance theory, untenable when it is stated in terms of choice. In both prescriptive and preferential systems, men are obliged to marry marriageable women and prohibited from marrying prohibited women. It is the definition of who is in the category of marriageable women which differs, not whether there is choice; it is how the lines are related, not whom the men are free to marry.

XVIII. The difficulties of dealing with types are clear, but they are easily forgotten. Just what is the 'type'? Is it a Weberian 'ideal type'? Is it an analytic construct which the anthropologist finds pedagogically useful? Is it a point on an evolutionary scale like 'preliterate', or 'use of fossil fuels'? Is it a summary of the most frequently encountered characteristics in a finite array of items

67

that corresponds to no one concrete case? What function has the segmentary type in Fortes's thinking or in his scheme of things? For Dumont, is it only a way of dividing those societies where alliance theory seems to hold from those in which it does not? Typologies have been used for more trivial purposes than these in the history of anthropology.

The difficulties of dealing with types are clear, but Needham's work is an illuminating instance of some of the pitfalls.

In 1956 he said, 'The greatest difficulty of all, however, is that we do not know what the facts are. There is no adequate account of unilateral cross-cousin marriage anywhere in the literature; and, until there is, there can be no great theoretical progress' (Needham, 1956, p. 108).

As if to contradict this grave pronouncement, Needham proceeded to publish more than 16 papers and a short book on this subject, discussing Eastern Sumba, Purum, Vaiphei, Kom, Lamet, Chawte, Aimol, Siriono, and Wikmunkan at greater or lesser length. These have all been literary analyses (Needham, 1957) of material largely available when Needham wrote his pronouncement of 1956.

The remarkable thing about the ethnography available to Needham up to 1956 (and possibly even now) is that according to him it has all been plagued by a host of errors made by the ethnographers. The ethnographers have made mistakes and failed to provide crucial information. For instance, Needham feels that there is enough evidence to show that the Siriono are matrilineal, but that the ethnographer failed to note it (Needham, 1961, 1962, p. 64; Coult, 1962; Needham, 1963b). For the Wikmunkan, 'I must say, too, that I should prefer to rely on his reports [those of Professor D. F. Thomson], for reasons which my analysis makes plain, than on those of the late Miss McConnell' (Needham, 1963b, p. 145). '. . . on this point Das' ethnography is contradictory and that the categorized totals of marriages above are wrong' (Needham, 1958a, p. 81). 'These are consistent with a lineal descent system, and given the general patrilineal character of Kuki society we may safely assume that the Vaiphei are patrilineal also' (Needham, 1959a, p. 401). 'ZS (ws) cannot be interpreted in this way, and is apparently incorrect' (Needham, 1960b, p. 103). Indeed, pages 102-104 of this paper are almost entirely devoted to sorting out the presumed inconsistencies reported by the ethnographer.

Errors and inadequacies of ethnographers are one side of the coin. The other side shows up when others have re-analyzed some of the same data. Needham's presentation can only then be appreciated for the true elegance and order which it imposes on the data. A closer look at the Purum, for instance, makes it appear to fit only very loosely into Needham's type (White, 1963, pp. 130-145; Leaf, 1963). A closer look at Lamet does not yield so neat a picture as one might have expected from Needham's 1960b paper. The material on the Pende is not so simply and decisively and undebatably 'preferential' as Needham claims, nor is the case of the Tismulan quite so clear (Needham, 1963, p. 58; Lane, 1962b).

The issue is simple. The inconsistencies, errors, inadequacies may in fact be inconsistencies, errors, inadequacies of the fieldwork and/or the reporting. Ethnographers *do* make mistakes. Informants *do* get their facts wrong. No one in the field can check every single bit of information he has collected. No ethnographer claims to infallibility.

The question, then, is this: Is this particular bit an inconsistency, an error in the data or not? Needham takes the ethnographic report and matches it against his model, his type. Every deviation of the ethnography from one or another element in the type suggests to Needham that *the ethnography* is wrong in one way or another. Needham never alters his type to accommodate the ethnography. Needham never changes his model to fit the data.

It seems, therefore, that Needham expects to find, free in nature, a concrete system which precisely replicates his type. If the type has characteristics X, Y, and Z in that order, then Needham expects to find that the Purum or the Lamet have characteristics X, Y, and Z in that order. Needham works with this type as if it were a kind of 'missing link', a real entity which a really good ethnographer who is a good hunter will be able to find – on Sumba perhaps, or among the Old Kuki. Once it is found we will *see* '. . . how the system really works' (Needham, 1958c, p. 323).

What else can we understand by such phrases as '. . . a prescriptive alliance system based on exclusive patrilateral cross-cousin marriage not only does not exist, but on both formal and pragmatic grounds cannot exist – and *this* is the answer to the problem of unilateral "choice" ' (Needham, 1962a, p. 118). To our astonishment, we are now told that the system cannot exist as a social system if, in fact, it cannot work. Livingston's demonstration that the Purum system could not actually work with the numbers of people reported now seems to be acknowledged to be true and just and the whole attack on it (Needham, 1960h) misconceived.

At what level does the system *exist*? For Needham, 'the system' seems to exist at the concrete level, at the manifest level, at the level of the explicit institutionalization of the categories and the rules relating those categories. There *must* be a prohibition on FaSiDa and a requirement to marry MoBrDa; these *must* be in unilineal descent units; MoBrDa *must be* terminologically distinguished from FaSiDa, etc. Any variation in the report is an error in the ethnography, not in the model.

For Needham, a society (Purum, Pende, Tismulan) is prescriptive *or* it is preferential. Needham can provide a list of those which are concretely and wholly in one or the other classification (Needham, 1962a, pp. 55-57).

Contrast this position with that of Lévi-Strauss. For the latter 'the system' is far more subtle. It exists and it is real. But its existence is only roughly manifest in the concrete categories and the socially institutionalized rules for relating these categories. Time, ecology, and a variety of factors affect the concrete manifestation of the principles.

Needham's typology is one of whole, concrete entities. If they exist as such, Needham feels that they ought to be discoverable and when they are found, they ought to be 'perfect crystals', so to speak. It seems apparent that Needham who has been to Sumba, Sarawak, and Malaya has not even been able to find these perfect specimens himself.

Needham's passionate dedication to his concrete types leads him into absurdities, into denying the existence of certain data which seem undeniable. His repeated assertions that patrilateral prescriptive systems 'cannot exist' (Needham, 1962, p. 118) can only be maintained if he insists on seeing a perfect specimen which, in its ethnographic report, is even more perfect than the matrilateral cases which have been so imperfectly reported. In addition to the Pende and Tismulan (Lane, 1962b), Salisbury's Siane (Salisbury, 1962), the Busuma, Iatmul, and perhaps others seem fit to the models advanced, provided there is no insistence on the kind of perfection in their concrete manifestation which Needham demands. Needham's effort to force the Siorono into a unilineal descent system because it has Crow-type terms is another example of the absurdity his typology requires of him. Needham feels that a proper alliance system cannot exist in the absence of unilineal descent groups. That Yalman's Sinhalese manage without unilineal descent groups either proves that Yalman (like Holmberg) simply failed to see what must have been there, or that this is, in fact, like the Pende and Tismulan, really a case in the other category – preferential – and can therefore be dismissed from consideration.

There is, however, still another and perhaps more important error that Needham commits by the use of his concrete types: this is the implicit assumption that each social norm and rule has one and only one function and, because each norm and rule has only one function, its particular shape can be *wholly* determined or explained by that function. The rules which categorize kinsmen, Needham implies, function so to order the social universe as to constitute and maintain a system of asymmetrical alliance. For it is Needham's assumption that kinship terms function only as the names by which social categories bearing a single mode of relationship with each other are designated.

Yet it seems clear that kinship terms have other functions than that of designating the categories to be related in an asymmetric alliance system. Among the Lamet or the Purum, for example, there may very well exist a system of asymmetric alliance, although the kinship terms may not be perfectly concordant with that system. Other loosely related systems occur too; subsystems of variant modes may occur within the major framework; alternate modes of designation and categorization may occur. As I have tried to show elsewhere (Schneider & Homans, 1955), the alternate terms of American kinship are, on the one hand, consistent with a single, overall pattern, yet vary within the framework of that pattern, whereas the Zuñi treatment of

71

FaSiDa as either FaSi or ESi varies across the lines of a basic framework (Schneider & Roberts, 1956). Alternate terms, as an order of data from a wide variety of different kinds of societies, from America to Zulu, from Zuñi to Truk, constitute the decisive bit of evidence against any simple, unicausal view of the determination of a terminological pattern.

In short, Needham's model differs in certain important respects from those of Leach and Lévi-Strauss. Needham expects that his model is a close approximation of the concrete shape and content of concrete societies. He thus expects to find a society which approximates in the closest terms the model he has built. Like the descent theory model of the segmentary system, Needham's prescriptive and preferential types are concrete types, they have exact counterparts in nature. So he has examined the literature and himself gone into the field. He has been able to show a large number of gaps and mistakes in the ethnographic reports because his model is perfect, but the work of the ethnographers is not. Though he speaks of principles at times, and though ideas like dualism and reciprocity are present in his work, he has moved, relentlessly almost, into the positivist position from which at first he had fled along with Lévi-Strauss. But he has backed into it at the end. His treatment of kinship terms is another example of this, for he acts as if the kin term system was a system determined entirely by the need to name categories whose only significance is their operation in a system of prescriptive alliance.

PART FOUR. CONCLUSION

XIX. I have set up what might seem to be two types; alliance theory and descent theory. By alliance theory I mean only what Lévi-Strauss, Leach, Needham, or Dumont have said, and by descent theory what Fortes, Goody, Gough, or Gluckman have said.

I do not pretend that all is peace and harmony within the ranks of those I group together. Early in Section IV, I quoted Needham on his differences with Lévi-Strauss and I have pointed out other differences when they seem relevant. I do not believe that Fortes agrees with everything which Goody has written, or vice versa.

I do not think that there is a 'thing' or a 'school' or a specific

72

body of doctrine apart from what each person has said. I have used the names 'alliance theory' and 'descent theory' on Dumont's suggestion and these words only mean that in certain carefully designated respects, Lévi-Strauss, Leach, Dumont, and Needham are in general agreement with each other and disagree with Fortes, Goody, Gough, and Gluckman, who are in closer agreement with each other on specific points than with the former.

My concern has been with the models these people use, with their internal consistency, and with certain of the implicit elements in the models. I have not tried to fit their models to the ethnographic facts. That is an entirely different problem from the one I have tried to deal with here.

The major criticism I have offered is that both the alliance theorists and the descent theorists have a tendency toward the development and propagation of whole-system, over-simple typologies. There has been a tendency to erect a typology and to defend it to the death against all comers; even against the facts where these prove stubborn.

This tendency toward the total-system typology is unevenly distributed among the theorists. Fortes is mildly addicted to his practice; Needham has a severe, and perhaps fatal case of it. Leach, despite his eloquent sermons (Leach, 1962a), is not entirely free of this vice himself (Leach, 1961).

I suspect that the addiction to such fruitless whole-system typologies is related to polemic tendencies. The greater the author's commitment to polemic goals, the greater the exaggeration into which he is forced, the greater the extremes of one sort or another he finds himself using, the greater the oversimplification of idea and expression. The time when Leach seems to accept the prescriptive-preferential typology as a serious possibility is when he is angrily after the scalp of Barbara Lane (Leach, 1961). In his more reasonable moments, he is not too seriously taken with that particular device for the classification of ethnographic butterflies (Leach, 1962a). The fact that Lane made some fair, cogent and important points may or may not be related to the magnitude of Leach's polemic explosion (also see Needham, 1963d).

One of the most serious difficulties with the descent theory model, and a difficulty of which the alliance theory model is not entirely free, is the failure to distinguish the segment as a conceptual entity from the segment as a concrete, physical entity in the total system.

I have tried to suggest in Sections X and XVI that there may be a single limiting case where the segment as a conceptual as well as a concrete entity would seem to be a workable model, but in fact, of course, even that model makes no sense. Even if the segment is totally self-sufficient except for a single function – that is, it must marry outside and thus must be linked by marriage with other like segments – that one link turns out, on closer inspection, to consist in a veritable network of highly differentiated modes of relationship. For the marriage, if it does not entail co-residence (and if it entails co-residence, the segment is not physically distinct), must at least entail visiting husbands and/or visiting wives, and these in turn, related to their children as well as their agnates, set up an intricate network of filiative bonds, and these, in their turn, proliferate into gift exchanges, favors, claims and counter claims, agnates versus affines, and the warmth of the mother's brother for his sister's son and daughter. Leach's down-to-earth discussion of local descent lines as the *real* things and not diagram lines, gives this good, hard feeling of a segment as a concrete entity (Leach, 1951). Evans-Pritchard's classic treatment of the Nuer (Evans-Pritchard, 1940) is one of the early statements of this confusion, for it is evident when Evans-Pritchard is faced with the odd fact that, although the lineages are territorial units, and although they seem to be as patrilineal as patrilineal can be, descent is traced through women and many people live matrilocally. In order to reconcile these apparent contradictions, we were treated to those special gems of paradoxical obfuscation for which Evans-Pritchard is justly famous, such as the remark that '. . . it is the clear, consistent, and deeply rooted lineage structure of the Nuer which permits persons and families to move about and attach themselves freely . . . to whatever community they choose by whatever cognatic or affinal tie they find it convenient to emphasize . . .' (Evans-Pritchard, 1951, p. 28) or, to go it one better, 'It would seem it may be partly just because the agnatic principle is unchallenged in Nuer society that the tracing of descent through women is so

74

prominent and matrilocality so prevalent' (Evans-Pritchard, 1951, p. 28).

The failure clearly to distinguish the segment as a conceptual entity from its concrete counterpart as a group leads to the special requirement that its modes of recruitment, and the rules governing membership, must be such as to permit the segment to be a physically distinct entity – perhaps, even, to assemble in its full force for some ceremony or other. Therefore, that mode of recruitment to group membership which yields a distinct, concrete entity should not be confused with others. The unilineal descent rule is believed to be such a mode of recruitment *par excellence*, for this allocates a whole man to a group (see Section X above). In order, therefore, to protect the model of a segment as a physically distinct entity, unilineal descent is separated from all other modes of recruitment and we are left with a new and wholly odd definition of descent as only the unilineal form; everything else must be called by some other name.

I find it strange and perverse that Rivers, Fortes, and Leach insist that it is not even possible to say that there are two different kinds of descent rules, one unilineal, the other not; that the one yields unambiguous group boundaries, the other yields ambiguous group boundaries; the one yields what are regarded as 'true social segments', the other not. Rivers, Fortes, and Leach (Leach, 1962b) require that we must not even call that second kind of descent 'descent'. We must banish its very name! As if calling it by another name would in fact banish it.

I have suggested, therefore, but perhaps too obliquely, that this is a perversion of the notion of descent, undertaken in the interest of protecting a typology of segmentary system, and of a model of a segment which is untenable to begin with. As an analytic scheme, it is misleading and thus harmful rather than useless.

Closely connected with this model of a segment is the notion that those forms of membership rule which permit any choice are different and yield different kinds of segment or group from those where no choice is permitted; that is, where the rule is ascriptive. Choice comes into the segmentary system model as an element opposed to ascription by 'true' unilineal descent, and it has a contrasting effect on group structure as well. Where choice is per-

David M. Schneider

mitted, it is believed that group boundaries are ambiguous and one must expect to encounter the entertaining dialogues which Leach offers us, of people patiently trying to unravel the tangled strands of their affiliation with different groups in terms of their enlightened self-interest (Leach, 1962b). I have tried to show that this is nonsense; that boundaries are ambiguous when the criteria for membership are ambiguous, not when choice is involved. I outlined a series of different kinds of choice condition, showing that the group boundary problem in each case is anything but ambiguous – indeed, quite as clear as in the purest case of 'true' (unilineal) descent.

In this section (XVII), I made the same case against Needham's use of choice as the criterion for distinguishing his prescriptive from his preferential types. My argument here was that Needham had confused his oppositional categories. In both preferential and prescriptive systems ego is obliged to marry a marriageable woman; he has no choice about that in either type, and the word 'choice' is misapplied here. In Needham's prescriptive type, the marriageable woman comes from a wife-giving unit whereas in the preferential type she does not, and this is what distinguishes Needham's two types, not the question of choice. (That the whole typology of preferential versus prescriptive is untenable for other reasons as well is beside the point here, which is that the use of choice only further confounds these issues.)

The point that choice is simply not a structurally relevant category applies to Lévi-Strauss's use of it too, for choice is basically a statement of an actor's course of action when the structure of the situation is taken as given. Lévi-Strauss, Needham, Leach, Fortes at least, and Gluckman (1950; see also Schneider, 1953a) in some of his writings, are primarily concerned with structure, not with individual action within the context of a structure. Choice does not say anything of significance or use about structure. This is what Parsons has properly called the confusion between the actor as the point of reference and the system as the object of reference.

I did not go into the matter in detail, but the problem of the ambiguity of boundaries, the rule of descent, the mode of recruitment are all closely linked with the problem of whether an alliance system requires unilineal descent. Yalman's paper on the

Sinhalese is of importance in two respects. First, it is a case where the system of alliance is perfectly clear, and where it works perfectly well without having, what Fortes and Leach insist be called 'true' or unilineal descent. The opposition between affinity and consanguinity, in the form of the unilineal segment or descent group, does not stand up as a necessary condition to such systems if Yalman's account is to be relied on. Ego-oriented systems do not lead to mires of confusion and boundary-ambiguity as Leach so vehemently claims. The second point of relevance is, of course, Needham's desperate efforts to make unilineal systems out of the Siriono and the Vaiphei, for instance. His failure to deal with the Sinhalese case in this respect is significant.

And this brings us back to the first major criticism. Instead of working with models made up of distinct pieces which are arranged and re-arranged into a variety of different permutations and combinations, Needham has saddled himself with a total-system model. Each little piece must be linked with every other little piece in a particular way to make a perfect constellation of a whole, crystal-clear system. The system must be lineal; the kin terms must be consistent with (patrilineal or matrilineal) lineal systems; the exchange units must be descent units, etc., etc., etc. So if the Siriono are not said to be matrilineal, then Holmberg must be wrong because as a total-system type, every piece must be in its proper place. Never once are we shown why a system, to be a prescriptive system, as a whole system, must be unilineal; why FaSiDa must be distinguished from MoBrDa.

Here Leach makes more sense than Needham. Where Needham is chained to his types, Leach is able to push alliance theory pieces as far as they can go without worrying about what is happening to a typology. Because of this, the structural role of marriage in segmentary systems now requires careful re-examination and restatement; the notion of filiation must be restated and redefined, though I expect it will survive; the sliding scale of corporateness, the residual rights and submerged rights, and imprecisely defined 'strengths' are now shown to be in dire need of repair. At the same time, by using Leach's technique of pushing parts of the alliance theory model into new and untried areas, clear defects in that model itself have become apparent. I have already referred to Yalman's Sinhalese kindred; Dumont

77

has already noted the problems raised by Barth's FaBrDa marriage material and his Pathan work.

Let me be very clear on this problem. The model which is a total-system model, which yields a typology, and where there is no specific aim or purpose for which that typology is constructed is, I think, demonstrably a mistake. Too much time, effort, and energy are spent in mending the model, in protecting it from new data, in insuring its survival against attacks. It is too late in the history of the social sciences to think we can go out among societies and, by keeping our eyes open, sort them into their natural classes. It is not possible to operate like those in the story of the blind men and the elephant and hope that if only we can put enough blind men on the elephant we will get a good factual description of the beast – the total elephant. A typology is for a problem, it is not for sorting of concrete societies into unchangeable, inherent, inalienable categories. (I agree completely with Leach in this matter, as should be clear by now (Leach, 1962a).)

Instead of typologies we need a series of relevant elements, like descent, classification, exchange, residence, filiation, marriage, and so on; these need to be rigorously defined as analytic categories and then combined and recombined into various combinations and permutations, in different sizes, shapes, constellations.

The model of defined parts can be constructed with, or without, Lévi-Strauss's kind of intellectualist or Hegelian assumptions, or the kind of positivism which Fortes requires. I have dwelt somewhat longer on some of the positivist difficulties than on the intellectualist problems, but each has its fair share of problems.

Finally, there is one point which needs stressing and which I only touched on. Alliance theory as a theory is capable of dealing with the symbol system as a system apart from, yet related to, the network of social relations. It has a way of dealing with problems of meaning which the descent theory of Radcliffe-Brown and Fortes does not have. Alliance theory, in the footsteps of Durkheim here as elsewhere, is cognizant of the importance of how the actor conceptualizes the structure ('how the natives think' perhaps) and the difference between this conceptualization and an outsider's analytic construct of the system as a system. Where Radcliffe-Brown rejected culture in favor of what he was pleased to call structure, and where Leach in an earlier work separated out cultural ornaments, alliance theorists have brought culture and social structure into an ordered relationship which even Needham's gross manipulations of the Purum data cannot obscure.

NOTES

1. Since its presentation to the Cambridge Conference, I have added Sections XVII, XVIII, and XIX, clarified minor portions of the argument, and profited from the suggestions of Paul W. Friedrich, F. K. Lehman, Melford Spiro, Richard F. Salisbury, and Fred Eggan. Professor Claude Lévi-Strauss made some helpful suggestions, which led me to delete some of the material from the earlier draft which was incorrect or unclear. In particular, he pointed out that I had misunderstood him if I regarded him as an 'idealist' in the sense of treating ideas as such as fundamental to social life. Rather, if I understand his position correctly now, he regards himself as an 'intellectualist' in the sense that *both* ideas and action derive from qualities of mind, and that neither action nor ideas has any particular priority. Murphy (1963) has described this most accurately, I think. I had hoped to revise and greatly expand Section II, discussing in detail the problems raised by Homans's and Lévi-Strauss's psychological reductionism and their emphasis on the actor's view of the system as distinct from the observer's view. But all of this proved another very long essay for which space was not provided here.

2. In fact, of course, Evans-Pritchard seems to have implied very strongly that it was the *idea* of the lineage quite as much as the actual groups; for it becomes apparent on close inspection that the lineages as actual groups are not nearly so enduring, nor so concrete, nor so strongly localized as might be inferred from a hasty reading of his monograph.

3. I have used the term 'corporate unit', since the definition of the word 'group' and its associations and meanings are so problematic. A modern nation has a corporate identity, but it is not possible for it to *act* in unison and concert and as a physically corporate group in the sense, let us say, of a small village assembling in its entirety for a religious ritual (Schneider, 1961).

ACKNOWLEDGEMENTS

Thanks are due to the following for permission to quote passages from published works:

Beacon Press, New York, and Merlin Press, London, in respect of *Totemism* by C. Lévi-Strauss, translated by Rodney Needham; the Editor of *Bijdragen tot de Taal-, Land-, en Volkenkunde* in respect of 'On Manipulated Sociological Models' by C. Lévi-Strauss and 'A Structural Analysis of Aimol Society' by Rodney Needham; Dr E. R. Leach and the Council of the Royal Anthropological Institute of Great Britain and Ireland in respect of 'On Certain Unconsidered Aspects of Double Descent Systems', *Man*, **62**, by E. R. Leach; The University of Chicago Press in respect of *Structure and Sentiment: A Test Case in Social Anthropology* by Rodney Needham, © 1962 by the University of Chicago.

REFERENCES

Names of journals are abbreviated as follows:
AA American Anthropologist
Bijdragen Bijdragen tot de taal-, land-, en volkenkunde
JPS Journal of the Polynesian Society
JRAI Journal of the Royal Anthropological Institute
SWJ Southwestern Journal of Anthropology

BEATTIE, J. H. M. 1957-58. Nyoro Kinship, Marriage and Affinity. *Africa* **27, 28.**

COULT, A. D. 1962. An Analysis of Needham's Critique of the Homans-Schneider Theory. *SWJ* **18.**

DE JOSSELIN DE JONG, J. P. B. 1952. *Lévi-Strauss' Theory on Kinship and Marriage.* Mededelingen van het Rijksmuseum voor Volkenkunde.

DUMONT, L. 1950. Kinship and Alliance among the Pramalai Kallar. *Eastern Anthropologist* **4.**

—— 1953a. The Dravidian Kinship Terminology as an Expression of Marriage. *Man* **53,** No. 54.

—— 1953b. Dravidian Kinship Terminology. *Man* **53,** No. 224.

—— 1957a. Hierarchy and Marriage Alliance in South Indian Kinship. *Occ. Pap. Roy. Anthrop. Inst.* No. 12.

—— 1957b. *Une Sous-caste de l'Inde du Sud.* Paris: Mouton.

—— 1959. A Structural Definition of a Folk Deity of Tamil Nad: Aiyanar, the Lord. *Contributions to Indian Sociology,* **3.**

—— 1960. Le mariage secondaire dans l'Inde du Nord. 6th Int. Congress Anthropology, Vol. 2.

—— 1961a. Descent, Filiation and Affinity. *Man* **61,** No. 11.

—— 1961b. Marriage in India: The Present State of the Question. *Contributions to Indian Sociology* **5.**

—— 1961c. Caste, Racism and 'Stratification': Reflections of a Social Anthropologist. *Contributions to Indian Sociology* **5.**

—— 1961d. Les Mariages Nayar Comme Faits Indiens, *L'Homme,* **1, 1.**

—— 1962. Le Vocabulaire de Parenté dans l'Inde du Nord. *L'Homme,* **2.**

DURKHEIM, E. 1947. *The Division of Labor in Society.* Glencoe, Ill.: The Free Press.

—— 1951. *Suicide.* Glencoe, Ill.: The Free Press.

EPLING, P. J. 1961. A Note on Njamal Kin-term Usage. *Man* **61**, No. 184.

EVANS-PRITCHARD, E. E. 1940. *The Nuer*. Oxford: Clarendon Press.
—— 1951. *Kinship and Marriage Among the Nuer*. Oxford: Clarendon Press.

FIRTH, R. 1957. A Note on Descent Groups in Polynesia. *Man* **57**, No. 2.

FORTES, M. 1953. The Structure of Unilineal Descent Groups. *AA* **55**.
—— 1959. Descent, Filiation, and Affinity. *Man* **59**, Nos. 309, 331.
—— 1962. Ritual and Office in Tribal Society. In Gluckman, M. (ed.), *Essays on the Ritual of Social Relations*. Manchester: Manchester University Press.

FORTUNE, R. R. 1933. A Note on Some Forms of Kinship Structure. *Oceania* **4**.

FREEMAN, J. D. 1961. On the Concept of the Kindred. *JRAI* **91**.

GLUCKMAN, M. 1950. Kinship and Marriage among the Lozi . . . and Zulu. In Radcliffe-Brown, A. R. and Forde, C. D., *African Systems of Kinship and Marriage*. London: Oxford University Press.

GOODENOUGH, W. 1955. A Problem in Malayo-Polynesian Social Organization. *AA* **57**.

GOODY, J. 1959. The Mother's Brother and the Sister's Son in West Africa. *JRAI* **89**.
—— 1961. The Classification of Double Descent Systems. *Current Anthrop.* **2**.
—— 1962. *Death, Property, and the Ancestors*. Stanford: Stanford University Press; London: Tavistock Publications.

GOUGH, E. K. 1952. Changing Kinship Usages in the Setting of Political and Economic Change Among the Nayars of Malabar. *JRAI* **82**.
—— 1955. Female Initiation Rites on the Malabar Coast. *JRAI* **85**.
—— 1956. Brahmin Kinship in a Tamil Village. *AA* **58**.
—— 1959. The Nayars and the Definition of Marriage. *JRAI* **89**.

HOMANS, G. C. 1962. *Sentiments and Activities*. New York: Free Press.

KROEBER, A. L. 1917. California Kinship Terminologies. *Univ. Calif. Public. in Amer. Archaeol. and Ethnol.* **12**.
—— 1948. *Anthropology*. New York: Harcourt, Brace.

LANE, B. S. 1960. Varieties of Cross-Cousin Marriage and Incest Taboos: Structure and Causality. In Dole, G. & Carneiro, R., *Essays in the Science of Society*. New York: Crowell.

LANE, B. S. 1961. Structural Contrasts Between Symmetric and Asymmetric Marriage Systems: A Fallacy. *SWJ* **17**.

81

F

LANE, R. & LANE, B. 1956. A Reinterpretation of the 'Anomalous' Six-Section Marriage System of Ambrym, New Hebrides. *SWJ* 12.

—— 1958. The Evolution of Ambrym Kinship. *SWJ* 14.

—— 1959. On the Development of Dakota-Iroquois and Crow-Omaha Kinship Terminologies. *SWJ* 15.

—— 1961. A Reconsideration of Malayo-Polynesian Social Organization. *AA* 63.

—— 1962a. Implicit Double Descent in South Australia and the Northeastern New Hebrides. *Ethnology* I.

—— 1962b. Patrilateral Cross-Cousin Marriage. *Ethnology* I.

LEACH, E. R. 1951. The Structural Implications of Matrilateral Cross-Cousin Marriage. *JRAI* 81.

—— 1957a. Aspects of Bridewealth and Marriage Stability among the Kachin and Lakher. *Man* 57.

—— 1957b. On Asymmetrical Marriage Systems. *AA* 59.

—— 1958. Concerning Trobriand Clans and the Kinship Category Tabu. In Goody, J. (ed.), *The Developmental Cycle in Domestic Groups*. Cambridge Papers in Social Anthropology, 1.

—— 1959. Social Change and Primitive Law. *AA* 61.

—— 1960. The Sinhalese of the Dry Zone of Northern Ceylon. In Murdock, G. P. (ed.), *Social Structure of Southeast Asia*. Viking Fund Pubs. 29. Chicago: Quadrangle.

—— 1961. Asymmetric Marriage Rules, Status Difference, and Direct Reciprocity. *SWJ* 17.

—— 1962a. *Rethinking Anthropology*. London: Athlone Press.

—— 1962b. On Certain Unconsidered Aspects of Double Descent Systems. *Man* 62, 214.

LEAF, M. 1963. 'Age' in Purum Social Structure. M.A. Thesis, Univ. of Chicago.

LEHMAN, F. K. 1963. *The Structure of Chin Society*. Illinois Studies in Anthropology No. 3.

LÉVI-STRAUSS, C. 1945. L'Analyse structurale en linguistique et en anthropologie. *Word* 1 (also in *Anthropologie Structurale*, 1958).

—— 1949. *Les Structures élémentaires de la parenté*. Paris: Presses Universitaires de France.

—— 1953. Social Structure. In Kroeber, A. L. (ed.), *Anthropology Today*. Chicago: University of Chicago Press.

—— 1955. The Structural Study of Myth. *J. Am. Folklore* 68.

—— 1956. Les Organisations dualistes existent-elles? *Bijdragen* 112.

—— 1960. On Manipulated Sociological Models. *Bijdragen* 116.

—— 1962a. *Le Totemisme aujourd'hui*. Paris: Presses Universitaires. (Trans. Needham, R., as *Totemism*. Boston: Beacon, 1963.)

— 1962b. *La pensée sauvage*. Paris: Plon.

LIVINGSTONE, F. A. 1959a. A Formal Analysis of Prescriptive Marriage Systems Among the Australian Aborigines. *SWJ* **15**.

— 1959b. A Further Analysis of Purum Social Structure. *AA* **61**.

MAUSS, M. 1954. *The Gift*. Trs. I. Cunnison, London: Cohen & West.

MAYBURY-LEWIS, D. 1960. The Analysis of Dual Organizations. *Bijdragen* **116**.

MURDOCK, G. P. 1949. *Social Structure*. New York: Macmillan.

— 1960. *Social Structure in S.E. Asia*. Viking Fund Pubs. No. 29. Chicago: Quadrangle.

MURPHY, R. F. 1963. On Zen Marxism: Filiation and Alliance. *Man* **63**, 21.

NEEDHAM, R. 1954a. Reference to the Dead among the Penan. *Man* **54**.

— 1954b. The System of Teknonyms and Death-names of the Penan. *SWJ* **10**.

— 1954c. A Penan Mourning-Usage. *Bijdragen* **110**.

— 1955. A Note on some Murut Kinship Terms. *J. Mal. Br. R. Asiatic Soc.* **28**.

— 1956a. Ethnographic Notes on the Siwang of Central Malaya. *J. Mal. Br. R. Asiatic Soc.* **29**.

— 1956b. Review of Homans and Schneider. *Am. J. Sociology* **66**.

— 1956c. A Note on Kinship and Marriage on Pantara. *Bijdragen* **112**.

— 1957. Circulating Connubium in Eastern Sumba. A Literary Analysis. *Bijdragen* **113**.

— 1958a. A Structural Analysis of Purum Society. *AA* **60**.

— 1958b. The Formal Analysis of Prescriptive Patrilateral Cross-Cousin Marriage. *SWJ* **14**.

— 1958c. Review of Dumont 'Une Sous-caste . . .'. *Bijdragen* **114**.

— 1959a. Vaiphei Social Structure. *SWJ* **15**.

— 1959b. An Analytical Note on the Kom of Manipur. *Ethnos* **3-4**.

— 1959c. Mourning-Terms. *Bijdragen* **115**.

— 1960a. Lineal Equations in a Two-section System. *JPS* **69**.

— 1960b. Alliance and Classification among the Lamet. *Sociologus* **10**.

— 1960c. Chawte Social Structure. *AA* **62**.

— 1960d. A Structural Analysis of Aimol Society. *Bijdragen* **116**.

— 1960e. Patrilateral Prescriptive Alliance and the Ungarinyin. *SWJ* **16**.

— 1960f. The Left Hand of the Mugwe. *Africa* **30**.

NEEDHAM, R. 1960g. Jataka, Pancatantra and Kodi Fables. *Bijdragen* **116**.

—— 1960h. Structure and Change in Asymmetric Alliance. *AA* **62**.

—— 1961a. Notes on the Analysis of Asymmetric Alliance. *Bijdragen* **117**.

—— 1961b. An Analytical Note on the Structure of Siriono Society. *SWJ* **17**.

—— 1962a. *Structure and Sentiment*. Chicago: University o Chicago Press.

—— 1962b. Genealogy and Category in Wikmunkan Society. *Ethnology* **I**.

—— 1962c. Notes on Comparative Method and Prescriptive Alliance. *Bijdragen* **118**.

—— 1963a. Prescriptive Alliance and the Pende. *Man* **63**.

—— 1963b. Some Disputed Points in the Study of Prescriptive Alliance. *SWJ* **19**.

—— 1963c. The Wikmunkan Mother's Brother: Inference and Evidence. *JPS* **72**.

—— 1963d. Symmetry and Asymmetry in Prescriptive Alliance. *Bijdragen* **119**.

PARSONS, T. 1949. *The Structure of Social Action*. Glencoe, Illinois: The Free Press.

POSPISIL, L. 1958. Social Change and Primitive Law. *AA* **60**.

RADCLIFFE-BROWN, A. R. 1952. *Structure and Function in Primitive Society*. London: Cohen & West.

—— 1953. Dravidian Kinship Terminology. *Man* **53**, No. 169.

RIVERS, W. H. R. 1914a. *Kinship and Social Organization*. London: Constable.

—— 1914b. *History of Melanesian Society*. 2 vols. Cambridge University Press.

—— 1924. *Social Organization*. New York: Knopf.

SALISBURY, R. F. 1956. Asymmetrical Marriage Systems. *AA* **58**.

—— 1962a. Unilineal Descent Groups in the New Guinea Highlands. *Man* **56**, No. 2.

—— 1962b. *From Stone to Steel*. Melbourne: Melbourne University Press.

SCHNEIDER, D. M. 1953a. A Note on Bridewealth and the Stability of Marriage. *Man* **53**, No. 75.

—— 1953b. Yap Kinship Terminology and Kin Groups. *AA* **55**.

—— 1957. Political Organization, Supernatural Sanctions and the Punishment for Incest on Yap. *AA* **59**.

—— 1961. The distinctive Features of Matrilineal Descent Groups. In Schneider, D. M. & Gough, K., *Matrilineal Kinship*. Berkeley: University of California Press.

—— 1962. Double Descent on Yap. *JPS* **71**.

SCHNEIDER, D. M. & HOMANS, G. C. 1955. Kinship Terminology and the American Kinship System. *AA* **57**.

SCHNEIDER, D. M. & ROBERTS, J. M. 1956. *Zuñi Kin Terms*. Notebook No. 3, Laboratory of Anthropology, University of Nebraska.

WHITE, H. 1963. *An Anatomy of Kinship*. Englewood Cliffs, N.J.: Prentice-Hall.

YALMAN, N. 1962. The Structure of the Sinhalese Kindred: A Re-Examination of the Dravidian Terminology. *AA* **64**.

I. M. Lewis

Problems in the Comparative Study of Unilineal Descent

I

INTRODUCTION

This paper seeks to examine some of the problems involved in comparing unilineal descent in different societies, problems which even if they cannot yet be fully resolved have to be considered if the study of unilineal descent is to proceed further. There is now, of course, an already considerable and indeed ever-increasing volume of writing, both regional and comparative, on segmentary lineage systems in particular and on unilineal descent in general, and some of the problems to which I wish to draw attention have been raised before though not, I think, sufficiently systematically. What I wish to deal with principally is the question of how unilineal descent varies in different unilineal descent systems, and how such variations can be assessed, or measured (if indeed this is possible), and also to focus attention on the implications of such variations. The sort of question which this essay seeks to inquire into is therefore: are some societies more or less 'strongly' patrilineal or matrilineal than others; and, if so, in what respects; and, further, by what criteria can such differences be objectively established? What, in short, are the implications of saying that one society is 'more, or less, strongly patrilineal (or matrilineal)' than another?

Traditionally, of course, patrilineal and matrilineal descent are opposed categories used for distinguishing tribal societies. And since Radcliffe-Brown's classic paper on patrilineal and matrilineal succession (Radcliffe-Brown, 1935), the range of types of descent system has been widened to include double unilineal systems, different types of bilateral system, and other variations with a plethora of barbaric titles. Double and bilateral

87

descent systems have been discussed considerably recently (Free-man, 1961; Goody, 1961; Leach, 1962) and I hasten to say that the object of this paper is not to add to that debate, although some of my points have perhaps some bearing on it. My concern, then, is with differences and variations in systems of unilineal descent which cannot be described or accounted for in terms of the parallel recognition of both patrilineal and matrilineal descent, however combined. For convenience I shall deal almost entirely with patrilineal descent, although the issues apply, I think, equally to descent traced matrilineally.[1] Finally, although the variations in the value given to descent discussed here do not depend upon the recognition of any form of bilateral or dual descent, the functional implications may, as I hope to show, be similar.

II

DESCENT IN SEGMENTARY LINEAGE SOCIETIES

The role of descent as an organizational principle in different societies naturally varies widely, but it is generally agreed that there are certain broad categories of rights and obligations which tend, in varying degrees and with varying emphasis, to be attached to and transmitted by descent. These are usually taken to relate to property, jural and political status, religion, and social status in the widest sense. And it is assumed, I think, that the most thorough-going kinship definition of a person's general social status and property-rights is provided for in lineage organ-ization. This is often simply taken for granted. Radcliffe-Brown (1950, p. 78), however, makes the point quite explicitly when he states that what 'mother-right' and 'father-right' have in com-mon is extreme emphasis on lineage; and this is surely also the reason for the title of Professor Fortes's fundamental survey of descent systems (Fortes, 1953). Indeed, all this is so obvious that it hardly needs saying. And yet, there are immediate implications which, though often noticed, have not hitherto been explored adequately. These derive from the functional aspects of lineage organization in different types of society.

Let me first take the case of those unilineal organizations

88

usually called segmentary lineage systems, for here the unilineal principle is all-pervasive, or almost so, and defines the individual's social status in the widest possible sense. As Freedman (1928, p. 138) puts it: 'The purest form of unilineal descent group is to be found in a society which is a segmentary system in its totality'. Let us examine the extent to which segmentary lineage organization varies among the Nuer (Evans-Pritchard, 1940a and b), the Tiv (L. Bohannan, 1952; Bohannan & Bohannan, 1953; L. Bohannan, 1958), the Cyrenaican Bedouin (Evans-Pritchard, 1949; Peters, 1960), and the Northern Somali (Lewis, 1961, 1962).

In all four societies a person's position in his community at large is defined first by his affiliation in the patrilineage to which he belongs by birth. There is moreover no doubt that these four peoples all possess an extremely highly developed patrilineal ideology, although there are differences in the extent to which each has a specific lineage terminology. What we seek to examine is the degree to which patrilineally defined segmentary lineage status determines the jural, political, and religious status of the individual in as absolute terms as possible. How exclusive, in other words is the patrilineal principle, and to what extent is it aided or reinforced by other principles of association and status ascription. And, of course, we have to remember that the unit of comparative analysis is the whole society in each case. We are, after all, comparing the Nuer, Tiv, Bedouin, and Somali as separate entities, and what we say must be modified if it applies only to a limited area of the society, or is restricted to certain levels of activity in it.

III

THE RANGE OF GENEALOGICAL ASCRIPTION

First, consider the range of socially significant genealogical articulation. The Tiv, Bedouin, and Somali have a single national or 'total' genealogy which embraces the whole society or culture in each case. Tiv genealogies go back to 'Tiv' (indeed they go back to 'Adam'), Bedouin pedigrees go back to an ancestress Sa'ada,[2] and Somali genealogies go back to 'Samaale' and beyond to

Arabian lineages. To reach their eponym Tiv count back about fifteen named generations, the Bedouin about a dozen, and the Somali sometimes thirty generations or more.

But although genealogical span has often been taken as an index of unilineality, it is not a very effective criterion, and certainly not an unambiguous one. Generational span has first to be set in relation both to the size of population and to the extent to which, at this level, there exists genealogically based corporate activity. The Tiv number about 800,000; the Cyrenaican Bedouin about 200,000; and the Northern Somali at least two and a half million. Yet unfortunately there are difficulties even with this sort of assessment, for there is no straight and invariable relationship between genealogical depth and population size because of the different manipulative processes which operate in different segmentary lineage societies (cf. L Bohannan, 1952; Peters, 1960, p. 32 ff; Lewis, 1961, pp. 144-152). The way in which genealogies relate to actual social and political process and the procedures of adjustment to which they are subject are by no means the same among the Tiv, Bedouin, and Somali. Hence we must conclude that genealogical depth, even in relation to size of population, is not in itself an unequivocal and cross-culturally valid measure of unilinearity.

Let us now consider the question of what the genealogies actually represent in social and political terms at this 'national' level. Do the three societies ever mobilize as effective political entities on a national scale; or is there any jural identity which has a national, all-embracing character.

Tiv fight their neighbours and indeed are engaged in a general movement of expansion, but apparently the whole society is never mobilized on a genealogical basis. The Tiv do not constitute a corporate political group, even transiently. Neither apparently do the Bedouin or the Somali. Indeed the Somali when inspired by diffuse general hostility (as, for example, towards the Amharas) do not express their unity in genealogical terms, but in terms of their national cultural identity.

As far as jural identity is concerned, each of the three societies would seem to possess a common code and means for the settlement of disputes on a society-wide basis. Moreover, legal issues are evaluated according to the segmentary lineage context in which they occur. As the Bohannans put it for the Tiv: 'The moral attitude to homicide – both in peacetime and time of war – is on a scale of values determined by the social distance (in lineage terms) between the people involved' (Bohannan & Bohannan, 1953, p. 26). For the Tiv, murder invokes several magical consequences; for the Bedouin and Somali, it raises the question of blood-money and vengeance. And all Somali, as all Bedouin, recognize the tariffs of compensation embodied in Muslim law.

In contrast to the Tiv, Bedouin, and Somali, the Nuer to not have a single national genealogy. But like the former they do not apparently combine on a national basis against their traditional enemies the Dinka. Their genealogically based politico-jural solidarity stops short at the 'tribe' and does not embrace the whole society.

Despite these differences in lineage coverage between the Nuer, on the one hand, and the Bedouin, Tiv, and Somali, on the other, the truth of course is that all four societies are essentially cultural entities rather than corporate political units. Yet there is a sense in which the genealogical placement of the individual within a national framework in the case of the Tiv, Bedouin, and Somali is more complete in these societies than it is among the Nuer. To this extent, and to the degree that jural identity is also involved, unilineal descent could be said to be more important, because more inclusive, among the Tiv, Bedouin, and Somali than amongst the Nuer.

IV

THE MAXIMUM CORPORATE GROUPING

Let us now consider the largest corporate politico-jural unit in each case. This among the Nuer is the 'tribe', which because of the association between 'dominant' clans and tribes has a genealogical structure. This unit Evans-Pritchard defines as the largest group within which there is both a means and a moral obligation to settle disputes. The external implications are that tribes may be divided by fighting and warfare, whereas, internally, among their segments fighting is institutionalized in terms of the blood-feud. In comparing the Tiv, Bedouin, Somali, and Nuer it is on the latter criterion – that of political unity as manifest in war – that we have to fasten. For, as has already been pointed out, the former jural criterion used by Evans-Pritchard to define the Nuer tribe in the case of the Tiv, Bedouin, and Somali applies to the whole society – at least in principle. With this qualification we can now examine Nuer tribes and the corresponding units in the other three cases.

Among the Nuer, a tribe has a maximum strength of about 45,000 souls, and the lineage unit associated with it, a genealogical span of ten generations. The equivalent Tiv unit has a genealogical span of about eight generations. Among the Bedouin, the corresponding unit seems to contain about 20,000 souls with a genealogical depth of again about eight generations. With the Somali the comparable unit may contain as many as 150,000 persons and the length of pedigree in this case is of the order of twenty generations. We can conclude, therefore, that of the four societies the Somali can boast the largest maximum politico-jural unit with the correspondingly longest genealogy. The implications of this conclusion are that among the Somali unilineal descent provides a basis for more extended corporate politico-jural solidarity than in the other three cases. In this respect, and in this respect alone, the Somali might be said to be the most patrilineal of the four societies.

Let us now consider the related problem of the degree to which, within the maximum politico-jural unit, lineage segmentation is functionally significant. In other words, within this unit, to what extent are ancestors in the genealogies points of corporate cleavage or aggregation? With the Nuer it seems that every level of genealogical differentiation in a tribe's associated 'dominant' clan is, in principle at least, structurally significant. There are, however, four main levels of corporate action within the tribe-clan and outside the family. Indeed, this pattern is so well known that it has become a kind of paradigm applied, somewhat holistically, to very many lineage societies. The Tiv, similarly, seem to have universal genealogical group differentiation, although four levels are apparently most significant. With the Bedouin the position is similar, although there is only a threefold differentiation within the 'tribe' and this exhausts the possibilities of genealogical division. There are three levels of division and three connecting ancestors between the founder of the tertiary section and the tribal eponym. The Somali, on the other hand, resemble the Nuer and Tiv, every ancestor being potentially at least a point of lineage division, but within the unit we are discussing there are two main levels of corporate action outside the family.

This discussion tells us little more than that there is a more flexible and potentially wider range of socially significant segmentation within the largest political unit in the case of the Tiv, Somali, and Nuer, than with the Bedouin. Because of the variable relationship between structural relations and genealogical organization, however, we cannot, I think, in this case draw any valid conclusions bearing on the functional significance of descent in this area of grouping.

The next consideration is that of the cultic significance of segmentation. Do these societies have religious cults which are consistently organized on a genealogical basis? Is a person's religious status defined by his lineage affiliation? To answer these questions we have to note first that none of the four societies practises ancestor worship in terms of Fortes's characterization of this form of religion (Fortes, 1960). The Nuer, Bedouin, and Somali worship a single deity. Among the Nuer, this deity or Spirit who is unique to them is seen as refracted into subsidiary spirit-entities by reference to the hierarchy of lineage segmentation.

The Bedouin and Somali, by contrast, both venerate ancestors as part of the Sufistic cult of saints and, although different levels of lineage grouping evoke different ancestors, this cult cannot, I believe, be described in terms of 'refractions' of God or Spirit in a manner analogous to Evans-Pritchard's description of Nuer religion. Moreover, lineage ancestors constitute only one class of the general category of saints, charismatic individuals who may be alive or dead, and who are regarded as intermediaries in the believer's relationship with God. Indeed, as I have argued elsewhere (Lewis, 1963), Muslim saints play a very similar role to saints in Catholicism and their existence, and the faith men place in their powers of mediation, enhance rather than detract from the lofty omnipotence of God. Thus it would seem correct to say that Nuer religion is more closely related to their segmentary lineage organization than is the case with the Bedouin or Somali.

93

With the two latter, and certainly in the case of the Somali, the significance of the ancestor cult increases as the degree of politico-jural cohesion decreases. There is a more vital cult of lineage ancestors at segmentary levels where politico-jural solidarity is weak than at levels of grouping where people share strong bonds of collaboration.

The Tiv have certainly a very different religious system, although again there is no comprehensive segmentary lineage ancestor cult. Thus, of the four societies, only in the case of the Nuer is the religious cult uniformly tied to lineage organization; and this, of course, is a very simplified (and perhaps distorting) way of referring to the realities of Nuer religion. Yet if we are to assess the significance of patrilineal descent in these four cases in relation to religion, we must, I think, conclude that the Nuer make more use of the unilineal principle for religious purposes than do the Bedouin, Tiv, or Somali.

To sum up our discussion so far: we can say that, although among the Somali the maximum genealogically defined politico-jural community (and the range of politically significant agnation) is greater than with the Nuer, Tiv, or Bedouin, lineage status has, apparently, more importance in religion for the Nuer than in the other three cases. Thus we might legitimately argue that, from the point of view of political and jural corporateness, descent is most important among the Somali. But from the point of view of religion, agnation is most significant among the Nuer. Before we can go beyond this to conclude that some of our four societies are in an overall sense more 'strongly' patrilineal than the others we must bring other criteria into the discussion.

V

THE UNIQUENESS OF DESCENT AS AN ORGANIZING
PRINCIPLE

The fundamental test of the functional importance of unilineal descent in a particular society must surely be the extent to which it is empirically the organizational basis for social activities in the widest sense. We have to inquire, therefore, to what extent the uniqueness of descent as a basis for social action is mitigated by the existence of other principles performing similar functions. Let us again consider the question of politico-jural collaboration.

Evans-Pritchard makes it very clear that among the Nuer the fundamental principle of grouping has a territorial basis and is in fact what Maine referred to as 'local contiguity'. Nuer politico-jural units are basically territorial entities, and descent is an aiding principle of social cohesion. Nevertheless, agnation is very important for, following a discussion of ecology and territorial grouping, Evans-Pritchard can say that: 'Tribal unity cannot be accounted for by any of the facts we have so far mentioned, taken alone, or in aggregate, but only by reference to the lineage system' (Evans-Pritchard, 1940b, p. 284). And the system of lineages of a 'dominant' clan enables Nuer to think of their tribe in the highly consistent form of clan structure. There is, moreover, a 'straight relationship' between political structure and the clan system of segments. Yet the Nuer themselves, Evans-Pritchard makes plain, conceive of their politico-jural cohesion primarily in territorial terms and the clan and lineage system comes into play to support the former.

These facts seem to indicate that here unilineal descent is a supplementary principle of aggregation, albeit one of great importance. With the Tiv, the position is, apparently very similar. Here territorially defined divisions of society are associated with lineage divisions and there is an 'almost one-to-one correlation between the territorial position of *utar* (territorial segments) and the genealogically defined order of segments' (Bohannan & Bohannan, 1953, p. 21). Moreover, agnates tend, more than among the Nuer where they are often dispersed, to reside together and there thus seems to be the regular consistency between territorial units and lineage segments which exists among the Nuer only in relation to 'dominant' clans and lineages. Again, it seems to me that we must conclude that descent amongst the Tiv is an aiding principle giving consistency and cohesion to what are essentially territorially defined groups. Territory (*tar*) is the primary referent of politico-jural cohesion.

The position with the semi-nomadic or transhumant Cyrenaican Bedouin is very similar. There is a general co-ordination between spatially defined territorial groupings and genealogical ties: 'The Cyrenaican genealogy is a conceptualization of a hierarchy of ordered territorial segments' (Peters, 1960, p. 31). Thus what Dr Peters calls the 'tertiary segment' of a tribe – the smallest political group whose members are bound by blood and the payment and receipt of blood-money – has its own homeland, water-supplies, pastures, and ploughland. In Bedouin society this is the vengeance group, a lineage unit with a span of five generations most of whose members live in their own homeland. Here again the fundamental bonds are surely those springing from common residence and association in their cultivable land-holdings and also in their summer grazing camps. Territorially based sentiments of loyalty are reinforced and given structural definition in lineage terms.

Thus in all three societies (Nuer, Tiv, and Bedouin) the basic politico-jural aggregates are primarily territorially defined, and the lineage organization, although existing to a variable extent as a system in its own right, serves to substantiate territorially founded relationships and provides the dominant idiom in which these are stated. The fundamentally territorial character of social and political association in general is indeed usually taken for granted, and has been assumed to apply as much to segmentary lineage societies as to other types of society (cf. Middleton & Tait, 1958, p. 5; Fortes & Evans-Pritchard, 1940, p. 10; Schapera, 1956, *passim*).

The position amongst the nomadic Somali, however, is very different. Here there are no fixed local groups, no permanent grazing areas, and no firm assertion of territorial ties. And although rights to water resources provide some limitation to the loci of pastoral movements, which are primarily dictated by the distribution of grazing, there are no stable territorial units. Local contiguity is not a principle of social collaboration. In these circumstances, the fundamental principle of association, the first 'given' as it were, is not territorial attachment but agnatic descent. Thus for the nomadic Somali descent has a primacy which it does not seem to possess among the Nuer, Tiv, and Bedouin. To this extent, I would argue that more is expected of descent as an organizational principle among the Somali than with the other three cases. Descent is therefore functionally more important in Somali society.

And yet, from another point of view it might be argued that the contrary is true. For the Nuer (Evans-Pritchard, 1940a, p. 198 ff), Tiv (L. Bohannan, 1952), and Bedouin (Peters, 1960), exemplify the classical principles of segmentary lineage organization where genealogies are, by different processes, adjusted to accord with political realities. The politico-jural ideology is uncompromisingly one of descent and 'co-ordinate segments which have come into existence as a result of segmentation are regarded as complementary and as formally equal' (Middleton & Tait, 1958, p. 7). So that even if social cohesion *derives* fundamentally from co-residence, the genealogical idiom is consistently maintained and genealogies are adjusted in step with changes in the balance of power (cf. Lewis, 1961, pp. 298-299). Among the Somali, however, where the rule of self-help places a premium on numerical supremacy, a specifically contractual principle is employed to achieve a balance of power in segmentary relations without resort to genealogical manipulation.[3] Small genealogically defined groups seek strength by alliance with stronger lineages by means of formal contractual agreements. Some contractual alliances do not always follow the principle of segmentary opposition, and sometimes indeed are in direct defiance of genealogical proximity.

Now, the Muslim Bedouin also employ a similar contractual principle, but this seems to be restricted in application to the level of the tertiary tribal segment whose agnatic members 'have agreed on the blood' (i.e. on the common obligation to pay and receive blood-compensation in concert). Notwithstanding this limited similarity between Somali and Bedouin, however, the latter manipulate their genealogies in order to maintain a consistent relationship between lineage and political solidarity. It could therefore be argued that, although agnation is perhaps a less fundamental principle among the Nuer, Tiv, and Bedouin than with the Somali, it nevertheless more consistently represents political relations and is consequently a more thorough-going basis for politico-jural relations.

There are however other facts to be considered. Both the Nuer and Tiv have an age-set system, a feature lacking amongst the Bedouin and Somali. What social functions, we must ask, are served by this organization in Nuer and Tiv society. While it is clear that in neither case are 'political relations between local

97

groups controlled by the holders of statuses in age-set or age-grade systems' (Middleton & Tait, 1958, p. 3; cf. Bernardi, 1952, p. 331), as among the Nilo-Hamites, yet age-sets do have some political functions. For the Nuer, Evans-Pritchard records that: 'the age-set system may, however, be regarded as a political institution, since it is, to a large extent, segmented tribally and since it divides a tribe – as far as its male members are concerned – into groups based on age, which stand in a definite relation to each other' (Evans-Pritchard, 1940b, p. 290). We are also told that the politico-territorial system and the age-set system are both consistent in themselves and to some extent overlap, but they are not interdependent (as the lineage and territorial systems are).

Tiv age-sets similarly seem to have a political dimension, being associated with territorial segments. It thus appears that the existence of an age-set organization amongst the Nuer and Tiv and its partial investment with political functions to some extent reduces the uniqueness of descent as a political principle in these societies. In this respect it might be argued that the role of descent as an exclusive organizational principle is weakened among the Nuer and Tiv in comparison with the Bedouin and Somali. And if we note a further Tiv principle, that of *ikul* treaties and market pacts which have some political functions, we have again to make a new assessment of the strength and importance of patriliny in the four cases.

VI

THE FACTORIZATION OF DESCENT

In what must seem an excessively rambling discussion, I have so far sought to show that if social function is the criterion, then in some respects unilineal descent is more important among the Bedouin and Somali than among the Nuer and Tiv, while in other respects this is not so. Perhaps for many it is labouring the obvious to say that it is in fact extremely difficult to establish that in any overall sense descent in one of a number of segmentary lineage societies is 'more important' than in others. The difficulty in making such statements arises of course because of the wide range of variables which cannot be held constant to set against the single criterion of unilinearity, and questions of judgement are involved which are not readily susceptible to simple measurement or enumeration.

But at least the facts so far surveyed indicate the extent of the problem and serve to underline the validity of Peters's statement (with reference to the Bedouin) that in such societies descent 'is not one thing, but many: it includes in its scope succession, status, inheritance, bride-wealth, blood-money, domestic and political behaviour, etc., and these can in turn be factorised into a number of components' (Peters, 1960, p. 49). The trouble – for comparative estimates of the extent or 'strength' of descent – is of course that the various components have different values and different functional importance in different societies. In some areas of social action the weighting is important and highly significant; in other respects it may be less so: yet how is one to arrive at an objective summation which gives a total evaluation characteristic of a particular society?

VII

LINEAGE ORGANIZATION IN STATES

So far, taking lineage as the epitome of unilineal descent, and segmentary lineage societies as the most thorough-going form of lineage organization, we have considered this type of system only. I want now to widen the frame of reference by examining the significance of descent in politically hierarchical societies which have, nevertheless, a lineage organization.

As has often been observed, such peoples as the Southern Bantu generally, the Ashanti, and the Yoruba provide examples of tribal states in which there is a lineage organization but where unilineal descent is relevant to property inheritance, status, and local organization, rather than to the political structure in a wider sense. In political contexts, at least in those above the minimal local level, the lineage system as a means of controlling external corporate relations is replaced by an hierarchical organization of political statuses, which may, of course, have a kinship pattern. Here we often have to distinguish between the presence or absence of politically corporate unilineal descent groups and such a principle of political kinship as perpetual succession (Cunnison, 1956). What is significant in this context is that in tribal states of this kind unililineal descent has only limited political functions.

Take the Zulu (Gluckman, 1940, 1950), for example. Here there is a patrilineal organization and lineages of up to nine generations in depth are, partially at least, residential units. Lineage segments provide the core organization of villages, and a number of villages so based in one neighbourhood form a recognized group in opposition to other similar groups. Segments are arranged in a genealogical structure, yet this does not pervade the whole social system and contributes, consequently, to social cohesion only at a limited level of grouping. The political superstructure of Zulu society is not an extension of this segmentary lineage organization. Hence with systems such as that of the Zulu it can be argued that in relation to political function unilineal descent is less important than it is among the Nuer and Tiv, etc. In this functional respect we might say that the Zulu are 'less' patrilineal than the Nuer. It would be more accurate, however, merely to say that patrilineal descent among the Zulu and Nuer has in some important respects different functions in each society.

Consider now lineage organization in South East China. Here, as Freedman (1958) has shown, we have a system where local units have a segmentary lineage structure; but where, although genealogies may be reckoned back for twenty-five generations and higher orders of lineage grouping emerge in ancestor worship, the whole society is not pervaded by the lineage principle. As with the Zulu and the other tribal states referred to above, there is here a political superstructure based on principles other than that of unilineal descent. As with the BaSoga (Fallers, 1954), as Freedman points out, in South-East China lineage and bureaucratic organizational principles are to some extent opposed. Here, then, is another example of a politically hierarchical system with a unilineal descent organization of limited political functions. In this respect South East Chinese society like that of the BaSoga, or the rather different Zulu system, is less unilineal than truly segmentary lineage societies.

With unilineally articulated 'segmentary states' such as the

Alur (Southall, 1954), we have something closer to the true or 'pure' segmentary lineage system and to that extent a more strongly unilineal type of organization.

VIII

THE CONSISTENCY OF THE DESCENT PRINCIPLE AND THE LOYALTIES CREATED BY IT

In the preceding sections we have been considering what, I suppose, might be called the functional exclusiveness of unilineal descent as a principle of social organization with special reference to politico-jural corporateness. It is now time to consider unilinearity from another, though not entirely unrelated, point of view, that of internal exclusiveness and self-consistency. We now have to ask the question: to what extent is the unilineal principle rigidly adhered to and traced through *real* blood ties; and further, how absolute are the loyalties of members of the unilineal group.

Where in patrilineally organized societies some of the links in descent are actually through women, it can be argued that the consistency of descent, and therefore the strength of patriliny in this sense, are weakened. Thus where as sometimes happens with the Nuer, Zulu, and Tiv, links through women are converted into patrilineal ties, this detracts from the exclusiveness and absoluteness of the patrilineal principle (cf. Schneider, 1961, p. 11). Differentiation by matrilateral, or uterine ties, in a patrilineally based system, does not, however, diminish the power of patriliny, for the recognition of such links follows from polygyny and merely takes advantage of what Fortes calls 'complementary filiation'. Is fictional agnation in patrilineal societies also to be regarded as abrogating the patrilineal principle?

It seems not generally regarded as having this effect: and yet, if a person can exchange one lineage status and loyalty for another, this surely implies a less exclusive system of descent than where this is impossible or very uncommon. And this raises the very important issue of the relative loyalties of unilineal kin and of affines. From what is generally assumed to be the Roman model of *patria potestas*, Radcliffe-Brown (1950, p. 78) argues that the extreme form of patrilineal descent requires that in marriage a woman is transferred completely from her father's *potestas* to that of her husband, the jural bonds between a woman and her siblings (and agnates) being finally severed by marriage.

Fortes takes the same position: 'In the limiting case, at the patrilineal pole, marriage may entail the almost complete severance of a woman from her natal family and the virtual extinction of her sisterhood and daughterhood' (Fortes, 1959, p. 20). Gluckman, likewise, in his stimulating discussion of descent and affinity among the Zulu and Lozi, argues that the strength of Zulu patriliny is to be seen in the severance of a woman's ties with her own natal kin when she marries, and her absorption (in a legal sense) into her husband's agnatic group (Gluckman, 1950, p. 182). And this, with the practice of the levirate, ghost marriage, and 'woman-to-woman marriage', as with the Nuer, for Gluckman demonstrates the power of Zulu patriliny. The same point of view is expressed by Freedman (1958, p. 134) in his analysis of lineage organization in South-East China where women, though never completely assimilated in their husband's group – for they retain their own surname – are very strongly identified by marriage with their husband's lineage. Here Freedman argues that the strength of Chinese patriliny can be seen in the relinquishing of female agnates and their incorporation in their husband's group; and again widow-inheritance is taken as an index of strong patriliny.

These evaluations of empirical data seem to stem largely from the acceptance of the Roman *gens* organization and *patria potestas* as the paradigm of patrilineal descent. Recently, in his discussion of the nature of matriliny, Schneider (1962, p. 11) has sought to give this interpretation a theoretical gloss. Schneider holds that, although in principle the strongest kind of descent group is that whose members are in no way assimilated into their affinal groups, the patrilineal group can dispense with its female members in exogamous marriage, acquiring in return wives from other groups, without in any way challenging the essential strength of patriliny. Women are only required for procreation, not, as with men in both patrilineal and matrilineal systems, for authority.

Without in any way attempting to dispute that what Fortes (1960) calls 'jural authority' is always predominantly vested in men, whatever the system of descent, there is another point of view which can, I think, be put with equal cogency. This proceeds from the assumption that unilineal descent (whether patrilineal or matrilineal) *may* define the status of all members of the descent group irrespective of sex. Thus in patrilineal systems sisters and daughters are, potentially at least, as much agnates as brothers and sons, although as women their overall social status is usually considerably inferior to that of men. Women then, may be members of their lineage, with their political and jural status firmly tied to it, even if they are perhaps only second-class citizens.

Thus, to refer to actual ethnographic data, in the case of the BaSoga (Fallers, 1957) although citizenship is not invariably tied to agnation and clientship is an important ascriptive principle, women are not strongly absorbed into their husband's groups by marriage but retain their natal patrilineal affiliation. Fallers argues that in this respect the Soga are more patrilineal than the Nuer or Zulu. Similarly Leach (1957) holds that a similar situation amongst the Lakher makes them no less patrilineal than the Jinghpaw whose marital institutions conform to those of the Zulu and Nuer. Likewise I consider that where, among the Somali, a woman is not fully absorbed into her husband's lineage but retains much of her pre-marital natal politico-jural status, this indicates strong patriliny rather than the reverse (Lewis, 1926, pp. 39-43). And this is true of both the northern nomadic Somali and of the southern part-cultivating Somali who have quite different patterns of marriage. The former tend to marry widely outside the group, whereas the latter most frequently marry patrilateral parallel cousins, or matrilateral cross-cousins.

In both cases, there is a high divorce rate, marriage is unstable, and a woman's life is *always* (before and after marriage) primarily the responsibility of her own natal kin. This is evident in the fact that when a married woman is killed, her bloodwealth is due not to the husband but to her own patrilineage. With the Cyrenaican Bedouin similarly a woman's patrilineal affiliation is never fully extinguished by marriage, and responsibility for her life rests ultimately with her own kin. Since among the Bedouin all marriages do not correspond to the preferential cousin pattern, these data, like those for the northern Somali, show that, contrary to Leach's suggestion (Leach, 1957, p. 55), this type of

103

descent is not invariably associated with preferential marriage. Indeed the Tswana (Schapera, 1950) provide an excellent example of the converse: they have a system of preferential cousin marriage like the Bedouin, and yet their system of descent follows the pattern of the Nuer and Zulu where marriage does incorporate women in their husband's group.

Thus in certain patrilineal societies, some with hierarchical political institutions and others without them, marriage does not incorporate a woman fully in the group of her husband. Among hierarchical systems, examples are provided by the Amba, Soga, Ruanda, Lakher, and Fulani; and, in uncentralized segmentary lineage societies, in the Tiv, Bedouin, Somali, and Tallensi. Since, as I have argued elsewhere (Lewis, 1962, pp. 41-43), these societies all have fairly high divorce rates, there seems to be a general correlation between unstable marriage and the extent to which a woman, after marriage, still retains strong legal ties with her own kin.

From the point of view of this paper, however, what is significant is that in some patrilineal societies, whether the unilineal principle permeates the political structure or not, and is therefore 'functionally strong' in this sense, descent links men and women in a different way from the Roman paradigm. We have therefore to recognize that, whereas in some societies women are little more than pawns in a patrilineal system, in other strongly patrilineal societies their patrilineal affiliation is little less binding than that of men.

Thus while it seems often to be assumed that the patrilineal group does not include women, indeed Radcliffe-Brown (1950, p. 41) states this quite explicitly, there are other patrilineal societies where women, although of markedly inferior status to men, have yet strong patrilineal rights and obligations. Such cases resemble matrilineal societies in that the sibling bond is strong between the sexes to the corresponding detriment of the marriage tie. A correlate of this type of patriliny, is, I suggest, the existence of strong matrilateral ties. And since these depend for their validity and force upon the attachment of women to their patrilineages of birth, I do not see how this can be regarded as detracting from the absoluteness and exclusiveness of patrilineal descent *per se*.

104

And here again we touch on the wider issue to which I have already referred: that the strength of patriliny cannot simply be assessed in relation to the extent to which matrilineal principles of grouping are, or are not, recognized. Nor, I believe, will a distinction between patriliny as a unilineal phenomenon, and 'father-right' as a jural principle, make the point of distinction adequately.[4] Institutional complexes (e.g. local contiguity, contract, age-sets, hierarchical political organization, etc.) separately, or in conjunction, may detract from the exclusiveness of patriliny just as effectively and significantly as the parallel recognition of matrilineal descent. In other words, patriliny cannot be weighed against matriliny in a functional vacuum. From this functional point of view some bilaterally organized societies or systems of dual descent may be just as strongly patrilineal, or matrilineal, as other societies where only one principle of descent is followed, but where other institutional principles are an important basis for the ascription of status.

A brief comparison of the Plateau Tonga (Colson, 1953) and the West African Yakö (Forde, 1950) will show very well what I mean. Matrilineal descent among both Tonga (who are classified as matrilineal) and among the Yakö (regarded as having double descent) seems to have a similar importance. In both societies matrilineal kin have corporate interests in cattle and movable goods; in marriage, for they are exogamous and pay and receive bridewealth in concert; and in the payment and receipt of damages. Moreover, matrilineal kin have common ritual duties. Among the Yakö recognition of the complementary principle of patrilineal descent is the basis for territorial allegiance and land-holding. But with the Tonga these interests are based on the principle of local contiguity, and social cohesion is maintained by the interaction of this principle with that of matrilineal descent. From this functional stand-point, therefore, matrilineal descent is no more important among the 'matrilineal' Tonga than it is among the Yakö characterized as having double descent. Nor are the Yakö any less matrilineal than the Tonga.

This example will perhaps suffice to indicate, in relation to what was said previously, how, if social function is the criterion, organizational principles other than descent have to be considered on the same plane of relevance as descent in character-

105

izing a social system. To this extent the labels 'matrilineal' and 'patrilineal' etc. are only fully meaningful when other principles of organization are taken into account in establishing the 'type' of a society.

IX

CONCLUSIONS

In discussing some of the problems which are encountered in the study of unilineal descent, I have followed Fortes and Evans-Pritchard's dictum (1940, p. 3) that 'comparative study ... has to be on an abstract plane where social processes are stripped of their cultural idiom and are reduced to functional terms'. From this point of view, the sort of taxonomic exercise performed by Fried (1957) where descent groups are classified in terms of matriliny or patriliny, corporateness, the presence or absence of ranking and stratification, and the character of exogamic proscriptions, seems to me of limited utility. For such criteria may have little direct relation to the functional realities of social organization. Moreover, in such a scheme of classification quite different functional situations may be lumped together and important underlying differences obscured. We need to know what unilineal descent entails in a society, in all its manifold implications, before we can attempt to characterize social systems in terms of 'strong' or 'weak' patriliny (or matriliny) and before we can draw meaningful analogies. Otherwise the criteria of our classification are little more than superficial cultural features which may have very limited functional significance.

Thus while many tribal social systems contain as one of their organizational principles the recognition of unilineal descent, the functional significance of this varies widely. Even in patrilineal segmentary lineage societies there are considerable differences in the functions assigned to descent as a principle of social cohesion and status ascription. Thus, as I have shown, in some respects patrilineal descent has a greater primacy among the Somali than with the Nuer, Tiv, or Bedouin, while in other functional respects the reverse is true. Similarly, if we examine the nature of social ties based on descent in relation to women as well as men, and compare descent with affinity, we find that some patrilineal systems resemble the Roman paradigm while others do not. And this, as it seems to me, quite fundamental difference in the character of agnation is not dependent upon whether a unilineal system is or is not of the segmentary lineage type. Patrilineal systems where men and women share similarly strong agnatic ties are found in both centralized and uncentralized political organizations. And the same is true of patrilineal descent systems of the Roman type.

Thus, if we focus attention on the character of the sibling bond, some kinds of patrilineal system have more in common with matrilineal systems than with other patrilineal organizations and the difference cannot be accounted for in terms of bilateral or dual descent. Moreover, if we take into account the contributions made to social cohesion and status ascription of institutional complexes other than descent, we have to acknowledge that to type some societies as patrilineal, or matrilineal, or as possessing bilateral or dual descent, without paying equal regard to the other operative principles of organization, may be highly misleading. Certainly at best it tells us surprisingly little. And here I feel we must recognize the validity of Leach's contention that: 'It may be that to create a class labelled matrilineal societies is as irrelevant for our understanding of social structures as the creation of a class of blue butterflies is irrelevant for the understanding of the anatomical structure of lepidoptera' (Leach, 1961, p. 4).

Finally, since descent has multiple characteristics in most societies, to say that one society is 'strongly' patrilineal or matrilineal, or is more patrilineal or matrilineal, than another, has in itself little meaning, except perhaps as an evaluation of native sentiment. From some points of view, as we have seen, the Tonga are no more matrilineal than the Yakö. Comparison of the strength of descent in different societies must, therefore, be with respect to specific functions or areas of status ascription. The degree of variation which is evident with even as few societies as have been discussed in this paper is striking. To emphasize this, significant points of difference for six of the patrilineal peoples discussed in this paper (the Tiv, Bedouin, Somali, Nuer, Zulu, and Chinese) are shown in the accompanying table.

Can one now simply add up the positive entries under each

107

aspect of descent in order to reach a characteristic score of patri-lineal 'strength' for each society? Few people, I imagine, would accept this, for it would assume that all the criteria accounted for are of equal significance. Thus when all the aspects into which descent can be factorized are considered, I see no simple way of making any total evaluation of the significance of descent in a

	Society					
	Tiv	*Bedouin*	*Somali*	*Nuer*	*Zulu*	*Chinese*
Inherent properties of descent:						
Unilinially consistent[1]	0	0	+	0	+	0
Binds men and women equally[2] . .	+	+	+	0	0	0
Functional aspects of descent:						
Embraces whole society[3]	+	+	+	0	0	0
Political cohesion .	+	+	+	+	0	0
Jural cohesion . .	+	+	+	+	+	+
Religious cohesion[4] .	0	0	0	+	+	+
Non-occurrence of other structural principles:						
Nil Local contiguity .	0	0	+	0	0	0
Nil Age-set organization	0	+	+	0	0	+
Nil Contractual collaboration . . .	0	0	0	+	+	+
Nil Centralized government . . .	+	+	+	+	0	0

NOTES

1. A positive entry here means that descent is exclusively (or virtually exclusively) traced through real agnatic kin; links through women are not made a basis for fictional agnatic ties.
2. A positive entry here indicates that women do *not* surrender their agnatic affiliation when they marry; men and women, more or less equally, retain their agnatic statuses of birth throughout life.
3. A positive entry here indicates that genealogical ascription embraces the entire society and culture; there is a single 'national' genealogy.
4. A positive entry here is meant to imply that religious beliefs and practice are to a significant extent organized on a lineage basis.

particular case, unless, perhaps, we adopt the typological pro-cedures of archaeology and speak of Nuer-type segmentary lineage societies, etc. And yet even here we are likely to be in difficulties, for the facts reviewed in this paper, if they do nothing else, at least illustrate abundantly that a system which is 'strongly' patrilineal or matrilineal in one respect is not necessarily so in another. Thus it is obvious that any comparative study of societies from the point of view of unilinearity must compare the specific functional respects in which unilineal descent is significant in each case. The lumping together of societies on the basis of patriliny or matriliny alone can only lead to confusion. The functional implications of descent are often much more significant than whether descent is traced in the patri- or matri-line.

NOTES

1. I realize, of course, that patrilineal descent and matrilineal descent are not 'mirror images' (to use Southall's expression) or, logical opposites, although I do not accept all the points of difference made by Schneider in his recent theoretical discussion of matriliny (Schneider, 1961).

2. This is not an indication of matriliny, but arises from the common practice of distinguishing segments within a patrilineage along the lines of uterine differentiation ('complementary filiation' in Fortes's terminology). All the patrilineal societies mentioned in this essay make use of this principle which, of course, follows from polygyny. (For the Bedouin, see Peters, 1960, p. 29.)

3. This is not to be taken as implying that Somali genealogies are accurate historical records. There is a general correlation between the numerical strength of a lineage and the number of generations in its pedigree. Since quite wide differences occur in the span of collateral lineages it seems that the genealogies of small groups are telescoped, while those of large groups ramify with increasing numbers and population strength. Thus names which are not significant points of ramification but merely serve to continue a single unilineal line tend to drop out of the genealogical record. Hence the genealogies of large groups are probably more accurate historically than those of smaller lineages. At the apex of Somali genealogies, where descent is traced from Arabia, a strongly mythical element enters and at this level genealogies have an altogether different character (cf. Lewis, p. 1962a).

4. As Leach (1957, p. 51) has pointed out, some matrilineal societies evince a certain degree of 'father-right', if by this term is meant the degree of jural authority which a father has over his children. In his discussion of Lozi and Zulu kinship and affinity, Gluckman (1950) uses the terms patriliny and 'father-right' more or less interchangeably, but seems to indicate that a valid distinction might be made between them. While granting that there are contexts in which a distinction could usefully be drawn, I do not see how the sorts of difference in patrilineal descent discussed here could be expressed in this way.

5. While urging that functional criteria are of extreme importance in establishing the nature of descent in different societies, I do not believe that simple and invariable correlations can be drawn between descent systems and socio-ecological conditions in an adaptive sense, as e.g. by Stewart (1955) or Sahlins (1961). Sahlins's contention, based on an apparently rather cursory survey of the literature, for instance, that segmentary lineage systems develop in tribes

expanding into an already occupied ecological niche seems to have little general validity. One of the greatest intrusive movements in North-East Africa was that of the Galla who employed an age-set organization of warriors in their movement of conquest. And although the Somali similarly expanded in their wake with a segmentary lineage organization, they later adopted an age-set warrior organization in their wars with the Galla. When their main movements of expansion ceased they abandoned the age-set organization which they had adopted and retained their segmentary lineage organization.

REFERENCES

BERNARDI, B. 1952. The Age-System of the Nilo-Hamitic Peoples. *Africa* 22: 316-332.

BOHANNAN, L. 1952. A Genealogical Charter. *Africa* 22: 301-315.

—— 1958. Political Aspects of Tiv Social Organization. In J. Middleton & D. Tait (eds.), *Tribes without Rulers*. London: Routledge & Kegan Paul.

BOHANNAN, L. & BOHANNAN, P. 1953. *The Tiv of Central Nigeria*. London: International African Institute.

COLSON, E. 1953. Social Control and Vengeance in Plateau Tonga Society. *Africa* 23: 199-212.

CUNNISON, G. 1956. Perpetual Kinship: A Political Institution of the Luapula Peoples. *Rhodes-Livingstone Journal* 20.

EVANS-PRITCHARD, E. E. 1940a. *The Nuer*. Oxford: Clarendon Press.

—— 1940b. The Nuer of the Southern Sudan. In Fortes, M. & Evans-Pritchard, E. E. (eds.), *African Political Systems*. London: Oxford University Press.

—— 1956. *Nuer Religion*. Oxford: Clarendon Press.

—— 1949. *The Sanusi of Cyrenaica*. Oxford: Clarendon Press.

FALLERS, L. A. 1954. *Bantu Bureaucracy*. Cambridge: Heffer.

—— 1957. Some Determinants of Marriage Stability in BuSoga. *Africa* 27: 106-123.

FORDE, C. D. 1950. Double Descent among the Yakö. In Radcliffe-Brown, A. R. & Forde, C. D. (eds.), *African Systems of Kinship and Marriage*. London: Oxford University Press.

FORTES, M. 1953. The Structure of Unilineal Descent Groups. *American Anthropologist* 55: 17-51.

—— 1959. Descent, Filiation and Affinity: A Rejoinder to Dr. Leach. *Man* 309 and 331.

—— 1960. Some Reflections on Ancestor Worship in Africa. Third International African Institute Seminar, Paper No. 19.

FORTES, M. & EVANS-PRITCHARD, E. E. 1940. *African Political Systems*. London: Oxford University Press.

FREEDMAN, M. 1958. *Lineage Organisation in Southeastern China.* London: Athlone Press.

FREEMAN, J. D. 1961. On the Concept of the Kindred. *Journal Royal Anthropological Institute* **92**: 192-220.

FRIED, M. H. 1957. The Classification of Corporate Unilineal Descent Groups. *Journal Royal Anthropological Institute* **87**: 1-30.

GLUCKMAN, M. 1940. The Kingdom of the Zulu of South Africa. In Fortes, M. & Evans-Pritchard, E. E. (eds.), *African Political Systems.* London: Oxford University Press.

—— 1950. Kinship and Marriage among the Lozi of Northern Rhodesia and the Zulu of Natal. In Radcliffe-Brown, A. R., and Forde, D. (eds.), *African Systems of Kinship and Marriage.* London: Oxford University Press.

GOODY, J. 1961. The Classification of Double Descent Systems. *Current Anthropology* **2**: 3-26.

LEACH, E. R. 1957. Aspects of Bridewealth and Marriage Stability among the Kachin and Lakher. *Man* **57**: 50-55.

—— 1961. *Rethinking Anthropology.* London: Athlone Press.

—— 1962. On Certain Unconsidered Aspects of Double Descent Systems. *Man* **62**: 130-134.

LEWIS, I. M. 1961. *A Pastoral Democracy.* London: Oxford University Press.

—— 1962a. Historical Aspects of Genealogies in Northern Somali Social Structure. *Journal of African History* **3**: 35-48.

—— 1962b. *Marriage and the Family in Northern Somaliland.* East African Studies No. 15, Kampala.

—— 1963. Dualism in Somali Notions of Power. *Journal Royal Anthropological Institute* **93**: 109-116

LLOYD, P. C. 1955. The Yoruba Lineage. *Africa* **25**: 235-252.

MAQUET, J. J. 1961. *The Premise of Inequality in Ruanda.* London: Oxford University Press.

MIDDLETON, J. & TAIT, D. (eds.). 1958. *Tribes Without Rulers.* London: Routledge & Kegan Paul.

PETERS, E. 1960. The Proliferation of Segments in the Lineage of the Bedouin in Cyrenaica. *Journal Royal Anthropological Institute* **90**: 29-53.

RADCLIFFE-BROWN, A. R. 1935. Patrilineal and Matrilineal Succession. *The Iowa Law Review* **20**: 283-303. Reprinted in Radcliffe-Brown, A. R. 1952. *Structure and Function in Primitive Society.* London: Cohen & West.

111

RADCLIFFE-BROWN, A. R. & FORDE, C. D. (eds.). 1950. *African Systems of Kinship and Marriage*. London: Oxford University Press.

SAHLINS, M. D. 1961. The Segmentary Lineage: An Organisation of Predatory Expansion. *American Anthropologist* **63**: 322-345.

SCHAPERA, I. 1956. *Government and Politics in Tribal Societies*. London: Watts.

SCHNEIDER, D. M. 1961. In Schneider, D. M. & Gough, K. (eds.), *Matrilineal Kinship*. University of California Press, 1-32.

SCHWAB, W. B. Kinship and Lineage among the Yoruba. *Africa* **25**: 352-374.

SOUTHALL, A. 1954. *Alur Society*. Cambridge: Heffer.

STENNING, D. J. 1959. *Savannah Nomads*. London: Oxford University Press.

STEWART, J. H. 1955. *Theory of Culture Change*. University of Illinois Press.

Barbara E. Ward

Varieties of the Conscious Model
The Fishermen of South China

INTRODUCTION

In the article entitled 'Social Structure' in *Anthropology Today*, Lévi-Strauss (1953, pp. 526-527) draws attention to the distinction between culturally produced models and observers' models. The former, constructs of the people under study themselves, he calls conscious models; the latter, unconscious models. Conscious models, he points out, may or may not exist for any particular phenomenon, may or may not provide useful insight, but, being part of the facts (and probably among the most significant facts), are in any case worthy of study. At best, they can 'furnish an important contribution to the understanding of the structures either as factual documents or as theoretical contributions similar to those of the anthropologist himself'.

Lévi-Strauss insists, in this same article, that though it has often been differently named ('ideal pattern', 'norm', for example) the concept of the conscious, or 'home-made' model is by no means a new one. Nor, he might have added, is it in any way novel to find it being employed in arguments about social continuity and social change, as, for example and most strikingly, by Leach in *Political Systems of Highland Burma* (1954). The present paper attempts to extend its use to a discussion of some of the problems of uniformity and variation posed by the unique temporal and spatial span of Chinese society and culture. In the course of this discussion the concept itself comes under examination.

THE FIRST PROBLEM

Anyone who has ever asked unsophisticated Chinese informants why they follow such and such a custom knows the maddeningly reiterated answer: 'Because we are Chinese'. At first one assumes

G

113

that this is simply a stock response to the uncultured foreigner or a way of fobbing off an impertinent outsider; after a time one realizes that most of one's informants do themselves see it as the correct explanation of almost all their own cultural behaviour and social organization. The conscious model of their own social system which they carry in their minds and which they use to explain, predict and justify their actual behaviour is labelled 'Chinese'. It is perhaps unnecessary to add that this insistence upon 'Chinese-ness' is accompanied by an unshakable conviction that all things Chinese are inherently superior.

Yet we are faced with a problem. What the people of one locality or time in the vast territory and history of the Chinese people think of as 'Chinese' in this sense may not necessarily be recognized as such by Chinese people elsewhere. For example, Southern Chinese fishermen have frequently expressed polite surprise to the writer on hearing that widows should not remarry, saying: 'We think you are mistaken. Certainly we Chinese always permit widows to marry again, perhaps it is one of your foreign customs to forbid them?' Yet there are many references in the literature to the existence of a ban on widow remarriage in traditional China. It would be possible to mention very many other examples of differences between different Chinese 'home-made' models. Even within a single village there can be quite marked distinctions between the conscious models carried by different sections of the population; yet each section, though aware of the difference, calls its own conscious model 'Chinese'. In other words, there is not one Chinese conscious model but several.

If this is so, then to talk as we commonly do of '*the* Chinese family' or '*the* traditional social structure of China' is as misleading at the level of ideal patterns as it has long been known to be misleading at the level of actual patterns of behaviour. Instead, we have to postulate a number of different Chinese ideal patterns varying in time and space with varying historical development and the demands of particular occupations and environments. Nevertheless, although there are and have been variations (and probably many more than is commonly believed) they are undoubtedly all variations on one easily recognizable theme. Important though it is to correct the popular view of a changeless

114

China, it still remains true that the most remarkable feature of Chinese civilization over its uniquely long history and wide geographical spread is its relative continuity and uniformity. The problem, then, is to provide such an explanation of continuity and uniformity as can at the same time accommodate an explanation of change and variation.

It is here that the concept of the conscious model may have some heuristic as well as descriptive value.

PRELIMINARY DISCUSSION

Historical reasons for this remarkable continuity and uniformity have often been stated. They are usually said to have been connected with the circumstances which made possible the long ascendency of a bureaucracy which, even in the most venal periods, remained open to talent. Entry into their ranks being through public, state-organized, written examinations in a narrow range of academic subjects, the bureaucrats were simply the most successful of a much larger category of the population, all of whom shared a similar education: the literati, or gentry. The facts that the bureaucrats controlled real power, that the needs of administration required that there could be no district without at least some bureaucrat in it, that the examinations were open to all, secured the China-wide prestige of the literati and their ideas. The fact that the examinations which they sat, and therefore the education which they underwent – often for more than twenty years of their lives – were almost exclusively concerned with the social ideas of Confucius on which they consciously modelled their own social norms, meant that in all parts of the country and at all times the literati held to what were essentially the same ideal patterns. In other words, it is likely that the conscious model of their own social system held by the Chinese literati (gentry) did in fact exhibit a very real continuity and uniformity, while at the same time its prestige was such that non-literati (whose ancestors and/or descendants might have been or might become literati) also aspired to follow it. Furthermore, all the actual sanctions of social order over literati and non-literati alike were in the last resort administered by bureaucrats, themselves literati, whose decisions and actions, inevitably

115

guided by the Confucian norms of their own conscious model, necessarily had a wide influence.

Recent historical scholarship (cp. Wright, 1960) has stressed not only that the interpretation of Confucian norms varied from time to time but also that there were always minorities even among the literati who rebelled against them; nevertheless, the statement that the long period of bureaucratic Imperial government was one in which the ideal patterns of the literati were remarkably uniform and stable is probably broadly true. There is equally little doubt that literati norms were widely approved by the non-literati, regarded as 'best' even by those who could neither follow them in practice nor even fully know them in detail, and used consciously as a measure of progress and a target to aim at by those who were engaged in social climbing or as an index of failure by those who were on the way down. In such circumstances as these it would be reasonable to postulate the development of a degree of agreement between the several Chinese traditional conscious models which could be ascribed, at least in part, to the overriding prestige of one particular conscious model (the literati one) and the authority in society at large of those who held it. One of the objects of the present paper is to examine the validity of this argument.

Assuming it to be valid, one would expect there to have developed most uniformity in those areas of social life which the literati model mapped in most detail and/or those over which they exercised most successful control. Conversely, the areas of greatest variety, whether in time or space, would be likely to be those for which literati norms were irrelevant. A simple example is the role of women. Non-literati China showed a fair variety of actual patterns and, no doubt, of conscious models too (we have already noted the question of the remarriage of widows); by comparison the literati scene was much simpler, for literati women were expected to play purely domestic roles in the narrow sense, and there was therefore little scope for variety. The ideal patterns appropriate to literati women were simply irrelevant to most of the women of different socio-economic levels, over whose daily lives the literati had in any case no control. This is not to say that the literati were not aware of these social differences. Of course they were, as their novels give ample

116

evidence. Their conscious models of Chinese society did not exclude the non-literati, but neither did they do anything to give them prestige, nor, usually, did they describe non-literati matters in any detail. And as very large areas of social living in fact fell outside the range of the literati's own practice, so, despite the very great influence of the relatively unchanging literati model, one can expect to find also considerable variety.

Now, in terms of groupings, the structures which the literati models mapped in most detail were those of family, lineage, and bureaucracy. But the bureaucracy exclusively and lineages essentially were literati structures. In China, non-literati, especially peasants, had no part in the one, and usually only a minor part in the other; overseas, neither existed. Thus one would expect local non-literati and overseas conscious models to show most agreement with their common (literati) model, and with each other, in matters of family structure. Where lineages exist, the conscious models of them are also likely to be fairly uniform, but other structures, being those less carefully or not at all described in the literati model, are likely to show much more variety.

A fairly wide reading of the literature, especially that on the overseas Chinese, has led me to think that a use of the concept of the conscious model somewhat on these lines can give quite valuable insight into the problem of variety-in-uniformity which the study of Chinese social systems inevitably poses, but only if the concept itself is fairly drastically reinterpreted. In what follows I attempt to illustrate this with reference to my own field material.

ILLUSTRATION: THE SOUTH CHINA FISHERMEN

The majority of the sea fishermen of Kwangtung (certainly the very large majority of the sea fishermen of Hong Kong) fall into the category *Tanka*, which is the Cantonese term for Cantonese-speaking boat-dwellers. The name, though used among themselves sometimes, is rightly regarded by the boat-people as a term of derision and disrepute. Until very recently, and to some extent still today, the boat-people have been despised, placed at the bottom of local systems of social stratification, and often

117

referred to as exemplars of loose sexual morality and other undesirable characteristics. They are frequently explained away as being not really Chinese, and I have heard well-educated Cantonese describing their non-Han descent, their non-Chinese language, and the special biological distinction which gives them six toes on each foot. Eyes and ears alone are enough to inform anyone who cares to notice that the boat-people, who very often go barefoot, have the normal complement of toes, and speak Cantonese – albeit usually with a 'broad' accent and always with the specialized vocabulary necessary to their specialized way of life. The non-Han descent question receives fuller treatment below, but briefly it can be argued here (1) that the boat-people's descent is probably neither more nor less 'non-Han' than that of most other Cantonese-speaking inhabitants of Kwangtung; (2) that there have been continuous additions to and departures from the boat population, which is therefore in no way 'racially' distinct; and (3) that such apparently physiological diacritica as can be discerned (for example, browner complexion, rolling gait, small leg muscles, and heavy shoulder development), together with nearly all the Tanka's social and cultural peculiarities, can be readily and much more economically ascribed to their aquatic mode of life. All boat-people I have ever met emphatically maintain that they are as 'Chinese' as any other Cantonese speakers, and habitually refer to themselves in the usual Cantonese phrase which can be translated: 'We people of China'. In Kwangtung Province they probably number between two and three million; in Hong Kong about 150,000, of whom about 100,000 live aboard fishing boats.

At first sight, the Tanka, particularly the fishing-boat-dwellers, seem to present such an extreme case of adaptation to environment, so entirely outside the range of literati experience, that, following the above argument, their socio-economic arrangements and their conscious models of them might be expected to depart quite radically from any of the usual Chinese patterns. Indeed, it would not be surprising if local land-lubberly opinion were right and the Tanka were to prove in the socio-cultural, if not in the 'racial' sense, 'un-Chinese'. The fact that until the last few decades very few Tanka received any education and that there were periods of Chinese history during which they

118

were forbidden to sit for the Imperial examinations lends plausibility to this suggestion. But observation does not bear it out. The fact is that, although their highly specialized water-borne way of life does pose certain problems which most Chinese do not have to face, there is precious little in Tanka social structure which cannot be paralleled elsewhere in China or in Chinese communities overseas.

Kau Sai, the community to which most of my most detailed observations apply, is a coastal village on one of the small islands which lie in the Port Shelter area on the eastern side of the British Crown Colony of Hong Kong. The present (1963) population comprises about 600 Tanka and three visiting non-Tanka schoolteachers. Nine Tanka households live ashore, the rest occupy some forty odd fishing boats, each with its permanent anchorage at the village. Except for the schoolteachers, all consider themselves Kau Sai people, and set a high valuation upon this claim. Most can, and do, quote genealogical information to show that they have been resident for at least four generations. The village contains a well-kept and well-patronized temple to a popular local sea deity, a newly built school, four or five small shops (selling mostly sweets, cigarettes, cakes, and soft drinks) and a new latrine, the hygienic nature of which is rightly a matter of immense local pride. There is a never-failing piped water supply, and ample space for net-drying and dyeing, fish-drying, etc. The village is most conveniently placed for each access to both fishing grounds and markets. Inshore purse-seining and inshore long-lining are the two main types of fishing practised. The average-sized boat measures about 30-35 feet overall and about 11 feet in the beam, and is mechanized with a small marine diesel engine. The numbers of people on board vary between three and fifteen, and include women and children.

Actual Kau Sai families are nuclear, patrilocal stem, or patrilocal extended (or in one or other stage of development towards or away from one of these climax states). Inshore long-lining of the small-scale kind practised from Kau Sai requires fewer able-bodied workers than purse-seining and can support fewer. There is no extended family among the long-liners. Inshore purse-seining, on the other hand, could not be carried on by a nuclear family alone. The additional complement may be made up with hired men, but this is unusual; Kau Sai purse-seiners all house families of the patrilocal extended type or parts of such families. Until very recently purse-seining always required the joint participation of two boats, which could quite easily provide living quarters for even a climax state extended family. Nowadays, with experience in mechanization, the actual fishing operations are usually performed by single vessels, the 'surplus' family members living still on the second junk which has thus become simply a house-boat. (There is a strong movement at present throughout all the boat communities of Hong Kong towards housing non-productive older people and children of school age and under ashore.) There are no female household heads in Kau Sai. All existing marriages have been patrilocal.

The most striking thing about this picture of the actual composition of families among these Kau Sai Tanka is the way in which, while agreeing remarkably closely with certain basic points in the descriptions of actual family composition elsewhere in China and among overseas Chinese, it shows an even nearer approach than many of them towards what is usually regarded as the Chinese ideal (i.e. the literati conscious model). As elsewhere there is a clear correlation between family size and family income; the larger the income the larger the family. As elsewhere, too, the mean size of families is around six. As elsewhere there is a strong emphasis upon patrilocality, patriliny, and the advantages of having many sons. But in Kau Sai this emphasis seems particularly strong. To take two examples only: there is no case of 'matrilocal' marriage, described for so many areas as existing though frowned upon, and there are no women heads of households.

It would of course be naïve to argue from these two facts that so far from being 'un-Chinese', as popular opinion so often believes, Tanka family structure is on the contrary rather closer in practice to the literati ideal than are the family structures of most other non-literati communities. It is true that the Tanka in Hong Kong at present are in general more conservative than most other local Chinese, but 'conservatism' is a descriptive term which by itself never explained anything. In any case, both 'matrilocal' marriages and female household heads are to be found among other Tanka in Hong Kong. Small passenger craft

120

in all the larger floating settlements of the Colony, including the main harbour, are very often owned and managed by females whose husbands are employed elsewhere. Among fishermen, even inshore fishermen as in Kau Sai, however, a female 'captain' is very rare. Whereas small-scale passenger transport in sheltered waters can be organized quite easily by a woman alone or with her unmarried daughters and younger sons, fishing on any scale above that of small hand-lining demands skills in handling men and boats at sea, in marketing procedures, including the organization of credit relationships, and in sheer physical strength which make it unsuitable for all but the most exceptional women. As for 'matrilocal' marriages, since it is known that in most Chinese communities only a relatively poor man will enter into such an alliance, their absence from Kau Sai is probably to be explained by the comparative prosperity of the village as a whole.

So one cannot explain the relative closeness of the actual patterns of Kau Sai family structure to the Chinese traditional ideal patterns as being simply a closer conscious following of the literati model. The sociological explanation is rather that the circumstances of a water-borne fisherman's life in Kau Sai seem to foster at least some of the same patterns as appear in that model. But this cannot be the whole story, for if technical and economic circumstances alone could account for Kau Sai's actual family structures we should be unable to explain their strong patrilineal and patrilocal bias. Male dominance can, and usually does, exist perfectly well in non-unilineal kinship systems or with matriliny. In Kau Sai, as we shall see, lineages can hardly be said to exist, yet patriliny is strongly entrenched. Why? It seems that after all the people's own explanation is right: 'because they are Chinese'. In other words, we are forced back to consider the conscious model again, for it is obvious that actual family structures in Kau Sai only make complete sense when they are seen as existing and developing within the framework of a strong patrilineal, patrilocal ideology. Kau Sai people do in fact hold a conscious model of family structure which is in essentials closely similar to that usually attributed to the traditional literati. They set a high value upon this model, and constantly invoke it as a yardstick for behaviour. Nearly all local gossip and discussion

121

centre upon it, and the very large majority of personal decisions are referred to it. It is a model for social action, which not only provides criteria for justification or criticism after an event, but also influences choice and decision beforehand. Conscious models which are less highly valued and less frequently used may well be of less significance, but in Kau Sai the conscious model of family structure is one of the crucial social facts.

THE SECOND PROBLEM:
WHAT IS A 'CONSCIOUS MODEL'?

I have earlier argued that one of the areas in which the prestige of the literati conscious model might be expected to have had most influence would be that of family structure because this was the one area which was common to both literati and non-literati, in the sense that all lived in families. Although it demonstrates that the conscious model alone does not explain the structure, Kau Sai material does suggest that in so far as the conscious model is significant this argument is likely to be borne out by the facts. Literati family norms, or some of them, do apply in Kau Sai, partly because they are appropriate to the technico-economic situation and partly because the people themselves give them high value and appeal to them every day. Does this then mean that it is useful, after all, to speak of a single China-wide conscious model of family structure? I think not; and for at least two reasons.

In the first place, by no means all the literati norms are to be found in either the observer's or the conscious models of Kau Sai family structure, nor are all aspects of the Kau Sai models in agreement with literati norms. We have already noted the re-marriage of widows, occurring normally (and, one should add, appropriately) and believed to be normative too in Kau Sai, but banned in theory and very frequently in practice by the literati. We have drawn attention also to the differing roles of women, and it is obvious that there must have been a whole host of details of literati family etiquette, etc., which would be quite outside the ken of Tanka boat-people. Then, secondly, the Tanka themselves are well aware that there are differences, and would not dare to claim the literati model for themselves. One of the difficulties of the early stages of fieldwork amongst them is always the need to overcome their conviction that they do not know the 'true' Chinese ways. 'We are not educated people, why do you come and ask us these things?' they say. Thus clarity is probably more nearly attained and the Kau Sai people's own ideas more nearly reflected by postulating two conscious models with a degree of consensus: a Kau Sai model and a literati model.

The question then arises: of whose consciousness are we speaking? So far as the Kau Sai model is concerned, there is no particular difficulty. The community is small, its members show a marked awareness of themselves as a local unit with common values. Although there are inevitably differences of opinion and differing degrees of knowledge, the general agreement on matters of, say, family structure is easily observable. It is otherwise with the literati model. Up till now we have simply assumed its existence, mentioning as evidence a shared educational system, common examinations, access to the same literature, literati control of the administration (which included the administration of justice), and so on. But this is evidence of a different order from that from which we can deduce the Kau Sai conscious model. Moreover, the traditional literati are long since dead, and we can hardly observe their collective consciousness now. All we can observe at the present time is the set of norms which are believed by present-day Chinese to have been the conscious models of the literati. We can assume that rather similar believed-in models existed also in the past, when they were presumably liable to 'correction' by existing local literati, in the light of their then existing conscious models, on the occasions in which they took the lead in village and clan affairs, acted as mediators in local disputes, and so on; and we may suppose that what we have earlier referred to as the 'overriding prestige' of the literati model may have exerted its influence in practice largely through such a process of 'correction'. In so far as Kau Sai today is concerned, what we have up till now called the literati conscious model is a postulate in the minds not of the literati but of the people in Kau Sai. It exists for them as an ideal, incompletely known, towards which they aspire but which they know they fall short of. For them it is, as it were, the 'real Chinese way' and therefore the best way of ordering social arrangements, and their own model, which is also

123

'Chinese' and better than anything non-Chinese, only approaches excellence in so far as it approximates the 'real Chinese-ness' of this believed-in literati model.

Thus the two conscious models we have postulated are brought into contact with each other simply because they both exist as ideas in the minds of the same (for us, Kau Sai) people. These people have other models in their minds, too. Tanka in Hong Kong know a good deal about the social arrangements of other local Chinese: Hakka, Cantonese of varying occupations and economic strata, Hoklo, and nowadays even Shanghainese. But the constructs they make about them are like observer's models, constructs about other social systems as the Tanka see them. They are not used as models for their own action, and they are rather the objects than the standards of criticism. On the other hand, when a Tanka has to deal with non-Tanka or gives up water-living and takes to paid employment ashore, he has ready to hand a fairly useful working model of non-Tanka Chinese structures by which to order his behaviour. Moreover, and this is the significant matter, he knows that non-Tanka Chinese also carry in their minds versions of the believed-in literati model which are essentially similar to his own, and that all regard it as the true Chinese way.

We are now in a position to restate the first naïve version of our argument. Whereas originally we postulated the existence of as many conscious models as there have been different groups in China, one of which, the literati model, had overriding influence over the others, we now suggest that every Chinese carries several conscious models in his mind. Some of these are like observer's models; they could be called internal observer's models, that is models of the socio-cultural arrangements of Chinese subgroups other than his own. He does not normally use them as models for action or standards of judgement, though he may do so if he has to change his own group membership and they may assist him in intergroup contacts. In addition he holds two other kinds of model: the one, which we may call the home-made or immediate model, is his own subgroup's model of its own socio-cultural system as they believe it to be, the other his subgroup's version of what they believe the 'true Chinese' literati model to have been. This may be called the believed-in traditional model, or the ideological model. Being based, however remotely, upon once existing relatively uniform literati practice, the ideological models held by different Chinese subgroups vary comparatively little. Their various immediate models, on the other hand, may well be expected to show wide differences between each other, especially in those areas which the believed-in traditions do not cover – for just as there are always large areas of a subgroup's ideological model which are irrelevant to its actual pattern of living and hence to its home-made (immediate) model, so there are likely to be more or less numerous parts of its immediate model which, like the actualities to which they refer, lie outside the range of its ideological model.

Strictly speaking, the only people who can observe differences between immediate models are outsiders (or social scientists); what a Chinese layman compares is his own immediate model of his own social arrangements with his own 'observer's' model of the other fellow's. As we have pointed out, such comparisons usually serve merely to confirm his belief in the superiority of his own group, but this conclusion is not reached in quite the same way as, say, the apparently similar conclusion that European social patterns are inferior. Foreign patterns are judged by criteria which the foreigners themselves do not and are not expected to share; the patterns of other Chinese groups are criticized according to criteria set by what are believed to be, and very largely are, agreed standards – the standards of the believed-in traditional (ideological) models. Therein, indeed, in the eyes of a Chinese lies the degree of 'Chinese-ness' of any other groups (or individuals) – how far do they or do they not conform to the ideological model which he not only believes in himself but believes them also to share? Only patterns of living which are so aberrant as to imply that this traditional ideology has never been accepted are dubbed 'non-Chinese'.

Thus it is plausible for a Cantonese landsman who criticizes Hakka, on the one hand, and Shanghainese, on the other, for not being 'really Chinese' to dismiss the water-people who speak his own language as completely non-Chinese because all that he ever sees of their way of life is obviously very far indeed from any literati derived ideological model. What he sees *is*, in this sense, 'un-Chinese': people living on boats, making a livelihood by

125

Barbara E. Ward

fishing or carrying cargo or, worse still, by carrying passengers – the last, being the most commonly seen by ordinary landsmen and therefore in their eyes the most 'typical', happens to be the one Tanka occupation with a high proportion of women managers, a grave departure from tradition. All in all, it would be surprising if the Tanka were not thought to practise all sorts of other non-Chinese traits (even matriliny has not infrequently been alleged), especially since the myth of non-Han descent is ready to hand and all landsmen are convinced that Tanka were never permitted to sit the Imperial examinations and so had no chance ever to have imbibed any education in literati norms. In their turn, the Tanka, measuring themselves and others by their own notion of the traditional, feel themselves entirely beyond criticism at sea, where literati-derived norms can have no place and they set their own standards, but, since they share the landsmen's views of their own ignorance, at a sad loss on land. 'Veritable dragons afloat', so runs one of their own sayings, 'but miserable worms ashore'.

FURTHER ILLUSTRATION

But let us return to Kau Sai.

The development of our original argument stated that what we are now calling the ideological model (the believed-in traditional model) would have most influence on those parts of any Chinese group's home-made model which dealt with family structures. We later claimed that the material from Kau Sai tended to confirm this view. The following brief consideration of non-family structures in Kau Sai may make this part of the discussion clearer.

We have suggested that Kau Sai family structure can only be understood if it is seen as existing in the framework of a strongly patrilineal ideology. In most parts of South China this traditionally found expression also in the actual existence of more or less strongly organized patrilineages together with highly developed conscious models of their structure, often written and usually ritualized. Leadership in these lineages was usually in the hands of their literati members, who were, of course, also responsible for their written rules. Thus for lineages there was usually quite a

126

close fit between conscious models and believed in traditional models. Kau Sai, however, a multi-surname village with no literati, has no lineages and, as far as I can ascertain, never has had any. In this, Kau Sai people are similar to other Tanka, to most Chinese in modern cities anywhere, and, indeed, to both rural and urban Chinese in many other parts of China and over- seas. The lack of permanent landed estates, the potential physical mobility afforded by boat-dwelling, the absence of literati from among them, and their economic dependence upon people who usually were not kinsmen in any sense – these were probably the factors which prevented the emergence of lineages among the Tanka. Kau Sai contains no ancestral halls, no genealogy books, and no corporate ancestor worship. Each family remembers its own dead on the usual formal occasions, but this ritual has (following Freedman, 1957) to be classed as memorialism rather than ancestor worship proper. There is no grouping intermediate between the family and the village, and the village is in no sense a kinship unit.

Paradoxically enough, the very fact that the Tanka have no lineages may be used to point up the strength of the influence of the believed-in traditional model of the family. The actual existence of a highly organized system of patrilineages necessarily affects family structure. Such a system may be said almost to dictate a patrilineal, patrilocal form of family, with biases towards polygyny and against both divorce and free widow remarriage; it goes with the careful control of women's repro- ductive powers and the treatment of women in general as jural minors. Thus it is arguable that where patrilineages exist family structures need not owe anything to any ideological model. Conversely, if in the absence of patrilineages family structures exhibit these, or many of these, characteristics, then it is reason- able to look for other influences – of which the existence of a prestigeful believed-in model may well be one. Our discussion of Kau Sai family structure, above, followed this line.

Beyond the field of family and lineage groupings we come to village structure. Our original argument predicts that where literati models are inapplicable, there wide variety is likely to be found. It is obvious that a settlement such as Kau Sai – without even a history of literati connexions, and with a highly specialized occupational basis which is linked with an unusual physical environment and gives the potentiality of almost unlimited physical mobility – is well outside the range of any literati-derived model. The kind of local grouping recorded as typical of Kwangtung and Fukien provinces (Freedman, 1958) is a single-surname village, its members comprising a single lineage (with the wives of the adult men and without their married sisters) under the leadership of its educated 'elders', the focus of village solidarity being an ancestral cult centred upon the lineage ancestral hall, to which there is usually attached a greater or lesser amount of lineage land. Kau Sai is not at all like that. It is, as we have just said, a multi-surname village, with no educated members. There is a tacit agreement that all heads of families are equal and a marked disinclination to assert any kind of personal leadership at the village level. A local deity ('shen') provides the focus of village solidarity, which is centred upon his temple. There is no corporate ancestor worship, no ancestral hall, and no landed property of any kind. Certainly, these are very considerable differences, and to that extent our argument is borne out; such studies as there are of villages in other parts of China and overseas show a number of other variations too.

Beyond the village we are no longer dealing with group structures. Each Kau Sai person has a series of dyadic relation-ships with other non-Kau Sai persons: market relationships, kinship and affinal relationships, and relationships connected with ritual and recreation. An anthropologist can observe a general congruence between the spatial areas in which these different relationships are concentrated. Borrowing an image from zoology, I propose to call the space so demarcated a 'territory'. Those who live within it do not form a social group in the sense that they ever act corporately, and though they are aware that they have much in common they do not think of themselves as a unit. The territory is simply a mappable area whose boundaries form the limits of most intense socio-economic interaction. Only a few social or economic relationships lead outside it, but its population is in effect merely the pool from which individual Kau Sai people draw their contacts.

This, of course, is my own observer's model. As an anthropologist I see Kau Sai as one of a number of very similar local groups situated within an area definable only in terms of the degree of intensity of the (dyadic) socio-economic relationships existing within it. The Hong Kong Government, on the other hand, sets Kau Sai, along with some of these other villages and many more not included in the territory, within the boundaries of an administrative District which in turn is encapsulated, along with other similar Districts, within a larger administrative area, the New Territories. The Governmental structure includes the positions of District Commissioner (for the New Territories), and District Officers (for the Districts), and a fairly regular system of Village Representatives and Rural Committees. Kau Sai people, though aware of these governmental notions, do not really share them.

Looking outwards from his own village, a Kau Sai man sees other fairly similar villages (the inferiorities of which he frequently remarks), the local market town, and the three major urban fish-market centres near the city of Victoria (Hong Kong island). There is also the District Office, which is situated in Kowloon. He does not see Kau Sai as in any way subordinate to any of these places, all relationships with which (including relationships with Government) he thinks of entirely in personal dyadic terms. In other words, like the anthropologist, he sees beyond the village level only sets and networks of dyadic relationships. His view differs from mine, however, in that he does not normally conceptualize what I have termed the territory – though if pressed he may be induced to recognize its existence. In so far as his own model sets Kau Sai within any embracing larger units, it selects only two or three rather vague entities, both thought of in cultural rather than in social structural terms: 'the water-people' (sometimes, also 'we water-people on the eastern side (of Hong Kong)') and 'the Chinese'.

Now, it is arguable that since the literati were so closely connected with the bureaucracy in traditional China their view of the place of village groups in the wider society was probably not far different from that of the Government of Hong Kong today. The boundaries of administrative districts, their nomenclature, and the titles of the officials of different ranks were of course different, but the model was of the same general bureaucratic type. But neither the Kau Sai home-made model nor the actuality have been influenced by it. How is this to be explained?

The difficulty is more apparent than real. The traditional Chinese bureaucratic apparatus stopped short of the village level at the town with the lowest magistrate's court ('yamen'). Non-literati villagers would have little contact with officialdom, and would do everything possible to make that little less. By no stretch of the imagination could the literati's bureaucratic patterns be regarded as models for peasant emulation as their family patterns could. We have stated that Kau Sai's relationships with the wider society today are not (from the point of view of Kau Sai people) conducted in group terms but as a series of dyadic relationships – and this was no doubt as true of its relationships with the bureaucracy in, say, the Ching dynasty as it is with the British administration today. There was thus no clash between theory and practice to force a change of view, and Kau Sai's own conscious (home-made) model of its position in the wider society could co-exist quite easily with what little its people knew of the literati model. They just did not meet.

If this part of the evidence for Kau Sai may be generalized for China as a whole, then it would seem to follow that here (in the relationships between villages and the wider society) is another area of social life in which relatively wide variety is to be expected. Few studies of Chinese villages to date have been concerned with extra-village relationships, but I should be surprised if in fact there was not much more uniformity at this level than at the level of internal village organization. At least three factors make this likely. In the first place, there were similarities in such economic and technological matters as means of transport, kinds of market, types of produce and so on all over China which must have set certain rather similar limitations to the possibilities of variation; second, and probably more significant, where relationships with the bureaucracy were concerned, one party to the relationship was everywhere very much the same; and, third, there was, of course, the strong influence of the believed-in traditional models of the proper way for conducting dyadic relationships, which being based on the pattern of family and kin relationships were relevant to everyone. That they were also largely effective and largely uniform – as from our argument we would expect – is well attested by the literature which over and over again describes the 'personalization' of all kinds of non-kinship relationship among the Chinese.

A word must be said about religion. Because formally the literati despised the popular cults we should expect perhaps the greatest variety of all to appear in this sphere. There is a good deal of evidence in support of this contention. In other words, there being no literati-derived model for religious behaviour outside the state and ancestral cults (which were uniform), the popular cults could develop to suit local fancy – and did.

THE PROCESS OF ASSIMILATION

Finally, because our data refer to people usually believed to be marginal, if not foreign, to Chinese society proper, it is necessary to turn to history. I have already mentioned the 'myth' of non-Han descent, and stated that in my opinion the present-day Tanka are neither more nor less 'non-Han' than most of the other Cantonese-speaking inhabitants of South China. It is interesting to note that the People's Government appears to agree with this view, for in the Census of 1953 the Tanka are not listed among the fifty separate ethnic groups of China. Nevertheless, as we have seen, popular opinion and most of the very scanty literature about the Tanka still explain their supposedly un-Chinese social structure and customs in terms of their ethnic distinctness. In this sense the story of non-Han descent is a myth – that is, it is a statement which, whether true or not, is used to explain or justify behaviour. (In this sense, too – the sense propounded by Leach (op. cit.) – the models we have so far been discussing are also myths.)

My views of the actual history of the Tanka follow fairly closely those of Wiens (1954) and Ch'en (1946). Wiens, basing his work on Eberhard, argues that the early Yueh culture of South China was not in reality a separate culture at all, but that the term 'Yueh' hid the product of a mixture of different cultures blended into a new individuality. The mixture, which comprised at least Yao and Tan (from which the compound word Tanka is derived) and T'ai or Chuang elements, had already occurred with the appearance of Yueh as a political concept, that is at the latest by the seventh century B.C.

Now, if Yueh culture already contained elements of Tan culture as early as the seventh century B.C., then there are three possibilities: either the Tan were already as much 'part of' the common culture and society of South China as anybody else, or at least some of the Tan were so, or, at the very least, Tan and Yueh culture cannot have been entirely foreign to each other. Even if only some of the Tan people had been absorbed by then – or none – it does not follow that a process of assimilation did not continue long after the seventh century B.C. We have, of course, ample evidence of continued assimilation in this part of China, particularly for the later centuries as Han culture, pushing steadily outwards, not only drew in what had been Yueh but also pressed upon the border peoples hitherto unassimilated to Yueh. There can be no reasonable doubt that the two and a half thousand years or so since Yueh first appeared as a political concept have given full opportunity for the Tan, less remote than the hill tribes and more mobile, to be assimilated to the surrounding people.

But the upholders of the traditional view claim that the opportunity was never taken; that though not remote physically the water-people have always remained so remote socially that they have been able to retain their original culture and social structure virtually unchanged for all this length of time. Quite apart from the fact that if this were so then the original Tanka socio-cultural system must have been quite presciently 'Chinese', I remain sceptical about the alleged segregation. The points usually mentioned are that the Tanka were not permitted to sit for the Imperial examinations, to live ashore, or to marry with landsmen. The implication is that these were official prohibitions, but although Imperial decrees did from time to time (by no means always) include 'boatmen' in the list of those ineligible for the examinations, it is certain that for at least the last two hundred years there have been no official disabilities. Intensive literary research has led one of the Tanka's recent students, Professor Ch'en Hsü Ch'ing, to the conclusion that it was probably always local prejudice rather than official policy that kept the Tanka out. A boatman who remained on his boat would necessarily find it almost impossible to become educated and certainly useless to marry a landsman's daughter, but a boatman who moved ashore could 'pass' without difficulty. Professor Ch'en asserts that there have always been many who did so, but that this has tended to go unnoticed because Tanka who have moved ashore successfully are no longer visibly Tanka at all and are careful to conceal their origins. Data from my own fieldwork in Hong Kong entirely support this view.

A point consistently overlooked in the traditional notion of Tanka separateness is that whatever their respective ethnic origins land- and water-people are and have long been inextricably closely interrelated through the facts of economics. The fishermen of Kau Sai, for example, are all involved in long-standing credit relationships with fish-dealers who are landsmen, and buy their boats, gear, and provisions from other landsmen – often also on credit. These are personalized relationships based as a rule upon long acquaintance (Ward, 1960) and requiring almost daily meetings, frequent mutual entertainment at the tea houses, and so on. In the face of so much daily intercourse with people whose ways of life they know to be of a kind they themselves must adopt if they are to gain any prestige in the wider society, the Tanka could only have maintained a markedly different system if they had resolutely rejected assimilation. There is considerable evidence of Southern hill tribes having done just that; there is no similar evidence (at least for several centuries) for any of the Tanka. And there is no doubt that today the contrary is true.

Moreover their system is not different.

And yet some non-Han, or at least non-literati, items have been retained, and even valued for their own sake. Such, for example, are the Tanka's ear-rings and bracelets, their using wooden figures rather than 'soul tablets' to represent their dead, and certain peculiarities of their marriage customs. Items of this general kind show much variation locally in other parts of China too: in Hong Kong alone one can see daily the unmistakably typical Hakka hats or Hoklo silver hair ornaments. Why is this? I can only suggest that these are all things which are capable of being used as 'badges' of identification by the groups concerned, self-conscious marks of differentiation and local pride – which can undoubtedly co-exist with a firm belief in the ultimate superiority of a 'real' Chinese tradition which is known to reject such 'barbarisms'. Many of the literati's own customs in such matters as these were in any case out of reach of the peasantry, because of sumptuary laws or expense. It is worth noticing, too, that such items as these can easily be changed if a family decides to give up its old way of life and start the upward climb; they are more and more being discarded by go-ahead, urbanized water-people in Hong-Kong at the present time.

We earlier referred to the remarriage of widows. This is far too widespread as a social fact in China to be a badge of differentiation nor is it on all fours with such purely cultural items as the wearing of jade bracelets. The 'rule' that a widow should not remarry was part of the literati ideal of the continuing patrilineal, patrilocal extended family. A continuing family household, with a secure economic background, can afford to support its widows; smaller households, breaking up every (or every other) generation, cannot. Since the actual numbers of continuing extended families were probably always few, so widow remarriage, even for members of the literati class, must have always been common. So it is not particularly surprising to find that Kau Sai people believe it to have been part of the traditional model.

We are arguing, then, that the very long history of assimilation affected the 'Tan' people no less than anyone else in South China, with the result that their social structure and culture have long been essentially 'Chinese'. And we would argue further that one of the main weapons by which Han civilization asserted its supremacy was its successful use of what we have called 'the believed-in traditional model'. We must add, too, that this was not due solely to the direct influence of the bureaucrats, though this played its part, or to their direct teaching, though that was important, but also to the more subtle influences of proverbs and legends, story-tellers, the drama and so on, and above all to the demands of social ambition – for since entry into the ranks of the literati was at all periods the major legitimate road to power and prestige, so almost all Chinese who were at all ambitious necessarily strove to acquire literati norms for themselves or their children. The gap was constantly, if irregularly, being narrowed – and always in the same direction.

SUMMARY AND CONCLUSION

The task set at the beginning of this paper was to discover a sociological formula which, while accounting for the uniquely widespread uniformity and long continuity of traditional Chinese society and culture, would at the same time explain the continued existence of quite considerable variation within it. Historically it seems fairly clear that one of the most significant influences for conformity was the relatively uniform and largely written conscious (normative) model of social life held by the literati classes from whom the administration was recruited. But this statement does nothing to explain the variations, and begs most of the sociological questions about how this influence actually worked. Illustrative material drawn from the writer's own fieldwork in what can fairly be considered a still largely 'traditional', though unusual, village in Hong Kong suggests that the concept 'conscious model' (more often referred to as 'ideal pattern' or 'norm': cp. Lévi-Strauss, 1953) requires rethinking.

The people of Kau Sai appear to have three different kinds of model of Chinese social arrangements in their consciousness. First there is their own notion of their own social and cultural system; this, again following Lévi-Strauss, we called the 'home-made' model; possibly for scientific use the term 'immediate model' might be more acceptable. Second, there is their version of what they believe to have been the traditional literati system; this we named the 'believed-in traditional model', or, better because of wider applicability, the 'ideological model'. It acts for them as their measure of what is truly Chinese, and wherever it is relevant it is, and has been, used as a corrective for their immediate model and so for their actual structure. Then, third, there are the various models they have constructed of the socio-cultural arrangements of other Chinese groups. These we called 'internal observers' models'. As a type they differ from observers' models proper (i.e. the models constructed by outsiders, including social scientists) only in that they are held by people who consider themselves members of the same wider society with those whom they are observing.

This breakdown into three kinds of conscious model then

allows us to see the process towards uniformity in China developing out of innumerable and continued shifts in the various immediate models of different local, occupational, and ethnic groups in the direction of their ideological models, which, being based on the relatively uniform actual literati structures, and often in the past subjected to correction by living literati (in the light of their own essentially similar ideological models), were in fact very much alike. Inevitably, however, ideological models derived from literati practice could not be entirely relevant to non-literati social life, which therefore had still a good deal of freedom to develop local idiosyncrasies in such fields as, for example, the sexual division of labour, village organization, and popular religion.

It is a striking fact that the one kind of structure which was lived in by all groups in China, and therefore the one to which the literati-derived ideological models were most universally relevant, was also the one to which these models gave the most value, namely: the family. Besides the patterns for family structures, the ideological models probably contained little that was of relevance to all actual group structures, though much (e.g. lineage patterns) which was relevant to many. However, since in setting the highest value upon family relationships they stressed also the rightness of 'familializing' all extra-family relationships, almost everything they contained about dyadic relationships of all kinds was relevant – and was given practical expression in the markedly similar cast of actual dyadic relationships throughout China.

Thus in speaking of the uniformity and continuity of the traditional Chinese social system it seems that what we are primarily referring to is the China-wide existence of essentially similar family structures and similar ('family-like') methods of organizing dyadic relationships outside the family. Less widespread, but probably more uniform where existing, were patrilineal lineage structures, and over all, of course, was the bureaucratic structure which, though it was lived in by and formed a detailed part of the immediate model of only some Chinese, nevertheless affected all because it was the administrative framework of the state. Outside these areas of social structure there was much variety, but because these were the areas which were most highly valued public opinion – scholarly as well as lay, and Chinese as well as foreign – has usually tended to overestimate the uniformities and underemphasize the variations.

Lévi-Strauss' substitution of the term 'conscious model' for 'ideal pattern' or 'norm' has the merit of getting away from the philosophical and verbal difficulties inherent in these two terms, but if it implies that there is ever one single version of their own social system constructed in the minds of all the individuals of any society it is misleading. We can and must contrast conscious models, existing as constructs in the minds of the people under study themselves, with observers' models constructed by outsiders, including social scientists, but it is probably always useful to think also in terms of at least the three different kinds of conscious model we have here distinguished as immediate models, ideological models, and internal observers' models. The degree to which any society exhibits widespread or lasting uniformities is likely to be connected with, among other things, the degree of similarity between the ideological models held by different subgroups and the narrowness of the gaps between ideological and immediate models on the one hand and between both these models and the actual structures on the other.

REFERENCES

CH'EN HSÜ CHING. 1936. *Tanka Researches*. Canton: Lingnan University Press (in Chinese).

FREEDMAN, MAURICE. 1957. *Chinese Family and Marriage in Singapore*. London: H.M.S.O.

—— 1958. *Lineage Organization in Southeastern China*. London: Athlone Press.

LEACH, E. R. 1954. *Political Systems of Highland Burma*. London: Bell.

LÉVI-STRAUSS, CLAUDE. 1953. Social Structure. In A. L. Kroeber (ed.), *Anthropology Today*. Chicago: University of Chicago Press.

WARD, BARBARA E. 1960. Cash or Credit Crops? *Economic Developments and Cultural Change* 8: 148-163.

WIENS, HEROLD JACOB. 1954. *China's March toward the Tropics*. Hamden, Conn.: Shoe String Press.

WRIGHT, ARTHUR F. (ed.). 1960. *The Confucian Persuasion*. Stanford, California: Stanford University Press.

Marshall D. Sahlins

On the Sociology of Primitive Exchange

In a discussion that has anthropological pretensions, 'provisional generalization' is no doubt a redundant phrase.[1] Yet the present venture needs a doubly cautious introduction. Its generalizations have developed out of a dialogue with ethnographic materials – many of these are appended Tylorian fashion as 'illustrative materials'[2] – but no rigorous tests have been applied. Perhaps the conclusions may be offered as a plea to ethnography rather than a contribution to theory, if these are not again the same thing. At any rate, there follow some suggestions about the interplay in primitive communities between forms, material conditions, and social relations of exchange.

I

MATERIAL FLOW AND SOCIAL RELATIONS

What are in the received wisdom 'noneconomic' or 'exogenous' conditions are in the primitive reality the very organization of economy.[3] A material transaction is usually a momentary episode in a continuous social relation. The social relation exerts governance: the flow of goods is constrained by, is part of, a status etiquette. 'One cannot treat Nuer economic relations by themselves, for they always form part of direct social relations of a general kind', Evans-Pritchard writes: '. . . there is always between them a general social relationship of one kind or another, and their economic relations, if such they may be called, must conform to this general pattern of behavior' (1940, pp. 90-91). The dictum is broadly applicable (cf. White 1959, pp. 242-245).

Yet the connection between material flow and social relations is reciprocal. A specific social relation may constrain a given movement of goods, but a specific transaction – 'by the same token' – suggests a particular social relation. If friends make gifts, gifts make friends. A great proportion of primitive exchange, much more than our own traffic, has as its decisive function this latter, instrumental one: the material flow underwrites or initiates social relations. Thus do primitive peoples transcend Hobbesian chaos. For the indicative condition of primitive society is the absence of a public and sovereign power: persons and (especially) groups confront each other not merely as distinct interests but with the possible inclination and certain right to physically prosecute these interests. Force is decentralized, legitimately held in severalty, the social compact has yet to be drawn, the state nonexistent. So peacemaking is not a sporadic intersocietal event, it is a continuous process within society itself. Groups must 'come to terms' – the phrase notably connotes a material exchange satisfactory on both sides:

'In these primitive and archaic societies there is no middle path. There is either complete trust or mistrust. One lays down one's arms, renounces magic and gives everything away, from casual hospitality to one's daughter or one's property. It is in such conditions that men, despite themselves, learnt to renounce what was theirs and made contracts to give and repay. But then they had no choice in the matter. When two groups of men meet they may move away or in case of mistrust or defiance they may resort to arms; or else they can come to terms' (Mauss, 1954, p. 79).

Even on its strictly practical side, exchange in primitive communities has not the same role as the economic flow in modern industrial communities. The place of transaction in the total economy is different: under primitive conditions it is more detached from production, less firmly hinged to production in an organic way. Typically, it is less involved than modern exchange in the acquisition of means of production, more involved with the redistribution of finished goods through the community. The bias is that of an economy in which food holds a commanding position, and in which day-to-day output does not depend on a massive technological complex nor a complex division of labor. It is the bias also of a domestic mode of production: of household producing units, division of labor by sex and age dominant, production that looks to familial requirements, and direct access by domestic groups to strategic resources. It is the bias of a social order in which rights to control returns go along with rights to use resources of production, and in which there is very limited traffic in titles or income privileges in resources. It is the bias, finally, of societies ordered in the main by kinship. Such characteristics of primitive economies as these, so broadly stated, are of course subject to qualification in specific instances. They are offered only as a guide to the detailed analysis of distribution that follows. It is also advisable to repeat that 'primitive' shall refer to cultures lacking a political state, and it applies only insofar as economy and social relations have not been modified by the historic penetration of states.

On a very general view, the array of economic transactions in the ethnographic record may be resolved into two types. First, those 'vice-versa' movements between two parties known familiarly as 'reciprocity' ($A \rightleftarrows B$). The second, centralized movements: collection from members of a group, often under one hand, and redivision within this group

$$\overset{A}{\underset{B \ C \ D}{\uparrow\uparrow\uparrow}} \supset \overset{A}{\underset{B \ C \ D}{\downarrow\downarrow\downarrow}}$$

This is 'pooling' or 'redistribution'. On an even more general view, the two types merge. For pooling is an organization of reciprocities, a system of reciprocities – a fact of central bearing upon the genesis of large-scale redistribution under chiefly aegis. But this most general understanding merely suggests concentration in the first place on reciprocity; it remains the course of analytic wisdom to separate the two.

Their social organizations are very different. True, pooling and reciprocity may occur in the same social contexts – the same close kinsmen pool their resources in household commensality, for instance, also individuals share things with one another – but the precise social relations of pooling and reciprocity are not the same. The material transaction that is pooling is socially a *within* relation, the collective action of a group. Reciprocity is a *between* relation, the action and reaction of two parties. Thus pooling is the complement of social unity and, in Polanyi's term, 'centricity'; whereas, reciprocity is social duality and 'symmetry'. Pooling stipulates a social center where goods meet and thence

141

flow outwards, and a social boundary too, within which persons (or subgroups) are cooperatively related. But reciprocity stipulates two sides, two distinct social-economic interests. Reciprocity can establish solidary relations, in so far as the material flow suggests assistance or mutual benefit, yet the social fact of sides is inescapable.

Considering the established contributions of Malinowski and Firth, Gluckman, Richards, and Polanyi, it does not seem too sanguine to say that we know fairly well the material and social concomitants of pooling. Also, what is known fits the argument that pooling is the material side of 'collectivity' and 'centricity'. Cooperative food production, rank and chieftainship, collective political and ceremonial action, these are some of the ordinary contexts of pooling in primitive communities. To review very briefly:

The everyday, workaday variety of redistribution is familial pooling of food. The principle suggested by it is that products of collective effort in provisioning are pooled, especially should the cooperation entail division of labor. Stated so, the rule applies not only to householding but to higher-level cooperation as well, to groups larger than households that develop about some task of procurement – say, buffalo-impounding in the Northern Plains or netting fish in a Polynesian lagoon. With qualifications – such as the special shares locally awarded special contributions to the group endeavor – the principle remains at the higher, as at the lower, household level: 'Goods collectively procured are distributed through the collectivity.'

Rights of call on the produce of the underlying population, as well as obligations of generosity, are everywhere associated with chieftainship. The organized exercise of these rights and obligations is redistribution:

'I think that throughout the world we would find that the relations between economics and politics are of the same type. The chief, everywhere, acts as a tribal banker, collecting food, storing it, and protecting it, and then using it for the benefit of the whole community. His functions are the prototype of the public finance system and the organization of State treasuries of to-day. Deprive the chief of his privileges and financial benefits and who suffers most but the whole tribe?' (Malinowski, 1937, pp. 232-233).

This use 'for the benefit of the whole community' takes various forms: subsidizing religious ceremony, social pageantry, or war; underwriting craft production, trade, the construction of technical apparatus and of public and religious edifices; redistributing diverse local products; hospitality and succor of the community (in severalty or in general) during shortage. Speaking more broadly, redistribution by powers-that-be serves two purposes, either of which may be dominant in a given instance. The practical, logistic function – redistribution – sustains the community, or community effort, in a material sense. At the same time, or alternatively, it has an instrumental function: as a ritual of communion and of subordination to central authority, redistribution sustains the corporate structure itself, that is in a social sense. The practical benefits may be critical, but, whatever the practical benefits, chiefly pooling generates the spirit of unity and centricity, codifies the structure, stipulates the centralized organization of social order and social action –

'. . . every person who takes part in the *aŋa* [feast organized by a Tikopia chief] is impelled to participate in forms of co-operation which for the time being go far beyond his personal interests and those of his family and reach the bounds of the whole community. Such a feast gathers together chiefs and their clansfolk who at other times are rivals ready to criticize and slander each other, but who assemble here with an outward show of amity. . . . In addition, such purposive activity subserves certain wider social ends, which are common in the sense that every person or nearly every person knowingly or unknowingly promotes them. For instance, attendance at the *aŋa* and participation in the economic contributions does in fact help to support the Tikopia system of authority' (Firth, 1950, pp. 230-231).

So we have at least the outline of a functional theory of redistribution. The central issues are now likely to be developmental ones, the specification by comparison or phylogenetic study of selective circumstances. The economic anthropology of reciprocity, however, is not at the same stage. One reason, perhaps, is a popular tendency to view reciprocity as balance, as unconditional one-for-one exchange. Considered as a material transfer, reciprocity is often not that at all. Indeed, it is precisely through scrutiny of departures from balanced exchange that one glimpses the interplay between reciprocity, social relations, and material circumstances.

Reciprocity is a whole class of exchanges, a continuum of forms. This is specially true in the narrow context of material transactions – as opposed to a broadly conceived social principle or moral norm of give-and-take. At one end of the spectrum stands the assistance freely given, the small currency of everyday kinship, friendship, and neighborly relations, the 'pure gift' Malinowski called it, regarding which an open stipulation of return would be unthinkable and unsociable. At the other pole, self-interested seizure, appropriation by chicanery or force requited only by an equal and opposite effort on the principle of *lex talionis*, 'negative reciprocity' as Gouldner phrases it. The extremes are notably positive and negative in a moral sense. The intervals between them are not merely so many gradations of material balance in exchange, they are intervals of sociability. The distance between poles of reciprocity is, among other things, social distance:

'Unto a stranger thou mayest lend upon usury; but unto thy brother thou shalt not lend usury' (Deuteronomy xxiii, 21).

'Native [Siuai] moralists assert that neighbors should be friendly and mutually trustful, whereas people from far-off are dangerous and unworthy of morally just consideration. For example, natives lay great stress on honesty involving neighbors while holding that trade with strangers may be guided by *caveat emptor*' (Oliver, 1955, p. 82).

'Gain at the cost of other communities, particularly communities at a distance, and more especially such as are felt to be aliens, is not obnoxious to the standards of homebred use and wont' (Veblen, 1915, p. 46).

'A trader always cheats people. For this reason intra-regional
144

trade is rather frowned upon while inter-tribal trade gives to the [Kapauku] businessman prestige as well as profit' (Pospisil, 1958, p. 127).

II

A SCHEME OF RECIPROCITIES

A purely formal typology of reciprocities is possible, one based exclusively on immediacy of returns, equivalence of returns, and like material and mechanical dimensions of exchange. The classification thus in hand, one might proceed to correlate sub-types of reciprocity with diverse 'variables' such as kinship distance of parties to the transaction. The virtue of this manner of exposition is that it is 'scientific', or so it would seem. Among the defects is that it is bogus, really just a metaphor of exposition, not a true history of experiment. It ought to be recognized from the beginning that the distinction of one type of reciprocity from another is more than formal. A feature such as the expectation of returns says something about the spirit of exchange, about its disinterestedness or its interestedness, the impersonality, the compassion. Any seeming formal classification conveys these meanings: it is as much a moral as a mechanical scheme. (That the recognition of the moral quality prejudges the relation of exchange to social 'variables', in the sense that the latter are then logically connected to variations in exchange, is not contested. This is a sign that the classification is good.)

The actual kinds of reciprocity are many in any primitive society, let alone in the primitive world taken as a whole. 'Vice-versa movements' may include sharing and counter-sharing of unprocessed food, informal hospitality, ceremonious affinal exchanges, loaning and repaying, compensation of specialized or ceremonial services, the transfer that seals a peace agreement, impersonal haggle, and so on and on. We have several ethno-graphic attempts to cope typologically with the empirical diversity, notably Douglas Oliver's scheme of Siuai transactions (1955, pp. 229-231; cf. Price, 1962, pp. 37 f; Spencer, 1959, pp. 194 f; Marshall, 1961; and others). In *Crime and Custom*, Malinowski wrote rather broadly and unconditionally about reciprocity; in the *Argonauts*, however, he developed a classification of Trobriand exchanges out of manifold variations in balance and equivalence (Malinowski, 1922, pp. 176-194). It was from this vantage-point, looking to the directness of returns, that the *continuum* which is reciprocity was revealed:

'I have on purpose spoken of forms of exchange, of gifts and counter-gifts, rather than of barter or trade, because, although there exist forms of barter pure and simple, there are so many transitions and gradations between that and simple gift, that it is impossible to draw any fixed line between trade on the one hand, and the exchange of gifts on the other. . . . In order to deal with these facts correctly it is necessary to give a complete survey of all forms of payment or present. In this survey there will be at one end the extreme cases of pure gift, that is an offering for which nothing is given in return [but see Firth, 1957, pp. 221, 222]. Then, through many customary forms of gift or payment, partially or conditionally returned, which shade into each other, there come forms of exchange, where more or less strict equivalence is observed, arriving finally at real barter' (Malinowski, 1922, p. 176).

Malinowski's perspective may be taken beyond the Trobriands and applied broadly to reciprocal exchange in primitive societies. It seems possible to lay out in abstract fashion a continuum of reciprocities, based on the 'vice-versa' nature of exchanges, along which empirical instances encountered in the particular ethnographic case can be placed. The stipulation of material returns, less elegantly, the 'sidedness' of exchange, would be the critical thing. For this there are obvious objective criteria, such as the toleration of material unbalance and the leeway of delay: the initial movement of goods from hand to hand is more or less requited materially and there are variations too in the time allowed for reciprocation (again see Firth, 1957, pp. 220-221). Put another way, the spirit of exchange swings from disinterested concern for the other chap through mutuality to self-interest. So expressed, the assessment of 'sidedness' can be supplemented by ethnographic observation in addition to those of immediacy and material equivalence: the initial transfer may be voluntary, involuntary, prescribed, contracted; the return freely bestowed,

146

exacted, or dunned; the exchange haggled or not, the subject of accounting or not; and so forth.

The spectrum of reciprocities proposed for general use is defined by its extremes and mid-point:

1. *Generalized reciprocity, the solidary extreme* ($A \xleftarrow{\longrightarrow} B$)

'Generalized reciprocity' refers to transactions that are putatively altruistic, transactions on the line of assistance given and, if possible and necessary, assistance returned. The ideal type is Malinowski's 'pure gift'. Other indicative ethnographic formulae are 'sharing', 'hospitality', 'free gift', 'help', and 'generosity'. Less sociable, but tending toward the same pole are 'kinship dues', 'chiefly dues', and *'noblesse oblige'*. Price (1962) refers to the genre as 'weak reciprocity' by reason of the vagueness of the obligation to reciprocate.

At the extreme, say voluntary food-sharing among near kinsmen – or for its logical value, one might think of the suckling of children in this context – the expectation of a direct material return is unseemly. At best it is implicit. The material side of the transaction is repressed by the social: reckoning of debts outstanding cannot be overt and is typically left out of account. This is not to say that handing over things in such form, even to 'loved ones', generates no counter-obligation. But the counter is not stipulated by time, quantity, or quality: the expectation of reciprocity is indefinite. It usually works out that the time and worth of reciprocation are not alone conditional on what was given by the donor, but also upon what he will need and when, and likewise what the recipient can afford and when. Receiving goods lays on a diffuse obligation to reciprocate when necessary to the donor and/or possible for the recipient. The requital thus may be very soon, but then again it may be never. There are people who even in the fullness of time are incapable of helping themselves or others. A good pragmatic indication of generalized reciprocity is a sustained one-way flow. Failure to reciprocate does not cause the giver of stuff to stop giving: the goods move one way, in favor of the have-not, for a very long period.

2. *Balanced reciprocity, the midpoint* ($A \xrightleftharpoons{} B$)

'Balanced reciprocity' refers to direct exchange. In precise

147

balance, the reciprocation is the customary equivalent of the thing received and is without delay. Perfectly balanced reciprocity, the simultaneous exchange of the same types of goods to the same amounts, is not only conceivable but ethnographically attested in certain marital transactions (e.g. Reay, 1959, pp. 95 f), friendship compacts (Seligman, 1910, p. 70), and peace agreements (Hogbin, 1939, p. 79; Loeb, 1926, p. 204; Williamson, 1912, p. 183). 'Balanced reciprocity' may be more loosely applied to transactions which stipulate returns of commensurate worth or utility within a finite and narrow period. Much 'gift-exchange', many 'payments', much that goes under the ethnographic head of 'trade' and plenty that is called 'buying-selling' and involves 'primitive money' belong in the genre of balanced reciprocity.

Balanced reciprocity is less 'personal' than generalized reciprocity. From our own vantage-point it is 'more economic'. The parties confront each other as distinct economic and social interests. The material side of the transaction is at least as critical as the social: there is more or less precise reckoning, as the things given must be covered within some short term. So the pragmatic test of balanced reciprocity becomes an inability to tolerate one-way flows; the relations between people are disrupted by a failure to reciprocate within limited time and equivalence leeways. It is notable of the main run of generalized reciprocities that the material flow is sustained by prevailing social relations; whereas, for the main run of balanced exchange, social relations hinge on the material flow.

3. *Negative reciprocity, the unsociable extreme* ($A \rightleftarrows B$)

'Negative reciprocity' is the attempt to get something for nothing with impunity, the several forms of appropriation, transactions opened and conducted toward net utilitarian advantage. Indicative ethnographic terms include 'haggling' or 'barter', 'gambling', 'chicanery', 'theft', and other varieties of seizure.

Negative reciprocity is the most impersonal sort of exchange. In guises such as 'barter' it is from our own point of view the 'most economic'. The participants confront each other as opposed interests, each looking to maximize utility at the other's expense. Approaching the transaction with an eye singular to the main chance, the aim of the opening party or of both parties is the unearned increment. One of the most sociable forms, leaning toward balance, is haggling conducted in the spirit of 'what the traffic will bear'. From this, negative reciprocity ranges through various degrees of cunning, guile, stealth, and violence to the finesse of a well-conducted horse-raid. The 'reciprocity' is, of course, conditional again, a matter of defense of self-interest. So the flow may be one-way once more, reciprocation contingent upon mustering countervailing pressure or guile.

It is a long way from a suckling child to a Plains Indians' horse-raid. Too long, it could be argued, the classification too widely set. Yet 'vice-versa movements' in the ethnographic record do grade into each other along the whole span. It is well to recall, nevertheless, that empirical exchanges often fall somewhere along the line, not directly on the extreme and middle points here outlined. The question is, can one specify social or economic circumstances that impel reciprocity toward one or another of the stipulated positions, toward generalized, balanced, or negative reciprocity? I think so.

III

RECIPROCITY AND KINSHIP DISTANCE

The span of social distance between those who exchange conditions the mode of exchange. Kinship distance, as has already been suggested, is especially relevant to the form of reciprocity. Reciprocity is inclined toward the generalized pole by close kinship, toward the negative extreme in proportion to kinship distance.

The reasoning is nearly syllogistic. The several reciprocities from freely bestowed gift to chicanery amount to a spectrum of sociability, from sacrifice in favor of another to self-interested gain at the expense of another. Take as the minor premise Tylor's dictum that kindred goes with kindness, 'two words whose common derivation expresses in the happiest way one of the main principles of social life'. It follows that close kin tend to share, to enter into generalized exchanges, and distant and non-kin to deal in equivalents or in guile. Equivalence becomes

149

compulsory in proportion to kinship distance lest relations break off entirely, for with distance there can be little tolerance of gain and loss even as there is little inclination to extend oneself. To nonkin – 'other people', perhaps not even 'people' – no quarter must needs be given: the manifest inclination may well be 'devil take the hindmost'.

All this seems perfectly applicable to our own society, but it is more significant in primitive society. Because kinship is more significant in primitive society. It is, for one thing, the organizing principle or idiom of most groups and most social relations. Even the category 'nonkin' is ordinarily defined by it, that is, as the negative aspect of it, the logical extreme of the class – nonbeing as a state of being. There is something real to this view; it is not logical sophistry. Among ourselves 'nonkin' denotes specialized status relations of positive quality: doctor-patient, policeman-citizen, employer-employee, classmates, neighbors, professional colleagues. But for them 'nonkin' principally connotes the negation of community (or tribalism); often it is the synonym for 'enemy' or 'stranger'. Likewise the economic relation tends to be a simple negation of kinship reciprocities: other institutional norms need not come into play.

Kinship distance, however, has different aspects. It may be organized in several ways, and what is 'close' in one of these ways need not be so in another. Exchange may be contingent on genealogical distance (as locally imputed), that is, on interpersonal kinship status. Or it may hinge on segmentary distance, on descent group status. (One suspects that where these two do not correspond the closer relation governs the reciprocity appropriate in dealings between individual parties, but this ought to be worked out empirically.) For the purpose of creating a general model, attention should also be given to the power of community in stipulating distance. It is not only that kinship organizes communities, but communities kinship, so that a spatial, coresidential term affects the measure of kinship distance and thus the mode of exchange.

'Brothers living together, or a paternal uncle and his nephews living in the same house were, as far as my observation goes, on much closer terms with each other than relatives of similar degrees living apart. This was evident whenever there was a question of borrowing things, of getting help, of accepting an obligation, or of assuming responsibilities for each other (Malinowski, 1915, p. 532; the reference is to the Mailu).

'Mankind [to Siuai] consists of relatives and strangers. Relatives are usually interlinked by both blood and marital ties; most of them live nearby, and persons who live nearby are all relatives. . . . Transactions among them should be carried out in a spirit devoid of commerciality – preferably consisting of sharing [i.e., "pooling" in terms of the present discussion], nonreciprocable giving, and bequeathing, among closest relatives, or of lending among more distantly related ones. . . . Except for a few very distantly related sib-mates, persons who live far away are not relatives and can only be enemies. Most of their customs are unsuitable for the Siuai, but a few of their goods and techniques are desirable. One interacts with them only to buy and sell – utilizing hard bargaining and deceit to make as much profit from such transactions as possible' (Oliver, 1955, pp. 454-455).

Here is one possible model for analyzing reciprocity: a tribal plan can be viewed as a series of more and more inclusive kinship-residential sectors, and reciprocity seen then to vary in character by sectoral position. The close kinsmen who render assistance are particularly near kinsmen in a spatial sense: it is in regard to people of the household, the camp, hamlet, or village that compassion is required, inasmuch as interaction is intense and peaceable solidarity essential. But the quality of mercy is strained in peripheral sectors, strained by kinship distance, so is less likely in exchanges with fellow tribesmen of another village than among covillagers, still less likely in the intertribal sector.

Kinship-residential groupings from this perspective comprise ever-widening comembership spheres: the household, the local lineage, perhaps the village, the subtribe, tribe, other tribes – the particular plan of course varies. The structure is a hierarchy of levels of integration, but from the inside and on the ground it is a series of concentric circles. Social relations of each circle have a specific quality – household relations, lineage relations, and so on – and except as the sectoral divisions be cut through by other

151

Marshall D. Sahlins

organizations of kinship solidarity – say, nonlocalized clans or personal kindreds – relations within each sphere are more solidary than relations of the next, more inclusive sector. Reciprocity accordingly inclines toward balance and chicane in proportion to sectoral distance. In each sector, certain modes of reciprocity are characteristic or dominant: generalized modes are dominant in the narrowest spheres and play out in wider spheres, balanced reciprocity is characteristic of intermediate sectors, chicane of the most peripheral spheres. In brief, a general model of the play of reciprocity may be developed by superimposing the society's sectoral plan upon the reciprocity continuum, something like this (*Figure 1*):

FIGURE 1—Reciprocity and Kinship Residential Sectors.

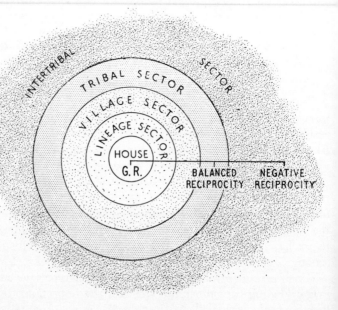

The plan does not rest alone upon the two terms of sectoral division and reciprocity variation. Something is to be said for the embedded third term, morality. 'Far more than we ordinarily suppose,' Firth has written, 'economic relations rest on moral foundations' (1951, p. 144). Certainly that must be the way the people see it – 'Although the Siuai have separate terms for "generosity", "cooperativeness", "morality" (that is, rule abiding), and "geniality", I believe that they consider all these to be closely interrelated aspects of the same attribute of goodness . . .' (Oliver, 1955, p. 78). Another contrast with ourselves is suggested, a tendency for morality, like reciprocity, to be sectorally organized in primitive societies. The norms are characteristically relative and situational rather than absolute and universal. A given act, that is to say, is not so much in itself good or bad, it depends on who the 'Alter' is. The appropriation of another man's goods or his woman, which is a sin ('theft', 'adultery') in the bosom of one's community, may be not merely condoned but positively rewarded with the admiration of one's fellows – if it is perpetrated on an outsider. The contrast with the absolute standards of the Judeo-Christian tradition is probably overdrawn: no moral system is exclusively absolute (especially in wartime) and none perhaps is entirely relative and contextual. But situational standards, defined often in sectoral terms, do seem to prevail in primitive communities and this contrasts sufficiently with our own to have drawn repeated comment from ethnologists. For instance:

'Navaho morality is . . . contextual rather than absolute. . . . Lying is not always and everywhere wrong. The rules vary with the situation. To deceive when trading with foreign tribes is a morally accepted practice. Acts are not in themselves bad or good. Incest [by its nature, a contextual sin] is perhaps the only conduct that is condemned without qualification. It is quite correct to use witchcraft techniques in trading with members of foreign tribes. . . . There is an almost complete absence of abstract ideals. Under the circumstances of aboriginal life Navahos did not need to orient themselves in terms of abstract morality. . . . In a large, complex society like modern America, where people come and go and business and other dealings must be carried on by people who never see each other, it is functionally necessary to have abstract standards that transcend an immediate concrete situation in which two or more persons are interacting' (Kluckhohn, 1959, p. 434).

The scheme with which we deal is tripartite: social, moral, and

153

Marshall D. Sahlins

economic. Reciprocity and morality are sectorally structured – the structure is that of kinship-tribal groupings.

But the scheme is entirely a hypothetical state of affairs. One can conceive circumstances that would alter the social-moral-reciprocal relations postulated by it. Propositions about the external sectors are particularly vulnerable. (For 'external sector' one can generally read 'intertribal sector', the ethnic peripherae of primitive communities; in practice it can be set where positive morality fades out or where intergroup hostility is the normal in-group expectation.) Transactions in this sphere may be consummated by force and guile, it is true, by *wabuwabu*, to use the near-onomatopoeic Dobuan term for sharp practice. Yet it seems that violent appropriation is a resort born of urgent requirements that can only, or most easily, be supplied by militant tactics. Peaceful symbiosis is at least a common alternative.

In these nonviolent confrontations the propensity to *wabuwabu* no doubt persists; it is built in to the sectoral plan. So if it can be socially tolerated – if, that is, countervailing peace-enforcing conditions are sufficiently strong – hard bargaining is the institutionalized external relation. We find then *gimwali*, the mentality of the market place, the impersonal (no-partnership) exchange of Trobriand commoners of different villages or of Trobrianders and other peoples. But still *gimwali* does suppose special conditions, some sort of social insulation that prevents the economic friction from kindling a dangerous conflagration. In the ordinary case, haggling is actually repressed, particularly, it appears, if the exchange of the border is critical to both sides, as where different strategic specialties move against each other. Despite the sectoral distance, the exchange is equitable, *utu*, balanced: the free play of *wabuwabu* and *gimwali* is checked in the interest of the symbiosis.

The check is delivered by special and delicate institutional means of border exchange. The means sometimes look so preposterous as to be considered by ethnologists some sort of 'game' the natives play, but their design manifestly immunizes an important economic interdependence against a fundamental social cleavage. (Compare the discussion of the *kula* in White, 1959, and Fortune, 1932.) Silent trade is a famous case in point – good relations are maintained by preventing any relations. Most

154

common are 'trade-partnerships' and 'trade-friendships'. The important thing in all varieties is a social suppression of negative reciprocity. Peace is built in, haggling outlawed, and, conducted as a transfer of equivalent utilities, the exchange in turn underwrites the peace. (Trade-partnerships, often developed along lines of classificatory or affinal kinship, particularly incapsulate external economic transactions in solidary social relations. Status relations essentially internal are projected across community and tribal boundaries. The reciprocity then may lean over backward, in the direction not of *wabuwabu* but something to the generalized side. Phrased as gift-giving, the presentation admits of delay in reciprocation: a direct return may indeed be unseemly. Hospitality, on another occasion returned in kind, accompanies the formal exchange of trade goods. For a host to give stuff over and above the worth of things brought by his partner is not unusual: it both befits the relation so to treat one's partner while he is traveling and stores up credits. On a wider view, this measure of unbalance sustains the trade partnership, compelling as it does another meeting.)

Intertribal symbiosis, in short, alters the terms of the hypothetical model. The peripheral sector is breached by more sociable relations than are normal in this zone. The context of exchange is now a narrower co-membership sphere, the exchange is peaceful and equitable. Reciprocity falls near the balance point.

Now the assertions of this essay, as I have said, developed out of a dialogue with ethnographic materials. It seems worth while to append some of these data to appropriate sections of the argument. Accordingly, Appendix A (below, pp. 186-200) sets out materials relevant to the present section, 'Reciprocity and Kinship Distance'. This is not by way of proof, of course – there are indeed certain exceptions, or seeming exceptions, in the materials – but by way of exposition or illustration. Moreover, since the ideas only gradually came over me and the monographs and articles had been in many instances consulted for other purposes, it is certain that data pertinent to reciprocity in the works cited have escaped me. (I hope this is sufficiently apologetic and that the ethnographic notes of Appendix A are of interest to someone besides myself.)

Whatever the value of these notes as exposition of the asserted

155

relation between reciprocity and kinship distance, they must also suggest to the reader certain limitations of the present perspective. Simply to demonstrate that the character of reciprocity is contingent upon social distance – even if it could be demonstrated in an incontestable way – is not to traffic in ultimate explanation, nor yet to specify when exchanges will in fact take place. A systematic relation between reciprocity and sociability in itself does not say when, or even to what extent, the relation will come into play. The supposition here is that the forces of constraint lie outside the relation itself. The terms of final analysis are the larger cultural structure and its adaptive response to its milieu. From this wider view one may be able to stipulate the significant sectoral lines and kinship categories of the given case, and to stipulate too the incidence of reciprocity in different sectors. Supposing it true that close kinsmen would share food, for example, it need not follow that the transactions occur. The total (cultural-adaptive) context may render intensive sharing dysfunctional and predicate in subtle ways the demise of a society that allows itself the luxury. Permit me to quote *in extenso* a passage from Fredrik Barth's brilliant ecological study of South Persian nomads. It shows so well the larger considerations that must be brought to the bar of explanation; in detail it exemplifies a situation that discounts intensive sharing:

'The stability of a pastoral population depends on the maintenance of a balance between pastures, animal population, and human population. The pastures available by their techniques of herding set a maximal limit to the total animal population that an area will support; while the patterns of nomadic production and consumption define a minimal limit to the size of the herd that will support a human household. In this double set of balances is summarized the special difficulty in establishing a population balance in a pastoral economy: the human population must be sensitive to imbalances between flocks and pastures. Among agricultural, or hunting and collecting people, a crude Malthusian type of population control is sufficient. With a growing population, starvation and death-rate rise, until a balance is reached around which the population stabilizes. Where pastoral nomadism is the predominant or exclusive pattern, the nomad population, if subjected to such a form of population control, would *not* establish a population balance, but would find its whole basis for subsistence removed. Quite simply, this is because the productive capital on which their subsistence is based is not simply land, it is animals – in other words *food*. A pastoral economy can only be maintained so long as there are no pressures on its practitioners to invade this large store of food. A pastoral population can therefore only reach a stable level if other effective population controls intervene *before* those of starvation and death-rate. A first requirement in such an adaptation is the presence of the patterns of private ownership of herds, and individual economic responsibility for each household. By these patterns, the population becomes fragmented with respect to economic activities, and economic factors can strike differentially, eliminating some members of the population [i.e., through sedentarization] without affecting other members of the same population. This would be impossible if the corporate organization with respect to political life, and pasture rights, were also made relevant to economic responsibility and survival' (Barth, 1961, p. 124).

Now, about the incidence of reciprocity in the specific case, here is something else to consider – the people may be stingy. Nothing has been said about sanctions of exchange relations nor, more importantly, about forces that countervail. There are contradictions in primitive economies: inclinations of self-interest are unleashed that are incompatible with the high levels of sociability customarily demanded. Malinowski long ago noticed this and Firth (1926) in an early paper on Maori proverbs skillfully brought to light the clash, the subtle interplay, between the moral dictates of sharing and hedonist personal interest. The widespread mode of family production for use, it might be remarked, acts to brake outputs at comparatively low levels even as it orients economic concern inward, within the household. The mode of production thus does not readily lend itself to general economic solidarity. Suppose sharing is morally called for, say by the destitution of a near kinsman, all the things that make sharing good and proper may not evoke in an affluent man the inclination to do it. And even as there may be little to gain by assisting others, there are no iron-clad guarantees of such social compacts as kinship. The received social-moral obligations prescribe an economic course, and the publicity of primitive life, increasing the risk of evoking jealousy, hostility, and future economic penalty, tends to keep people on course. But, as is well known, to observe that a society has a system of morality and constraints is not to say that everyone acquiesces in it. There may be *biša-baša* times, 'particularly in the late winter, when the household would hide its food, even from relatives' (Price, 1962, p. 47).

That *biša-baša* is the pervasive condition of some peoples is not embarrassing to the present thesis. The Siriono, everyone knows, parley hostility and crypto-stinginess into a way of life. Interestingly enough, the Siriono articulate ordinary norms of primitive economic intercourse. By the norm, for instance, the hunter should not eat the animal he has killed. But the *de facto* sector of sharing is not merely very narrow, 'sharing rarely occurs without a certain amount of mutual mistrust and misunderstanding; a person always feels that it is he who is being taken advantage of', so that 'The bigger the catch the more sullen the hunter' (Holmberg, 1950, pp. 60, 62; cf. pp. 36, 38-39). The Siriono are not thereby different in kind from the run of primitive communities. They simply realize to an extreme the potentiality elsewhere less often consummated, the possibility that structural compulsions of generosity are unequal to a test of hardship. But then, the Siriono are a band of displaced and deculturated persons. The whole cultural shell, from rules of sharing through institutions of chieftainship and Crow kinship terminology, is a mockery of their present miserable state.

IV

RECIPROCITY AND KINSHIP RANK

It is by now apparent – it is made apparent by the illustrative materials of Appendix A – that in any actual exchange several circumstances may simultaneously bear upon the material flow. Kinship distance, while perhaps significant, is not necessarily decisive. Something may be said for rank, relative wealth and need, the type of goods whether food or durables, and still other 'factors'. As a tactic of presentation and interpretation, it is useful to isolate and separately consider these factors. Accordingly, we move on to the relation between reciprocity and kinship rank. But with this proviso: propositions about the covariation of kinship distance or of kinship rank and reciprocity can be argued separately, even validated separately to the extent to which it is possible to select instances in which only the factor at issue is in play – holding 'other things constant' – but the propositions do not present themselves separately in fact. The obvious course of further research is to work out the power of the several 'variables' during combined plays. At best only the beginnings of this course are suggested here.

Rank difference as much as kinship distance supposes an economic relation. The vertical, rank axis of exchange – or the implication of rank – may affect the form of the transaction, just as the horizontal kinship-distance axis affects it. Rank is to some extent privilege, *droit du seigneur*, and it has its responsibilities, *noblesse oblige*. The dues and duties fall to both sides, both high and low have their claims, and feudal terms indeed do not convey the economic equity of kinship ranking. In its true historic setting *noblesse oblige* hardly cancelled out the *droits du seigneur*. In primitive society social inequality is more the organization of economic equality. Often, in fact, high rank is only secured or sustained by o'ercrowing generosity: the material advantage is on the subordinates' side. Perhaps it is too much to see the relation of parent and child as the elemental form of kinship ranking and its economic ethic. It is true, nevertheless, that paternalism is a common metaphor of primitive chieftainship. Chieftainship is ordinarily a relation of higher descent. So it is singularly appropriate that the chief is their 'father', they his 'children', and economic dealings between them cannot help but be affected.

The economic claims of rank and subordination are interdependent. The exercise of chiefly demand opens the way to solicitation from below, and vice versa – not uncommonly a moderate exposure to the 'larger world' is enough to evoke native reference to customary chiefly dues as local banking procedure (cf. Ivens, 1927, p. 32). The word then for the economic relation between kinship ranks is 'reciprocity'. The reciprocity, moreover, is fairly classed as 'generalized'. While not as sociable as the run

159

of assistance among close kinsmen, it does lean toward that side of the reciprocity continuum. Goods are in truth *yielded* to powers-that-be, perhaps on call and demand, and likewise stuff may have to be *humbly solicited* from them. Still the rationale is often assistance and need, and the supposition of returns correspondingly indefinite. Reciprocation may be left until a need precipitates it, it bears no necessary equivalence to the initial gift, and the material flow can be unbalanced in favor of one side or the other for a long time.

Reciprocity is harnessed to various principles of kinship rank. Generation-ranking, with the elders the privileged parties, may be of significance among hunters and gatherers not merely in the life of the family but in the life of the camp as a whole, and generalized reciprocity between juniors and seniors a correspondingly broad rule of social exchange (cf. Radcliffe-Brown, 1948, pp. 42-43). The Trobrianders have a name for the economic ethic appropriate between parties of different rank within common descent groups – *pokala*. It is the rule that 'Junior members of a sub-clan are expected to render gifts and services to their seniors, who in return are expected to confer assistance and material benefits on the juniors' (Powell, 1960, p. 126). Even where rank is tied to genealogical seniority and consummated in office-power – chieftainship properly so called – the ethic is the same. Take Polynesian chiefs, office-holders in large, segmented polities: supported on the one hand by various chiefly dues, they are freighted, as many have observed, with perhaps even greater obligations to the underlying population. Probably always the 'economic basis' of primitive politics is chiefly generosity – at one stroke an act of positive morality and a laying of indebtedness upon the commonalty. Or, to take a larger view, the entire political order is sustained by a pivotal flow of goods, up and down the social hierarchy, with each gift not merely connoting a status relation but, as a generalized gift not directly requited, compelling a loyalty.

In communities with established rank orders, generalized reciprocity is enforced by the received structure, and once in operation the exchange has redundant effects on the rank system. There is a large range of societies, however, in which rank and leadership are in the main achieved; here reciprocity is more or

160

less engaged in the *formation* of rank itself, as a 'starting mechanism'. The connection between reciprocity and rank is brought to bear in the first case in the form, 'to be noble is to be generous', in the second case, 'to be generous is to be noble'. The prevailing rank structure influences economic relations in the former instance; the reciprocity influences hierarchical relations in the latter. (An analogous feedback occurs in the context of kinship distance. Hospitality is frequently employed to suggest sociability – this is discussed later. John Tanner, one of those 'feral Whites' who grew to manhood among the Indians, relates an anecdote even more to the point: recalling that his Ojibway family was once saved from starvation by a Muskogean family, he noted that if any of his own people ever afterwards met any of the latter 'he would call him "brother", and treat him as such' (Tanner, 1956, p. 24).)

The term 'starting mechanism' is Gouldner's. He explains in this way how reciprocity may be considered a starting mechanism:

'. . . it helps to initiate social interaction and is functional in the early phases of certain groups before they have developed a differentiated and customary set of status duties. . . . Granted that the question of origins can readily bog down in a metaphysical morass, the fact is that many concrete social systems [– perhaps "relations and groups" is more apt –] do have determinate beginnings. Marriages are not made in heaven. . . . Similarly, corporations, political parties, and all manner of groups have their beginnings. . . . People are continually brought together in new juxtapositions and combinations, bringing with them the possibilities of new social systems. How are these possibilities realized? . . . Although this perspective may at first seem somewhat alien to the functionalist, once it is put to him, he may suspect that certain kinds of mechanisms, conducive to the crystallization of social systems out of ephemeral contacts, will in some measure be institutionalized or otherwise patterned in any society. At this point he would be considering "starting mechanisms". In this way, I suggest, the norm of reciprocity provides one among many starting mechanisms' (Gouldner, 1960, pp. 176-177).

161

Economic imbalance is the key to deployment of generosity, of generalized reciprocity, as a starting mechanism of rank and leadership. A gift that is not yet requited in the first place 'creates a something between people': it engenders continuity in the relation, solidarity – at least until the obligation to reciprocate is discharged. Secondly, falling under 'the shadow of indebtedness', the recipient is constrained in his relations to the giver of things. The one who has benefited is held in a peaceful, collaborative, circumspect, and responsive position in respect to his benefactor. The 'norm of reciprocity', Gouldner remarks, 'makes two interrelated minimal demands: (1) people should help those who have helped them, and (2) people should not injure those who have helped them' (1960, p. 171). (Or, as Hobbes put it: 'As justice dependeth on antecedant covenant; soe does GRATITUDE depend on antecedant grace; that is to say, antecedant free gift; and is the fourth law of nature; which may be conceived in this form, *that a man which receiveth benefit from another of mere grace, endeavour that he which giveth it, have no reasonable cause to repent him of his good will.*') These demands are as compelling in the highlands of New Guinea as in the prairies of Peoria – 'Gifts [among Gahuka-Gama] have to be repaid. They constitute a debt, and until discharged the relationship of the individuals involved is in a state of imbalance. The debtor has to act circumspectly towards those who have this advantage over him or otherwise risk ridicule' (Read, 1959, p. 429). The esteem that accrues to the generous man all to one side, generosity is usefully enlisted as a starting mechanism of leadership *because it creates followership*. 'Wealth in this finds him friends,' Denig writes of the aspiring Assiniboin, 'as it does on other occasions everywhere' (Denig, 1928-29, p. 525).

Apart from highly organized chiefdoms and simple hunters and gatherers, there are many intermediate tribal peoples among whom pivotal local leaders come to prominence without yet becoming holders of office and title, of ascribed privilege and of sway over corporate political groups. They are men who 'build a name' as it is said, 'big-men' they may be reckoned, or 'men of importance', or 'bulls' who rise above the common herd, who gather followers, who achieve authority. The Melanesian 'big-man' is a case in point. So too the Plains Indian 'chief'. The process of gathering a personal following and that of ascent to the summits of renown is marked by calculated generosity – if not true compassion. Generalized reciprocity is more or less enlisted as a starting mechanism.

In diverse ways, then, generalized reciprocity is engaged with the rank order of the community. Yet we have already character- ized the economics of chieftainship in other transactional terms, as redistribution (or large-scale pooling). At this juncture the evolutionist question is posed: 'When does one give way then to the other, reciprocity to redistribution?' This question, however, may mislead. Chiefly redistribution is not different in principle from kinship-rank reciprocity. It is, rather, based upon the reciprocity principle, a highly organized form of that principle. Chiefly redistribution is a centralized, formal organization of kinship-rank reciprocities, an extensive social integration of the dues and obligations of leadership. The real ethnographic world does not present us with the abrupt 'appearance' of redistribution. It presents approximations and kinds of centricity. The apparent course of wisdom is to hinge our characterizations – of rank- reciprocities vs. a system of redistribution – on formal differences in the centralization process, and in this way to resolve the evolutionist issue.

A big-man system of reciprocities may be quite centralized and a chiefly system quite decentralized. A thin line separates them, but it is perhaps significant. Between centricity in a Melanesian big-man economy such as Siuai (Oliver, 1955) and centricity in a North-west Coast chiefdom such as the Nootka (Drucker, 1951), there is little to choose. A leader in each case integrates the economic activity of a (more or less) localized following: he acts as a shunting station for goods flowing reciprocally between his own and other like groups of society. The economic relation to followers is also the same: the leader is the central recipient and bestower of favors. The thin line of difference is this: the Nootka leader is an office-holder in a lineage (house group), his following is this corporate group, and his central economic position is ascribed by right of chiefly due and chiefly obligation. So centricity is built into the structure. In Siuai, it is a personal achievement. The following is an achievement – a result of generosity bestowed – the leadership an achievement, and the whole structure will as such dissolve with the demise of the pivotal big-man. Now I think that most of us concerned with 'redistributive economies' have come to include Northwest Coast peoples under this head; whereas assigning Siuai that status would at least provoke disagreement. This suggests that the political organization of reciprocities is implicitly recognized as a decisive step. Where kinship-rank reciprocity is laid down by office and political grouping, and becomes *sui generis* by virtue of customary duty, it takes on a distinctive character. The distinctive character may be usefully named – chiefly redistribution.

A further difference in economies of chiefly redistribution is worth remarking. It is another difference in centricity. The flow of goods both into and out of the hands of powers-that-be is for the most part unintegrated in certain ethnographic instances. Subordinates in severalty and on various occasions render stuff to the chief, and often in severalty receive benefits from him. While there is always some massive accumulation and large-scale handout – say during rites of chieftainship – the prevailing flow between chief and people is fragmented into independent and small transactions: a gift to the chief from here, some help given out there. So aside from the special occasion, the chief is continuously turning over petty stocks. This is the ordinary situation in the smaller Pacific island chiefdoms – e.g. Moala (Sahlins, 1962), apparently Tikopia – and it may be generally true of pastoralist chiefdoms. On the other hand, chiefs may glory in massive accumulations and more or less massive dispensations, and at times too in large stores on hand congealed by pressure on the commonalty. Here the independent act of homage or *noblesse oblige* is of less significance. And if, in addition, the social scale of chiefly redistribution is extensive – the polity large, dispersed, and segmented – one confronts a measure of centricity approximating the classical magazine economies of antiquity.

Appendix B (pp. 200-215, below) presents illustrative ethnographic materials on the relation between rank and reciprocity. (See the citation from Malo under B.4.2 and from Bartram under B.5.2 on magazine economies of various scale.)

V

RECIPROCITY AND WEALTH

According to their [the Yukaghir] way of thinking, 'a man who possesses provisions must share them with those who do not possess them' (Jochelson, 1926, p. 43).

'This habit of share and share alike is easily understandable in a community where everyone is likely to find himself in difficulties from time to time, for it is scarcity and not sufficiency that makes people generous, since everybody is thereby ensured against hunger. He who is in need to-day receives help from him who may be in like need tomorrow' (Evans-Pritchard, 1940, p. 85).

One of the senses of previous remarks on rank and reciprocity is that rank distinctions, or attempts to promote them, tend to extend generalized exchange beyond the customary range of sharing. The same upshot may come of wealth differences between parties, often anyhow associated with rank differences.

If one is poor and one's comrade is rich, well, there are certain restraints on acquisitiveness in our dealings – at least if we are to remain comrades, or even acquaintances, for very long. There are particularly restraints on the wealthier, if not a certain *richesse oblige*.

That is to say, given some social bond between those who exchange, differences in fortune between them compels a more altruistic (generalized) transaction than is otherwise appropriate. A difference in affluence – or in capacity to replenish wealth – would lower the sociability content of balanced dealing. As far as the exchange balances, the side that cannot afford it has sacrificed in favor of the side that did not need it. The greater the wealth gap, therefore, the greater the demonstrable assistance from rich to poor that is necessary just to maintain a given degree of sociability. Reasoning further on the same line, the inclination toward generalized exchange deepens where the economic gap amounts to oversupply and undersupply of customary requirements and, especially, of urgent stuff. The thing to look for is food-sharing between haves and have-nots. It is one thing to demand returns on woodpecker scalps, yet one spares a dime – brother! – for even a hungry stranger.

The 'brother' is important. That scarcity and not sufficiency makes people generous is understandable, functional, 'where everyone is likely to find himself in difficulties from time to time'. It is most understandable, however, and most likely, where kinship community and kinship morality prevail. That whole economies are organized by the combined play of scarcity and differential accumulation is no secret to economic science. But then the societies involved do not wrest a livelihood as limited and uncertain as the Nuer's (and many another primitive group's), nor do they meet hardship as kinship communities. It is such circumstances precisely that make invidious accumulation of fortune intolerable and dysfunctional. And if the affluent do not play the game, they ordinarily can be forced to disgorge, in one way or another:

'A Bushman will go to any lengths to avoid making other Bushmen jealous of him, and for this reason the few possessions the Bushmen have are constantly circling among members of their groups. No one cares to keep a particularly good knife too long, even though he may want it desperately, because he will become the object of envy; as he sits by himself polishing a fine edge on the blade he will hear the soft voices of the other men in his band saying: "Look at him there, admiring his knife while we have nothing." Soon somebody will ask him for his knife, for everybody would like to have it, and he will give it away. Their culture insists that they share with each other, and it has never happened that a Bushman failed to share objects, food, or water with other members of his band, for without very rigid co-operation Bushmen could not survive the famines and droughts that the Kalahari offers them' (Thomas, 1959, p. 22).

Should the condition of poverty be extreme, as for food collectors such as these Bushmen, it is best that the inclination to share out one's abundance be made lawful. Here it is a technical condition that some households day in and day out will fail to meet their requirements. The vulnerability to food shortage can be met by instituting continuous sharing within the local community. I think this the best way to interpret tabus that prohibit hunters from eating game they bring down, or the less drastic and more common injunction that certain large animals be shared through the camp – ' "the hunter kills, other people have", say the Yukaghir' (Jochelson, 1926, p. 124). Another way to make food-sharing the rule, if not a rule, is to freight it heavily with moral value. If this is the case, incidentally, sharing will break out not merely in bad times but especially in good. The level of generalized reciprocity 'peaks' on the occasion of a windfall: now everyone can cash in on the virtues of generosity:

'They gathered almost three hundred pounds [of tsi nuts]. . . . When the people had picked all they could find, when every possible bag was full, they said they were ready to go to Nama, but when we brought the jeep and began to load it they were already busy with their endless preoccupation, that of giving and receiving, and had already begun to give each other presents of tsi. Bushmen feel a great need to give and receive food, perhaps to cement relationships with each other, perhaps to prove and strengthen their dependence upon each other; because the opportunity to do this does not occur unless huge quantities of food are at hand, Bushmen always exchange presents of foods that come in huge quantities, these being the meat of game antelope, tsi nuts, and the nuts of the mangetti trees, which at certain seasons are scattered abundantly all through the mangetti forests. As we waited by the jeep Dikai gave a huge sack of tsi to her mother. Her mother gave another sack to Gao Feet's first wife, and Gao Feet gave a sack to Dikai. Later, during the days that followed, the tsi was distributed again, this time in smaller quantities, small piles or small bagfuls, after that in handfuls, and, last, in very small quantities of cooked tsi which people would share as they were eating . . .' (Thomas, 1959, pp. 214-215).

The bearing of wealth differences upon reciprocity, of course, is not independent of the play of rank and kinship distance. Real situations are complicated. For instance, wealth distinctions probably constrain assistance in some inverse proportion to the kinship distance of the sides to exchange. It is poverty in the in-group particularly that engenders compassion. (Conversely, helping people in distress creates very intense solidarity – on the principle of 'a friend in need . . .'.) On the other hand, material distinctions between distant relatives or aliens may not commensurately, or even at all, incline the affluent party to be charitable. If the interests had been opposed to begin with, well now the desperate traffic will bear more.

The observation is frequently made that any accumulation of wealth – among such and such people – is followed hard upon by its disbursement. The *objective* of gathering wealth, indeed, is often that of giving it away. So, for example, Barnett writes of Northwest Coast Indians that 'Accumulation in any quantity by borrowing or otherwise is, in fact, unthinkable unless it be for the purpose of immediate redistribution' (1938, p. 353). The general proposition may be allowed that the material drift in primitive societies tends on the whole away from accumulation towards insufficiency. Thus: 'In general it may be said that no one in a Nuer village starves unless all are starving' (Evans-Pritchard, 1951, p. 132). But in view of foregoing remarks there must be qualification. The incline toward have-nots is steeper for more urgently than for less urgently required goods, and it is steeper within local communities than between them.

Supposing some tendency to share in favor of need, even if qualified by community, it is possible to draw further inferences about economic behavior in general scarcity. During lean food seasons the incidence of generalized exchange should rise above average, particularly in the narrower social sectors. Survival depends now on a double-barreled quickening of social solidarity and economic cooperation (see Appendix C, e.g. C.1.3). This social and economic consolidation conceivably could progress to the maximum: normal reciprocal relations between households are suspended in favor of pooling of resources for the duration of emergency. The rank structure is perhaps mobilized and engaged, either in governance of pooling or in the sense that chiefly food reserves are now put into circulation.

Yet the reaction to depression 'all depends': it depends on the social structure put to test and on the duration and intensity of the shortage. For the forces that countervail are strengthened in these *biša-baša* times, the tendency to look to household interests especially, and also the tendency for compassion to be more-than-

168

proportionately expended on close kin in need than on distant kin in the same straits. Probably every primitive organization has its breaking-point, or at least its turning-point. Every one might see the time when cooperation is overwhelmed by the scale of disaster and chicanery becomes the order of the day. The range of assistance contracts progressively to the family level; perhaps even these bonds dissolve and, washed away, reveal an inhuman, yet most human, self-interest. Moreover, by the same measure that the circle of charity is compressed that of 'negative reciprocity' is potentially expanded. People who helped each other in normal times and through the first stages of disaster display now indifference to each others' plight, if they do not exacerbate a mutual downfall by guile, haggle, and theft. Put another way, the whole sectoral scheme of reciprocities is altered, compressed: sharing is confined to the innermost sphere of solidarity and all else is devil take the hindmost.

Implicit in these remarks is a plan of analysis of the normal sectoral system of reciprocities in the given case. The prevailing reciprocity scheme is some vector of the quality of kin-community relations and the ordinary stresses developing out of imbalances in production. But it is the emergency condition that concerns us now. Here and there in the illustrative materials to this section we see the two predicted reactions to depressed food supplies, both more sharing and less. Presumably the governing conditions are the community structure on one side and the seriousness of shortage on the other.

A final remark under the head of reciprocity and wealth. A community will, if suitably organized, 'tighten' not only under economic threat but in the face of other present danger, of external political-military pressure, for example. In this connection, two notes on the economics of native war parties are included in the illustrative materials appended to the present section (Appendix C: C.1.10 and C.2.5). They illustrate an extraordinary intensity of sharing (generalized reciprocity) between haves and have-nots during preparations for attack. (Likewise, the experience of recent wars would show that transactions move a long way from yesterday's dice game in the barracks to today's sharing of rations or cigarettes on the front line.) The sudden outbreak of compassion is consistent with what has been said of

169

sociability, sharing, and wealth differences. Generalized reciprocity is not merely the sole exchange congruent with the now serious interdependence, it strengthens interdependence and so the chances of each and all to survive the noneconomic danger.

Ethnographic data relevant to the propositions of this section may be found in Appendix C (pp. 215-225).

VI

RECIPROCITY AND FOOD

The character of the goods exchanged seems to have an independent effect on the character of exchange. Staple foodstuffs cannot always be handled just like anything else. Socially they are not quite like anything else. Food is life-giving, urgent, ordinarily symbolic of hearth and home, if not of mother. By comparison with other stuff, food is more readily, or more necessarily, shared; barkcloth and beads more readily lend themselves to balanced gift-giving. Direct and equivalent returns for food are unseemly in most social settings: they impugn the motives both of the giver and of the recipient. From this several characteristic qualities of food transfers appear to follow.

Food dealings are a delicate barometer, a ritual statement as it were, of social relations, and food is thus employed instrumentally as a starting, a sustaining, or a destroying mechanism of sociability:

'Food is something over which relatives have rights, and conversely relatives are people who provide or take toll on one's food' (Richards, 1939, p. 200).

'The sharing of food [among the Kuma] symbolizes an identity of interests.... Food is never shared with an enemy.... Food is not shared with strangers, for they are potential enemies. A man may eat with his cognatic and affinal relatives and also, people say, with the members of his own clan. Normally, however, only members of the same subclan have an unequivocal right to share each other's food.... If two men or the members of two sub-subclans have a serious and lasting quarrel, neither they nor their descendants may use one another's fires....When

170

affinal relatives come together at marriage, the formal presentation of the bride and the pork and the valuables emphasizes
the separate identity of the two clans, but the people actually
participating in the ceremony share vegetable food informally,
unobtrusively, as they might share it with intimate com-
panions within the subclan. This is a way of expressing their
common interest in linking the two groups. Symbolically, they
belong now to a single group and so are "brothers", as affinal
relatives should be' (Reay, 1959, pp. 90-92).

Food offered in a generalized way, notably as hospitality, is
good relations. As Jochelson says, putting it for the Yukaghir
with near-Confucian pith: 'hospitality often turns enemies into
friends, and strengthens the amicable relations between groups
foreign to one another' (1926, p. 125). But then, a complementary
negative principle is implied, that food not offered on the suitable
occasion or not taken is bad relations. Thus the Dobuan syndrome
of suspicion of everyone save the nearest kinfolk finds its clearest
expression in the social range of food-sharing and commensality –
'Food or tobacco is not accepted except within a small circle'
(Fortune, 1932, p. 170; on rules proscribing commensality, cf.
pp. 74-75; Malinowski, 1915, p. 545). Finally there is the principle
that one does not exchange things for food, not directly that is,
among friends and relatives. Traffic in food is traffic between
foreign interests. (Look how a novelist quite simply suggests that
one of his characters is a real bastard: 'He brought his blankets to
the bare house, took silent supper with the Boss family, insisted
on paying them – he could not understand why they pretended
reluctance when he offered to pay them; food cost money; they
were not in the restaurant business, but food cost money, you
could not deny that' – MacKinlay Kantor.)

In these principles of instrumental food exchange there seems
little variation between peoples. Of course, the extent to which
they are employed, and which of them are employed, vary with
the case. Dobuans proscribe intervillage visiting and hospitality,
no doubt for good and sufficient reasons. Elsewhere, circumstances ranging from economic interdependence through political
strategy enjoin both visiting and the hospitable entertainment
of visitors. A detailed look at the circumstances would be beyond

the present purview: the point is that where some coming to sociable terms with visitors is desirable, hospitality is an ordinary way of doing it. And the Dobuan syndrome is by no means typical. Ordinarily, 'Savages pride themselves in being hospitable to strangers' (Harmon, 1957, p. 43).

Consequently the sphere of generalized exchange in food is sometimes wider than the sphere of generalized exchange in other things. This tendency to transcend the sectoral plan is most dramatized in the hospitality afforded trade partners, or any kinsmen from afar, who make visits the occasion for exchanging presents (see examples in Appendix A). Here are people whose dealings in durables are consciously balanced out – or even potentially run on *caveat emptor* – by some miracle charitably supplying one another with food and shelter. But then hospitality counters the *wabuwabu* lurking in the background and provides an atmosphere in which direct exchange of presents and trade goods can be equitably consummated.

There is logic in an undue tendency to move food by generalized reciprocity. Like exchange between rich and poor, or between high and low, where food is concerned a greater inclination to sacrifice seems required just to sustain the given degree of sociability. Sharing needs to be extended to more distant relatives, generalized reciprocity broadened beyond ordinary sectoral limits. (It might be recalled from the Appendices to previous sections that generosity is distinctively associated with food dealing.)

About the only sociable thing to do with food is to give it away, and the commensurably sociable return, after an interval of suitable decency, is the return of hospitality or assistance. The implication is not only a rather loose or imperfect balance in food dealing, but specifically a restraint on exchanges of food for other goods. One notes with interest normative injunctions against the sale of food among peoples possessed of primitive currencies, among certain Melanesian and California tribes for instance. Here balanced exchange is run of the mill. Money tokens serve as more or less general equivalents and are exchanged against a variety of stuff. But not *food*stuff. Within a broad social sector where money talks for other things, staples are insulated against pecuniary transactions and food shared perhaps but rarely sold.

172

Food has too much social value – ultimately because it has too much use value – to have exchange value.

'Food was not sold. It might be given away, but being "wild stuff" should not be sold, according to Pomo etiquette. Manufactured articles only were bought and sold, such as baskets, bows and arrows' (Gifford, 1926, p. 329; cf. Kroeber, 1925, p. 40, on the Yurok – same sort of thing).

'[To the Tolowa-Tututni] food was only edible, not saleable' (Drucker, 1937, p. 241; cf. DuBois, 1936, pp. 50-51).

'The staple articles of food, taro, bananas, coconuts, are never sold [by Lesu], and are given to kindred, friends, and strangers passing through the village as an act of courtesy' (Powdermaker, 1933, p. 195).

In a similar way, staple foodstuffs were excluded from balanced trading among Alaskan Eskimo – 'The feeling was present that to trade for food was reprehensible' – and even luxury foods that were exchanged between trade partners were transferred as presents and apart from the main trading (Spencer, 1959, pp. 204-205).

It would seem that common foodstuffs are likely to have an insulated 'circuit of exchange', separate from durables, particularly 'wealth'. (See Firth, 1950; Bohannan, 1955; Bohannan & Dalton, 1962, on 'spheres of exchange'.) Morally and socially this should be so. For a wide range of social relations, balanced and direct food-for-goods transactions (conversions) would rend the solidary bonds. Distinctive categorizations of food vs. other goods, i.e. 'wealth', express the sociological disparity and protect food from dysfunctional comparisons of its worth – as among the Salish:

'Food was not classed as "wealth" [i.e. blankets, shell ornaments, canoes, etc.]. Nor was it treated as wealth . . . "holy food", a Semiahmoo informant called it. It should be given freely, he felt, and could not be refused. Food was evidently not freely exchanged with wealth. A person in need of food might ask to buy some from another household in his community, offering wealth for it, but food was not generally offered for sale' (Suttles, 1960, p. 301; Vayda, 1961).

But an important qualification must in haste be entered. These food and nonfood spheres are sociologically based and bounded. The immorality of food-wealth conversions has a sectoral dimension: at a certain socially peripheral point the circuits merge and thus dissolve. (At this point, food-for-goods exchange is a 'conveyance' in Bohannan and Dalton's usage.) Food does not move against money or other stuff within the community or tribe, yet it may be so exchanged outside these social contexts, and not merely under duress but as use and wont. The Salish *did* customarily take food, 'holy food', to affinal relatives in other Salish villages and received wealth in return (Suttles, 1960). Likewise, Pomo *did* 'buy' – at any rate gave beads for – acorns, fish, and like necessities from other communities (Kroeber, 1925, p. 260; Loeb, 1926, pp. 192-193). The separation of food and wealth cycles is contextual. Within communities these are insulated circuits, insulated by community relations; they are kept apart where a demand of return on necessities would contradict prevailing kinship relations. Beyond this, in the intercommunity or intertribal sector, the insulation of the food circuit may be worn through by frictions of social distance.

(Foodstuffs, incidentally, are not ordinarily divorced from the circuit of labor assistance. On the contrary, a meal is in the host of primitive societies the customary return for labor solicited for gardening, housebuilding, and other domestic tasks. 'Wages' in the usual sense is not at issue. The feeding amounts to an extraordinary extension to other relatives and to friends of the household economy. Rather than a tentative move toward capitalism, it is perhaps better understood by a principle something to the opposite: that those who participate in a productive effort have some claim on its outcome.)

VII

ON BALANCED RECIPROCITY

We have seen generalized reciprocity in play in instrumental ways, notably as a starting mechanism of rank distinction and also, in the form of hospitality, to mediate relations between persons of different communities. Balanced reciprocity likewise finds instrumental employments, but especially as formal social compact. Balanced reciprocity is the classic vehicle of peace and alliance contracts, substance-as-symbol of the transformation from separate to harmonious interests. Group prestations are the dramatic and perhaps the typical form, but there are instances too of interpersonal compact sealed by exchange.

Here it is useful to recall Mauss's dictum: 'In these primitive and archaic societies there is no middle path.... When two groups of men meet they may move away or in case of mistrust or defiance they may resort to arms; or else they can come to terms.' And the terms ought to balance, insofar as the groups are 'different men'. The relations are too tenuous to long sustain a failure to reciprocate – ' "Indians notice such things" ' (Goldschmidt, 1951, p. 338). They notice a lot of things. Goldschmidt's Nomlaki Indians in fact articulate a whole set of glosses and paraphrases of Maussian principle, among them:

> 'When enemies meet they call to one another. If the settlement is friendly they approach closer and spread out their goods. One man would throw something in the middle, one man from the other side would throw in something for it and take the traded material back. They trade till one side has traded everything. The ones that have some left make fun of those who have run out, bragging about themselves.... This trade takes place on the border line' (Goldschmidt, 1951, p. 338).

Balanced reciprocity is willingness to give for that which is received. Therein seems to be its efficacy as social compact. The striking of equivalence, or at least some approach to balance, is a demonstrable foregoing of self-interest on each side, some renunciation of hostile intent or of indifference in favor of mutuality. Against the preexisting context of separateness, the material balance signifies a new state of affairs. This is not to deny that the transaction is ever consequential in a utilitarian sense, as it may well be – and the social effect perhaps compounded by an equitable exchange of different necessities. But whatever the utilitarian value, and there need be none, there is always 'moral' purpose, as Radcliffe-Brown remarked of certain Andaman transactions:

175

'to provide a friendly feeling . . . and unless it did this it failed of
its purpose'.

Among the many kinds of contract closed as it were by
balanced exchange, the following seem most common:

1. *Formal friendship or kinship*

These are interpersonal compacts of solidarity, pledges of
brotherhood in some cases, friendship in others. The alliance may
be sealed by exchange of identical goods, the material counterpart of some exchange of identities, but at any rate the transaction is likely to balance and the exchange is of distant for close
relationship (e.g. Pospisil, 1958, pp. 86-87; Seligman, 1910,
pp. 69-70). An association once so formed may well become more
sociable over time, and future transactions both parallel and
compound this trend by becoming more generalized.

2. *Affirmation of corporate alliances*

One may place in this category the various feasts and entertain-
ments reciprocally tendered between friendly local groups and
communities, such as certain of the interclan vegetable-heap
presentations in the New Guinea Highlands or inter-village social
feasts in Samoa or New Zealand.

3. *Peace-making*

These are the exchanges of settlement, of cessation of dispute,
feud, and warfare. Both interpersonal and collective hostilities
may be thus quieted by exchange. 'When an equivalence is
struck' parties to an Abelam argument are satisfied: ' "talk is
thrown away" ' (Kaberry, 1941-42, p. 341). That is the general
principle.

One may wish to include wergeld payments, compensations for
adultery, and other forms of compounding injury in this category,
as well as the exchanges that terminate warfare. They all work on
the general principle, the principle of fair trade. (Spencer provides an interesting Eskimo example: when a man received compensation from the abductor of his wife the two men 'inevitably'
become friendly, he writes, 'because they had conceptually
effected a trade' (1959, p. 81). (See also Denig, 1928-29, p. 404;
Powdermaker, 1933, p. 197; Williamson, 1912, p. 183; Deacon,

1934, p. 226; Kroeber, 1925, p. 252; Loeb, 1926, pp. 204-205; Hogbin, 1939, pp. 79, 91-92; etc.).

4. *Marital alliance*

Marriage prestations are of course the classic form of reciprocity as social compact. I have little to add to the received anthropological discussion, except a slight qualification about the character of reciprocity in these transactions, and even this may be superfluous.

It does seem to miss the point, however, to view marital exchange either as 'total' or as perfectly balanced prestation. The transactions of marriage, and perhaps contingent future affinal exchange as well, are ordinarily not exactly equal. For one thing, asymmetry of exchange is commonplace: women move against hoes or cattle, *toga* against *oloa*, fish against pigs. In the absence of some secular convertability, or of a mutual standard of value, the transfer seems to an extent one of incomparables; neither equivalent nor total, the transaction may be of incommensurables. In any event, and even where the same sorts of things are exchanged, one side or the other may be conceived to benefit unduly, at least for the time being. This lack of precise balance is socially of the essence.

First, unequal benefit sustains the alliance as perfect balance could not. Truly, the people concerned – and/or the ethnographer – might muse that in the fullness of time accounts between affines even out. Or losses and gains may be cancelled by cyclical or statistical patterns of alliance. Or some balance in goods, at least, may obtain in the total political economy, where the flow of payments upwards (against a flow of women downwards) through a series of ranked lineages is reversed by redistribution from the top (cf. Leach, 1951). Yet it is socially critical that over a long term, and perhaps forever, the exchange between two groups united by a marriage has not been balanced. In so far as the things transferred are of different quality, it may be difficult ever to calculate that the sides are 'even-steven'. This is a social good. The exchange that is symmetrical or unequivocally equal carries some disadvantage from the point of view of alliance: it cancels debts and thus opens the possibility of contracting out. If neither side is 'owing' then the bond between them is comparatively fragile. But if accounts are not squared, then the relationship is maintained by virtue of 'the shadow of indebtedness', and there will have to be further occasions of association, perhaps as occasions of further payment.

Secondly, and directly related, an asymmetrical exchange of different things lends itself to alliance that is complementary. The marital bond between groups is not always, maybe not even usually, some sort of fifty-fifty partnership between homologous parties. One group surrenders a woman, another gets her; in a patrilineal context the wife-receivers have secured continuity, something at the expense of the wife-givers, at least on this occasion. There has been a differential transfer: the groups are socially related in a complementary and asymmetrical way. Likewise, in a ranked lineage system the giving of women may be a specification of the set of subordinate-superordinate relations. Now in these cases, the several rights and duties of alliance are symbolized by the differential character of transfers, are attached to complementary symbols. Asymmetrical prestations secure the complementary alliance once again as perfectly balanced, symmetrical, or all-out total prestations would not.

The casual received view of reciprocity supposes some fairly direct one-for-one exchange, balanced reciprocity, or a near approximation of balance. It may not be inappropriate, then, to footnote this discussion with a respectful demur: that in the main run of primitive societies, taking into account directly utilitarian as well as instrumental transactions, balanced reciprocity is not the prevalent form of exchange. A question might even be raised about the stability of balanced reciprocity. Balanced exchange may tend toward self-liquidation. On one hand, a series of honorably balanced dealings between comparatively distant parties builds trust and confidence, in effect reduces social distance, and so increases the chances for more generalized future dealings – as the initial blood-brotherhood transaction creates a 'credit rating', as it were. On the other hand, a renege acts to sever relations – as failure to make returns breaks a trade-partnership – if it does not actually invite chicanery in return. May we conclude that balanced reciprocity is inherently unstable? Or perhaps that it requires special conditions for continuity?

The societal profile of reciprocity, at any rate, most often inclines toward generalized modes. In the simpler hunting groups the generalized assistance of close kinship seems usually dominant; in neolithic chiefdoms this is supplemented by kinship-rank obligations. There are nonetheless societies of certain type in which balanced exchange, if not exactly dominant, acquires unusual prominence. Interest attaches to these societies, not alone for the emphasis on balanced reciprocity, but for what goes with it.

The well known 'labor exchange' in Southeast Asian hinterland communities brings these immediately to mind. Here is a set of peoples who, placed against the main run of primitive societies, offer departures in economy, and social structure as well, that cannot fail to kindle a comparative interest. The well-described Iban (Freeman, 1955, 1960), Land Dayak (Geddes, 1954, 1957; cf. Provinse, 1937) and Lamet (Izikowitz, 1951) belong in the class – some Philippine peoples may as well, but I am uncertain how far the analysis about to be suggested will work for the Philippines.

Now these societies are distinctive not only for uncommon internal characteristics of economy but for unusual external relations – unusual, that is, in a strictly primitive milieu. They are hinterlands engaged by petty market trade – and perhaps also by political dominance (e.g. Lamet) – to more sophisticated cultural centers. From the perspective of the advanced centers, they are backwaters serving as secondary sources of rice and other goods (cf. VanLeur, 1955, especially pp. 101 f, for some hints about the economic significance of hinterland provisioning in Southeast Asia). From the hinterlands view, the critical aspect of the intercultural relation is that the subsistence staple, rice, is exported for cash, iron tools, and prestige goods, many of the last quite expensive. It is suggested – with all the deference that must be supplied by one who has no research experience in the area – it is suggested that the peculiar social-economic character of Southeast Asian hinterland tribes is congruent with this unusual employment of household subsistence surpluses. The implication of an external trade in rice is not merely an internal ban on sharing it, or a corresponding requirement of quid-pro-quo in intra-community dealings, but departure from ordinary characteristics of primitive distribution in virtually all respects.

179

The engagement with the market makes a key minimal demand: that internal community relations permit household accumulation of rice, else the amounts required for external exchange will never be forthcoming. This stipulation must prevail in the face of limited and uncertain modes of rice production. The fortunate households cannot be responsible for the unfortunate; if internal leveling is unleashed then the external trade relations are simply not sustained.

The set of consequences for the economy and polity of the hinterland tribal communities appear to include: (i) Different households, by virtue of variations in number of effective producers, amass different amounts of the subsistence-export staple. The productive differences range between surfeit above and deficit below family consumption requirements. These differences, however, are not liquidated by sharing in favor of need. Instead (ii) the intensity of sharing within the village or tribe is low, and (iii) the principal reciprocal relation between households is a closely calculated balanced exchange of labor service. As Geddes remarks of the Land Dayak: '. . . co-operation beyond the household, except on business lines where every service must have an equal return, is at a low level' (1954, p. 34). Balanced labor-exchange, of course, maintains the productive advantage (accumulation capacity) of the family with more adult workers. The only goods that customarily move in generalized reciprocity are game and perhaps large domestic animals sacrificed in family ceremonies. Such items are widely distributed through the community (cf. Izikowitz, 1951), much as hunters would share them, but the sharing of meat is not as decisive in structuring interfamilial relations as the lack of sharing decreed by export of staples. (iv) Even household commensality may be rather rigidly supervised, subjected to accounting of each person's rice dole in the interest of developing an exchange reserve, hence less sociable than ordinary primitive commensality (compare, for example, Izikowitz, 1951, pp. 301-302 with Firth, 1936, pp. 112-116). (v) Restricted sharing of staples, demanded by articulation with the siphoning market, finds its social complement in an atomization and fragmentation of community structure. Lineages, or like systems of extensive and corporate solidary relations, are incompatible with the external drain on household staples and the corresponding posture of self-interest required *vis-à-vis* other households. Large local descent groups are absent or inconsequential. Instead, the solidary relations are of the small family itself, with various and changing interpersonal kin ties the only such nexus of connection between households. Economically, these extended kin ties are weak ones:

'A household is not only a distinct unit, but one which minds its own business. Perforce, it has to do so, because it has with other households no formal relations, sanctioned by custom, on which it can rely for certain support. Indeed, the absence of such structured relationships is a condition of the society as at present organized. In the main economic affairs, cooperation with others is based upon contract and not primarily upon kinship. . . . As a result of this situation, ties which persons have with others in the community tend to be widespread, but limited to sentiment and sociability, often sadly so' (Geddes, 1954, p. 42).

(vi) Prestige apparently hinges upon obtaining exotic items – Chinese pottery, brass gongs, etc. – from the outside in exchange for rice or work. Prestige does not, obviously cannot, rest on generous assistance to one's fellows in the manner of a tribal big-man. The exotic goods figure internally as ceremonial display items and in marriage prestations – thus insofar as status is linked to them it is principally as possession and ability to make payments, again not through giving them away. ('Wealth does not help a man to become chief because it gives him power to distribute largesse. Riches rarely incline a Dayak to charity, although they may to usury', Geddes, 1954, p. 50.) No one then obligates others very much. No one creates followers. As a result there are no strong leaders, a fact which probably contributes to the atomization of the community and may have repercussions on the intensity of land use (cf. Izikowitz, 1951).

In these Southeast Asian communities, the prevalence of balanced reciprocity does seem connected with special circumstances. But then the circumstances suggest that it is not legitimate to involve these peoples in the present context of tribal economics. By the same token, their use in debating issues of primitive economics, as Geddes uses the Land Dayak to argue

181

against 'primitive communism', seems not quite cricket. Perhaps they are best classed with peasants – so long as one does not thereupon suggest, as is unfortunately often done under the label 'economic anthropology', that 'peasant' and 'primitive' belong together in some undifferentiated type of economy distinguished negatively as whatever-it-is that is outside the province of orthodox economic analysis.

There are, however, incontestable examples of societal emphasis on balanced reciprocity in primitive settings. Primitive monies serving as media of exchange at more or less fixed rates argue this. The monies amount to the suggested special mechanisms for maintaining balance. It is worthwhile to inquire into their incidence and their economic and social concomitants.

Yet this is not to be hazarded without some formal definition of 'primitive money', a problem approaching the status of a classic dilemma in comparative economics. On one side, any thing that has a 'money use' – as we know money uses: payments, exchange, standard, etc. – may be taken for 'money'. If so, probably every society enjoys the dubious benefits, inasmuch as some category of goods is usually earmarked for certain payments. The alternative is less relativistic and therefore seems more useful for comparative generalizations: to agree on some minimal use and quality of the stuff. The strategy, as Firth suggests, is not to question ' "What is primitive money?" but "What is it useful to include in the category of primitive money?" ' (1959, p. 39). His specific suggestion, which as I understand it centrally involves the medium-of-exchange function, does indeed appear useful. ('My own view is that to entitle an object to be classified as money, it should be of a generally acceptable type, serving to facilitate the conversion of one object or service into terms of another and used as a standard of value thereby,' Firth, 1959, pp. 38-39).

Let 'money' refer to those objects in primitive societies that have token value rather than utility and that serve as means of exchange. The exchange use is limited to certain categories of things – land and labor are ordinarily excluded – and is brought to bear only between parties of certain social relation. In the main it serves as an indirect bridge between goods ('C-M-C') rather than commercial purposes ('M-C-M'). These limitations would

182

justify the phrase 'primitive money'. If all this is agreeable, it further appears that pristine developments of primitive money are not broadly spread through the ethnographic scene, but are restricted to certain areas: especially western and central Melanesia, aboriginal California, and certain parts of the South American tropical forest. (Monies may also have developed in pristine contexts in Africa, but I am not expert enough to disentangle their distribution from archaic civilizations and ancient 'international' trade.)

This is also to say that primitive money is associated with an historically specific type of primitive economy, an economy with a marked incidence of balanced exchange in peripheral social sectors. It is not a phenomenon of simple hunting cultures – if I may be permitted, cultures of a band level. Neither is primitive money characteristic of the more advanced chiefdoms, where wealth tokens though certainly encountered tend to bear little exchange load. The regions noted – Melanesia, California, South American tropical forest – are (or were) occupied by societies of an intermediate sort, such as have been called 'tribal' (Sahlins, 1961; Service, 1962) or 'homogeneous' and 'segmented tribes' (Oberg, 1955). They are distinguished from band systems not merely for more settled conditions of life – often associated with neolithic vs. paleolithic production – but principally for a larger and more complex tribal organization of constituent local groupings. The several local settlements of tribal societies are bound together both by a nexus of kin relations and by cross-cutting social institutions, such as a set of clans. Yet the relatively small settlements are autonomous and self-governing, a feature which in turn distinguishes tribal from chiefdom plans. The local segments of the latter are integrated into larger polities, as divisions and subdivisions, by virtue of principles of rank and a structure of chieftainships and subchieftainships. The tribal plan is purely segmental, the chiefdom pyramidal.

This evolutionary classification of social-cultural types is admittedly loose. I hope not to raise an issue over it, for it has been offered merely to direct attention to contrasting structural features of primitive-money areas. They are precisely the kinds of features that, given previous argumentation, suggest an unusual incidence of balanced reciprocity. A greater play of

183

balanced exchange in tribal over band societies is argued in part by a greater proportion of craft goods and services in the societal economic output. Foodstuffs, while still the decisive share of a tribal economic product, decline relatively. Transactions in durables, more likely to be balanced than food transactions, increase. But more important, the proportion of peripheral-sector exchange, the incidence of exchange among more distantly related people, is likely to be considerably greater in tribal than in band societies. This is understandable by reference to the more definite segmental plan of tribes, which is also to say more definite sectoral breaks in the social structure.

The several residential segments of tribes are comparatively stable and formally constituted. And a corporate political solidarity is as characteristic of the tribal segment as it is lacking in flexible camp-and-band arrangements of hunters. Tribal segmental structure is also more extensive, including perhaps internal lineage groupings in the political segments, the set (and sometimes segmentary subsets) of political segments, and the tribal-foreigner division. Now the accretion over band organization is particularly in peripheral structure, in the development of the intratribal and intertribal sectors. Here is where exchange encounters increase, whether these be instrumental, peace-making exchanges or frankly materialistic dealings. The accretion in exchange then is in the social areas of balanced reciprocity.

A chiefdom, in further contrast, liquidates and pushes out peripheral sectors by transforming external into internal relations, by including adjacent local groups within enclaving political unions. At the same time, the incidence of balanced reciprocity is depressed, in virtue of both the 'internalization' of exchange relations and their centralization. Balanced exchanges should thus decline in favor of more generalized with the attainment of a chiefdom level. The implication for primitive money is perhaps illustrated by its absence in the Trobriands, despite the fact that this island of chiefdoms is set in a sea of money-using tribes, or by the progressive attentuation in exchange-uses of shell beads moving northward from tribal California to protochiefdom British Columbia.

The hypothesis about primitive money – offered with due
184

caution and deference – is this: it occurs in conjunction with unusual incidence of balanced reciprocity in peripheral social sectors. Presumably it facilitates the heavy balanced traffic. The conditions that encourage primitive money are most likely to occur in the range of primitive societies called tribal and are unlikely to be served by band or chiefdom development. But a qualification must in haste be entered. Not all tribes provide circumstances for monetary development and certainly not all enjoy primitive money, as that term is here understood. For the potentiality of peripheral exchange is maximized only by some tribes. Others remain relatively inner-directed.

First, peripheral sectors become scenes of intensive exchange in conjunction with regional and intertribal symbiosis. An areal ecological regime of specialized tribes, respective families and communities of which are in trade relation, is probably a necessary condition for primitive money. Such regimes are characteristic of California and Melanesia – about South America I am not prepared to say – but in other tribal settings symbiosis is not characteristic and the intertribal (or interregional) exchange sector comparatively underdeveloped. Perhaps just as important are circumstances that put premiums on delayed exchange and so on tokens that store value in the interim. The outputs of interdependent communities, for example, may be unavoidably unbalanced in time – as between coastal and inland peoples, where an exchangeable catch of fish cannot always be met by complementary inland products. Here a currency acceptable on all sides very much facilitates interdependence – so that shell beads, say, taken for fish at one time can be converted for acorns at another (cf. Vayda, 1954; Loeb, 1926). Big-man leadership systems, it would seem from Melanesia, may likewise render delayed balanced exchange functional. The tribal big-man operates on a fund of power consisting of food, pigs, or the like, stuffs with the common quality that they are not easy to keep around in large amounts over long periods. But, at the same time, the extractive devices for accumulating these political funds are underdeveloped, and collection of goods for a climactic giveaway would have to be gradual and thus technically difficult. The dilemma is resolvable by monetary manipulations: by converting wealth into tokens and by calculated deployment of money in loans and exchange, so that a time will come when a massive call on goods can be made and the whole pile of stuff, given away, converted into status. That's the way the money goes.

VIII

AN AFTERTHOUGHT

It is difficult to conclude with a dramatic flourish. The essay has not a dramatic structure – its main drift seems downhill. And a summary would be needlessly repetitive.

But there is a curiosity worth remarking. Here has been given a discourse on economics in which 'economizing' appears mainly as an exogenous factor! The organizing principles of economy have been sought elsewhere. To the extent they have been found outside man's presumed hedonist propensity, a strategy for the study of primitive economics is suggested that is something the reverse of economic orthodoxy. It may be worth while to see how far this heresy will get us.

APPENDIX A

Notes on Reciprocity and Kinship Distance

A.1.0   *Hunters and Gatherers* – Generally: sectoral breaks in reciprocity not always as definite as for neolithic peoples, but variation in reciprocity by interpersonal kinship distance apparent. Generalized reciprocity often consists of specific obligations to render goods to certain kinsmen (kinship dues) rather than altruistic assistance. Notable differences between the handling of foods and durables.

A.1.1   *Bushmen* – The Kung term lack of generosity or failure to reciprocate 'far-hearted' – a felicitous choice of words, from our perspective.

    Three social-material breaking points in reciprocity are apparent in Marshall's (1961) paper on Kung exchange: (i) a range of close kin in the camp with whom meat is shared, often as customary obligation; (ii) more distant kin within the camp and other Bushmen, with whom economic relations are characterized by 'gift-giving' of durables in a more balanced fashion and transactions in meat that approximate 'gift-giving'; (iii) 'trade' with Bantu. Marshall's materials are rich and indicate the play of various social considerations and sanctions determining specific transactions. Large game moves through a camp in several waves. Initially it is pooled in the hunting party by the taker, with shares going also to the arrow. 'In the second distribution [here we move into reciprocity proper] close kinship is the factor which sets the pattern of the giving. Certain obligations are compulsory. A man's first obligation at this point, we were told, is to give to his wife's parents. He must give to them the best he has in as generous portions as he can, while still fulfilling other primary obligations, which are to his own parents, his spouse, and offspring [note, these cook and eat meat separately]. He keeps a portion for himself at this time and from it would give to his siblings, to his wife's siblings, if they are present, and to other kin, affines, and friends who are there, possibly only in small quantities by then. Everyone who receives meat gives again, in another wave of sharing, to his or her parents, parents-in-law, spouses, offspring, siblings, and others. The meat may be cooked and the quantities small. Visitors, even though they are not close kin or affines, are given meat by the people whom they are visiting' (Marshall, 1961, p. 238). Beyond the range of close kin, giving meat is a matter of individual inclination in which friendship, obligation to return past favors and other considerations come into account. But this giving is definitely more balanced: 'In the later waves of sharing when the primary distribution and the primary kinship obligations have been fulfilled, the giving of meat from one's own portion has the quality of gift-giving. !Kung society requires at this point only that a person should give with reasonable generosity in proportion to what he has received and not keep more than an equitable amount for himself in the end, and that the person who receives a gift of meat must give a reciprocal gift some time in the future' (p. 239). Marshall reserves 'gift-giving' to the exchange of durables; this occurs also, and importantly, between Kung of different bands. One should neither refuse such gifts nor fail to make a return. Much of the gift-giving is instrumental, having principally social effects. Even asking

187

for thing, claimed one man, ' "formed a love" between people. It means "he still loves me, that is why he is asking".' And Marshall adds laconically, 'At least it forms a something between people, I thought' (p. 245). 'Gift-giving' is distinguishable from 'trade' both in form of reciprocity and social sector. 'In reciprocating [a gift] one does not give the same object back again but something of comparable value. The interval of time between receiving and reciprocating varied from a few weeks to a few years. Propriety requires that there be no unseemly haste. The giving must not look like trading' (p. 244). The mechanics of trading are not specified. 'Negotiation' however is mentioned; the implication is of haggle. The social sphere is in any case clear: 'The !Kung do not trade among themselves. They consider the procedure undignified and avoid it because it is too likely to stir up bad feelings. They trade with Bantu, however, in the settlements along the B.P. border. . . . The odds are with the Bantu in the trading. Big, aggressive, and determined to have what they want, they easily intimidate the Bushmen. Several !Kung informants said that they tried not to trade with Herero if it was possible to avoid it because, although the Tswana were hard bargainers, the Herero were worse' (p. 242).

Intense generalized reciprocity within Bushman camps and bands – especially food-sharing – is also indicated by Thomas (1959, pp. 22, 50, 214-215) and Schapera (1930, pp. 98-101, 148). Interband exchange, however, is characterized as 'barter' by Schapera (1930, p. 146; cf. Thomas's amusing anecdote of the trouble that developed between a man and woman of different groups over an unrequited gift presented to the father of the former by the woman's father, 1959, pp. 240-242).

Theft reported unknown to them (Marshall, 1961, pp. 245-246; Thomas 1959, p. 206). However, Schapera implies it exists (1930, p. 148).

A.1.2   *Congo Pygmies* – In general, the scheme of reciprocity looks very much like the Bushmen's, including a rather impersonal exchange with 'Negroes' (Putnam, 1953, p. 322; Schebesta, 1933, p. 42; Turnbull, 1962). Hunting spoils, large game especially, are shared out in the camp, on a kinship-distance basis it appears – Putnam implies that first the family shares, then the 'family group' gets shares (1953, p. 332; cf. Schebesta 1933, pp. 68, 124, 244).

A.1.3   *Washo* – 'Sharing obtained at every level of Washo social organization. Sharing also decreased as kinship and residence distances increased' (Price, 1962, p. 37). It is difficult to say where 'trade' leaves off and 'gift-giving' begins, but 'In trade there tended to be immediate reciprocation while gift exchange often involved a time lapse. Trade also tended to be competitive and to increase with less intense social ties. Trade involved explicit negotiation and social status was secondary as a factor in the transaction' (p. 49).

A.1.4   *Semang* – Sharp sectoral break in reciprocity at the 'family group' (band) border: 'Each family contributes from its own food, already cooked and prepared, to every other family. If one family on any particular day is unusually well supplied, they give generously to all kindred families, even if it leaves them with too little. If other families not belonging to the group are in the camp, they do not share, or only to a very small extent, in the distribution' (Schebesta, n.d., p. 84).

A.1.5   *Andamans* – Radcliffe-Brown's (1948) account suggests a higher level of generalized reciprocity within the local group, particularly in food dealings and in transactions between junior and senior generations (cf. pp. 42-43), and more balanced forms of reciprocity between people of different bands, particularly in durables. The exchange of presents is characteristic of interband meetings, an exchange that could amount to swapping local specialties. In this sector, 'It requires a good deal of tact to avoid the unpleasantness that may arise if a man thinks he has not received things as valuable as he has given' (p. 43, cf. pp. 83-84; Man, n.d., p. 120).

A.1.6   *Australian Aborigines* – A number of formal, compulsory kin dues and also formal precedence-orders for sharing food and other goods with relatives of the camp (see Elkin, 1954, pp. 110-111; Meggitt, 1962, pp. 118, 120, 131, 139, etc.; Warner, 1937, pp. 63, 70, 92-95; Spencer & Gillen, 1927, p. 490).

A strong obligation to share out food in the horde (Radcliffe-Brown, 1930-31, p. 438; Spencer & Gillen, 1927, pp. 37-39).

Yir-Yiront exchange seems to parallel the Bushman scheme (above). Sharp notes that reciprocity varies on both sides of the set of customary kin dues, toward balance beyond and toward generalized reciprocity in the narrowest sphere of closest kin. Giving to persons outside the range of those

189

entitled dues 'amounts to compulsory exchange. . . . But there is also irregular giving, though within a relatively narrow social range, for which the incentives seem to be chiefly sentimental, and which may be considered altruistic; this may lead to a desire to acquire property in order to give it away' (Sharp, 1934-35, pp. 37-38).

On the connection between assistance and close kinship: Meggitt observes of the Walbiri that '. . . a man who has several spears parts with them willingly; but, should he have only one, his son or father should not ask for it. If he is asked, the man usually gives the single article to an actual or close father or son, but he refuses distant "fathers" and "sons" ' (Meggitt, 1962, p. 120).

Balanced reciprocity, in various specific guises, is characteristic of the well-known interband and intertribal trade exchange, which is often effected by trade partners who are classificatory kin (see, for example, Sharp, 1952, pp. 76-77; Warner, 1937, pp. 95, 145).

A.1.7   *Eskimo* – High level of generalized reciprocity in the camp, associated by Birket-Smith with 'the fellowship of the settlement'. This concerns food in the main, particularly large animals, and especially during the winter season (Birket-Smith, 1959, p. 146; Spencer, 1959, pp. 150, 153, 170; Boas, 1884-85, p. 562; Rink, 1875, p. 27).

Taken all in all, Spencer's study of the North Alaskan Eskimo suggests significant differences between the reciprocity appropriate among kinsmen, among trade partners and among non-kin who are also not trade partners. These variations concern durables, especially trade goods. Non-kin within the camp would presumably be given some food if they are short, but trade goods are exchanged with them, as well as with outsiders (who are not trade partners), in an impersonal 'bidding' transaction (reminiscent of Brazilian Indians' 'trade game'). Trade partnerships are formed – on quasi-kin or institutional-friendship lines – between coastal and inland men; the exchange is of local specialties. Partners deal without haggle, indeed try to extend themselves, yet without balance (or near balance) in exchange the partnership would dissolve. Trade relations are specifically distinguished by Spencer from kinship-generalized reciprocity. Thus kinsmen do not need to enter into partnership, he says, for 'A relative would always be of assistance, an arrangement which pointed primarily to the sharing of food and granting of shelter' (Spencer, 1959, pp. 65-66). Again: 'One would not form a partnership with a brother, the theory being that one secured assistance and aid from one's close relatives in any case' (p. 170).

A.1.8   *Shoshoni* – When a family did not have a great deal to share out, as when only seeds or small animals had been taken, that given out was to close relatives and neighbors (Steward, 1938, pp. 74, 231, 240, 253). There seems to have been a fairly high level of generalized reciprocity in the village, which Steward links to the 'high degree of [kin] relationship between village members' (p. 239).

A.1.9   *Northern Tungus* (mounted hunters) – Much sharing within the clan, but food sharing most intense within the few families of a clan that nomadized together (Shirokogoroff, 1929, pp. 195, 200, 307). According to Shirokogoroff, gift-giving among Tungus was not reciprocal, and Tungus resented Manchu expectations on this head (p. 99); however, he also wrote that gifts were given to guests (over and above ordinary hospitality) and these items should be reciprocated (p. 333). Reindeer sold only outside the clan; inside, pass as gifts and assistance (pp. 35-36).

A.2.0   *Oceania* – The sectoral system of reciprocities is often more clear and more definite, especially in Melanesia. In Polynesia it is overridden by centralization of reciprocities in chiefly hands or by redistribution (see Section IV, pp. 158-164 above).

A.2.1   *'Gawa (Busama)* – A full set of data illustrative of the present thesis. Hogbin contrasts maritime intertribal trade through partnerships and inland trade with unrelated peoples, saying of the latter exchange: 'The parties seem slightly ashamed, however, and conclude their arrangements outside the village. [Note the literal exclusion of impersonal exchange from the 'Gawa village:] Commerce it is considered, should be carried on away from where people live, preferably alongside the road or the beach (the native-owned store at Busama is located fifty yards from the nearest dwelling). The Busama sum up the situation by saying that the maritime people give one another presents but insist on a proper return from the bushmen. The basis of the distinction is that on the coast activities are confined to relatives, but so few of the beach folk have kinsmen in the hill country that most transactions take place of necessity between comparative strangers. [Hogbin mentions

191

elsewhere that the bush trade is recent.] A certain amount of migration and intermarriage has taken place around the sea-board, and every coastal native has kinsmen in some of the other shore villages, especially those close at hand. When trading by sea it is with these, and these only, that he makes exchanges. Kinship ties and bargaining are considered to be incompatible, and all goods are handed over as free gifts offered from motives of sentiment. Discussion of values is avoided, and the donor does the best he can to convey the impression that no thought of a counter gift has entered his head. Yet at a later stage, when a convenient opportunity arises, hints are dropped of what is expected, whether pots, mats, baskets, or food. . . . Most of the visitors go home with items at least as valuable as those with which they came. Indeed, the closer the kinship bond the greater the host's generosity is, and some of them return a good deal richer. A careful count is kept, however, and the score is afterwards made even. . . . [The account goes on to give examples and to note that failure to balance will cause termination of the partnership. Now, contrast the foregoing with reciprocity in the intravillage sector:] It is significant that when a Busama acquired a string bag from a fellow villager, as has recently become possible, he always gives twice what he would pay to a more distant relative [i.e., trading partner] on the north coast. "One is ashamed," the people explain, "to treat those with whom one is familiar like a tradesman" ' (Hogbin, 1951, pp. 83-86). The variation in reciprocity by linear-kinship distance is also worth noting: 'A presentation [of a pig] from a close relative imposes the usual obligation to return an animal of equivalent size on some future occasion, but no money changes hands either when the original gift is made or later. A similar obligation exists between distant kinsmen, but in this case each pig has also to be paid for at its full market price. The transaction is in line with earlier practice, except that dog's teeth then served as payment. The members of the purchasers' group help him nowadays with a few shillings, just as formerly they would have given him a string or two of teeth' (p. 124).

A.2.2   *Kuma* – Generalized reciprocity within such small-scale descent groups as the 'sub-subclan'–'a bank and a labour force for its members' (Reay, 1959, p. 29) – and the subclan (p. 70). The interclan sector is characterized by balanced exchange, by 'the general emphasis on exact reciprocity between groups' (p. 47, see also pp. 55, 86-89, 126). In the external sector, balance is appropriate between trade-partners, but without a partnership the transaction inclines toward negative reciprocity: 'In Kuma trading, there are two distinct forms: institutionalized transactions through trading partners, and casual encounters along the trade routes. In the former, a man is content to conform to the ruling scale of values ... but in the latter he haggles for a bargain, trying to gain a material advantage. The term for "trading partner" is, most significantly, a verb form, "I together I-eat." ... He is, as it were, drawn into the "in-group" of clansmen and affines, the people who should not be exploited for private ends' (pp. 106-107, 110). Hospitality runs alongside the balanced exchange of trade goods between partners, and 'to exploit a partner for material gain is to lose him' (p. 109). Nonpartnership exchange is mostly a recent development.

A.2.3   *Buin Plain, Bougainville* – Sectoral distinctions in reciprocity among the Siuai have been indicated in previous textual citations. A few further aspects can be mentioned here. First, on the extremely generalized reciprocity appropriate among very close kinship: 'Gift-giving among close relatives over and beyond the normal expectations of sharing ['sharing' as Oliver defines it is the 'pooling' of the present essay] cannot entirely be reduced to conscious expectation of reciprocity. A father might rationalize the giving of tidbits to his son by explaining that he expected to be cared for by the latter in his old age, but I am convinced that some giving between, say, father and son does not involve any desire or expectation for reciprocation' (Oliver, 1955, p. 230). Loans of productive goods normally brought over-and-above returns ('interest'), but not from close relatives (p. 229). Exchange between distant relatives and trade partners is *ootu*: it is characterized by approximate equivalence but is distinguished from 'sales' involving shell money (as the sale of craft goods) by the possibility of deferring payments in *ootu* (pp. 230-231). In trade-partner transactions, also, giving above going rates is creditable, so that balance is achieved perhaps only over the long term (see pp. 297, 299, 307, 350-351, 367-368).

Sectoral variations in the economy of the Buin neighbors of the Siuai (the Terei, apparently) so impressed Thurnwald that he suggested the existence of three 'kinds of economics: (1) the husbandry [pooling] within the family . . . ; (2) the inter-individual and inter-familial help among near relatives and members of a settlement united under a chief; (3) the inter-communal relations manifested by barter between individuals belonging to different communities or strata of society' (Thurnwald, 1934-35, p. 124).

A.2.4   *Kapauku* – The difference in reciprocity between interregional and intraregional sectors of the Kapauku economy has been noted in textual citation (above). Also notable is the fact that kinship and friendship ties lower customary rates of exchange in Kapauku shell-money dealings (Pospisil, 1958, p. 122). The Kapauku data are rendered obscure by an inappropriate economic terminology. So-called 'loans', for example, are generalized transactions – ' "take it without repayment in the immediate future" ' (p. 78, see also p. 130) – but the social context and extent of these 'loans' is not clear.

A.2.5   *Mafulu* – Excepting pig-exchange, which the ethnographer discounts as a ceremonial affair, 'Exchange and barter is generally only engaged in between members of different communities and not between those of the same community' (Williamson, 1912, p. 232).

A.2.6   *Manus* – Affinal exchanges, ordinarily between Manus of the same or different villages, are distinguished by long-term credit, compared with the short-term credit of trade friendship or market exchange (Mead, 1937, p. 218). Trade-friendship exchange, while more or less balanced, is in turn to be differen-tiated from the more impersonal 'market' exchange with Usiai bushfellows. The trade friendships are developed with people of distant tribes, sometimes on long-standing kinship ties. Some credit is extended trade friends, as well as hospitality, but market exchange is direct: the Usiai are viewed as furtive and hostile, 'whose eye is ever on driving a sharp bargain, whose trade manners are atrocious' (Mead, 1930, p. 118; see also Mead, 1934, pp. 307-308).

A.2.7   *Chimbu* – 'Mutual help and sharing characterize relations among subclan members. A man may call upon a fellow sub-clansman for help whenever he needs it; he may ask any wife or daughter of a member of his subclan to give him food when she has some. . . . However, it is only the most prominent men who can count on such services from persons outside their own subclan' (Brown & Brookfield, 1959-60, p. 59 ; on the exception of 'prominent men', compare pp. 162-164 and 200-215 on Reciprocity and Kinship Rank). The pig-exchanges and other exchanges between clans argue balance in the external sector here, as elsewhere in the New Guinea Highlands (compare, for example, Bulmer, 1960, pp. 9-10).

A.2.8 *Buka Passage* – The total of internal reciprocity seems limited by comparison with external trade, but there are some indications of generalized exchange in internal sectors as contrasted with balanced, though not haggled, external exchange. In Kurtatchi village, requests from own sibmates of the same sex for areca or coconuts are honored without repayment though the recipients are open to counter request; otherwise, no giving of something for nothing – save that near relatives may take a man's coconuts (Blackwood, 1935, pp. 452, 454; compare p. 439 f on trade).

A.2.9 *Lesu* – 'Free gifts' (generalized reciprocity) are especially rendered relatives and friends, most especially certain types of kinsmen. These gifts are food and betel. Between villages and moieties there are various balanced transactions (Powdermaker, 1933, pp. 195-203).

A.2.10 *Dobu* – As is well known, a very narrow sector of economic trust and generosity, including only *susu* and household. Outside of this, theft a possibility. Intervillage affinal exchanges more or less balanced, with village mates helping the sponsoring *susu* meet its obligations (Fortune, 1932).

A.2.11 *Trobriands* – The sociology of the reciprocity continuum described by Malinowski is only partly sectoral; rank considerations (compare below) and affinal obligations notably intrude. 'Pure gift,' however, is characteristic of family relations (Malinowski, 1922, pp. 177-178); 'customary payments, re-paid irregularly, and without strict equivalence' include *urigubu* and contributions to a kinsman's mortuary-ceremony fund (p. 180); 'gifts returned in economically equivalent form' (or almost equivalent form) include intervillage presentations at visits, exchanges between 'friends' (apparently these are especially or exclusively outside the village), and, it seems, the 'secondary' trade in strategic goods between kula partners (pp. 184-185); 'ceremonial barter with deferred payment' (not haggled) is characteristic between kula partners and between partners in the inland-coastal, vegetables vs. fish exchange (*wasi*) (pp. 187-189; cf. p. 42); 'trade,

195

pure and simple', involving haggling, mainly in nonpartner exchange between members of 'industrial' and other villages within Kiriwina (pp. 189-190). The last type is *gimwali*; it is characteristic also of vegetable-fish exchange in the absence of partnership and overseas exchange accompanying *kula*, again in the absence of partnership (cf. pp. 361 f).

A.2.12 *Tikopia* – Near kinsmen and neighbors are privileged economically (e.g. Firth, 1936, p. 399; 1950, p. 203) and are expected to render economic assistance in various ways (e.g. Firth, 1936, p. 116; 1950, p. 292). The necessity of a *quid pro quo* seems to increase with kinship distance – thus 'forced exchange' (also known ethnographically as 'coercive gift') is a transaction of the more distant sector: 'The importance of the social category comes out . . . in cases such as when a man wants a coconut-grating stool. If he knows of a close kinsman who has an extra one, he goes and asks for it and should get it without ceremony. "You give me a stool for myself; your stools are two." It is said that the kinsman "rejoices" to give it because of the tie between them. Sooner or later he in turn comes and asks for something he fancies and this too will be handed over freely. Such freedom of approach obtains only between members of a small kinship group and depends upon the recognition of a principle of reciprocity. If a man is going to apply to someone not of his own kin, a "different man" as the Tikopia say, then he cooks food, fills a large basket, and tops it off with an ordinary piece of bark-cloth or even a blanket. Armed with this he goes to the owner and asks for the article. He is usually not refused' (Firth, 1950, p. 316).

A.2.13 *Maori* – A large part of the internal circulation, here of the village especially, was centralized in chiefly hands – it was generalized enough but run on the principles of chiefly due and *noblesse oblige* (cf. Firth, 1959). The external exchanges (intervillage, intertribal) involved more direct and equivalent reciprocation, although prestige of course accrued to liberality (cf. Firth, 1959, pp. 335-337, 403-409, 422-423). Maori proverb: In winter a relation, in autumn a son; 'signifying "he is only a distant relative at the time of cultivation when there is heavy work to be tackled, but in the time after harvest when all is finished, and there is plenty of food to be eaten, he calls himself my son" ' (Firth, 1926, p. 251).

A.3.0 *Notes from here and there.*

A.3.1 *Pilagá* – Henry's well-known study (1951) of food-sharing in

196

a Pilagá village is here cited with caution. We have to deal
with a disrupted and resettled population. Also, during the
period of Henry's observations a great portion of the men were
away working on sugar plantations. It was, moreover, the
'hungry time' of the Pilagá year. 'Thus we are dealing with an
economic system from which a considerable number of productive persons had been withdrawn, and during a period of
scarcity, with the society functioning at low ebb' (Henry,
1951, p. 193). (The intense food-sharing under these miserable
conditions is consistent with propositions developed below
on the relation between reciprocity and need.) I assume that
most if not all the instances of sharing were of the generalized
reciprocal sort, the giving out of larger stocks that had come
to hand, rendering assistance and the like. The assumption is
consistent with examples offered by Henry and with the lack
of balance he records in individuals' outgo and income. Trade
with other groups, reported by Henry to have occurred, is not
considered in the study in question. The principal value of this
study for the present discussion is its specification of the
incidence of food-sharing by social distance. The obligation to
share food is highest among those closest in kinship-residential
terms. 'Membership in the same household [a multifamily and
multidwelling group making up a section of the village] constitutes a very close tie; but membership in the same household
plus a close kinship tie is the closest of bonds. This is objectified
in food-sharing, those having the closest bond sharing food
most often' (p. 188). The conclusion is supported by analysis
of particular cases. (In one of these, the association between
sharing and close relations was working the other way around –
a woman was sharing food heavily with a man whom she
wanted to, and eventually did, marry.) 'The cases reviewed so
far concerning distribution within the household [section of
the village] may be summarized as follows: the answer to the
question, *to which individual or family did each individual or
family give most often?* can be answered only through quanti-
tative analysis of the behavior of individuals and families.
When this is done four points emerge: (1) The Pilagá distributes most of his product to members of his own household.
(2) He does not distribute equally to all. (3) A variety of
factors enter to prevent his distributing equally to all; (*a*)
differences in genealogical ties, (*b*) differences of obligations
among the people of the household with respect to their

197

obligations outside it, (c) stability of residence, (d) dependency needs, (e) marital expectations, (f) fear of shamans, and (g) special food taboos. (4) When common residence and close genealogical ties combine, the highest rate of interchange of products between families so related is present' (p. 207). The sectoral incidence of food-sharing is shown in the following chart (adapted from Henry's *Table IV*, p. 210).

Family	Per cent of Times Sharing Food with Families in		
	Own household section of village	The other household section of the village	Outsiders, of other villages
I	72	18	10
II	43	0	7
III	81	16	3
IV	55	34	11

The other section of the village, for which Henry did not have as numerous records – because they were wandering about the forest a good deal – does not show the same trend (also *Table IV*). The second column is in three of four instances larger than the first – more sharing across the village than within the 'household' section. But this section of the village is not comparable to the other (tabulated above) because in the former people were 'more closely integrated [i.e. closely related] than those at the other end, thus much of what takes the form of *distribution*, the transfer of produce from the producer to another person, in No. 28's part of the village [tabulated above], takes the form of *commensality* at No. 14's end of the village. Hence the percentage of product distributed by No. 14's people to persons within the section . . . appears low, while that distributed to other classes [sectors] seems high' (p. 211; Henry's emphases). Since Henry does not consider commensality among different families of the same 'household' as food-sharing, the seeming exception may be in fairness disregarded.

A.3.2 *Nuer* – Intensive food-sharing, hospitality, and other general-ized reciprocities in Nuer smaller local groups (hamlet sections of the village) and cattle camps (Evans-Pritchard, 1940, pp. 21, 84-85, 91, 183; 1951, pp. 2, 131-132; Howell, 1954, p. 201). Not much exchange in the intratribal (extra-village) sector except the instrumental transactions of bridewealth and feud settlement (as compensations, of their nature balanced). Nuer specifically distinguish internal reciprocity from trade with Arabs by the directness (temporally) of the latter exchange (Evans-Pritchard, 1956, p. 223f). Relations with neighboring tribes, especially Dinka, notoriously appropriative, amounting in the main to seizure of loot and territory through violence.

A.3.3   *Bantu of North Kavirondo* – Intensive informal hospitality among neighbors. Exchanges of balanced sort are principally in durables, with craftsmen, but the rates most favor neighbor-clansmen, are higher for the clansman who is not a neighbor, most dear for strangers (Wagner, 1956, pp. 161-162).

A.3.4   *Chukchee* – Certain amount of generosity and assistance within Chukchee camps (see citations in Sahlins, 1960). Theft from the herds of other camps common (Bogoras, 1904-09, p. 49). Aboriginal trade between maritime and reindeer Chukchee, and some trade across the Bering Straits: apparently the trade more or less balanced; some of it was silent and all of it conducted with considerable mistrust (Bogoras, 1904-09, pp. 53, 95-96).

A.3.5   *Tiv* – Clear differentiation at least between external ('market') and internal spheres. A 'market' distinguishable from the several varieties of gift: the last imply 'a relationship between the two parties concerned which is of a permanence and warmth not known in a "market", and hence – though gifts should be reciprocal over a long period of time – it is bad form overtly to count and compete and haggle over gifts' (Bohannan, 1955, p. 60). A 'market' is competitive and exploitative: 'In fact, the presence of a previous relationship makes a "good market" impossible: people do not like to sell to kinsmen since it is bad form to demand as high a price from kinsmen as one might from a stranger' (p. 60).

A.3.6   *Bemba* – A centralized system of reciprocities (chiefly redistribution) is, analogously to Polynesia, the main part of the larger economy; a very limited inter-tribal exchange sector (Richards, 1939, pp. 221 f). Various dues to close relatives by kin type (pp. 188 f). Apart from hospitality to visiting kinsmen, chiefs and, nowadays, strangers, food-sharing is ordinarily characteristic in a narrow circle of close kin – but apparently in a wider circle during scarcities (pp. 108-109, 136 f, 178-182, 186, 202-203). The money that has been introduced is not much used in internal exchange, but when it is, 'People buying from relatives pay less than the normal rate, and usually add some service to the transaction' (p. 220). '. . . I have often seen women take a pot of beer and conceal it in a friend's granary on the reported arrival of some elderly relative. To refuse hospitality with a pot of beer sitting on the hearth would be an impossible insult, but a bland assertion that "Alas, Sir, we poor wretches. . . . We have nothing to eat here" is sometimes necessary. This would not be done in the case of a near relative, but only with a more distant kinsman of a classificatory type, or one of the well-known "cadgers" of a family' (p. 202).

APPENDIX B

Notes on Reciprocity and Kinship Rank

These materials deal with kinship-rank reciprocities both in simple form and in the context of chiefly redistribution.

B.1.0   *Hunting-Gathering Peoples.*

B.1.1   *Bushmen* – 'No Bushman wants prominence, but Toma [a band headman] went further than most in avoiding prominence; he had almost no possessions and gave away everything that came into his hands. He was diplomatic, for in exchange for his self-imposed poverty he won the respect and following of all the people there' (Thomas, 1959, p. 183). 'We did hear people say . . . that a headman may feel that he should lean well to the generous side in his giving, for his position as headman sets him out from the others a little and he wants whatever attention this attracts not to be envious. Someone remarked that this could keep a headman poor' (Marshall, 1961, p. 244).

B.1.2   *Andamans* – 'Generosity is esteemed by the Andaman Islanders as one of the highest of virtues and is unremittingly practiced by the majority of them,' Radcliffe-Brown writes (1948, p. 43). He notes that the person who does not work and must needs be given food sinks in esteem, while Man remarked that the generous person rises in esteem (Man, n.d., p. 41). There is a definite generation-status influence on reciprocity. Although at least sometimes appearing as givers of food – on occasions of collective sharing of game – elders are privileged in regard to juniors: 'It is considered a breach of good manners ever to refuse the request of another. Thus if a man be asked by another to give him anything that he may possess, he will immediately do so. If the two men are equals a return of about the same value will have to be made. As between an older married man and a bachelor or a young married man, however, the younger would not make any request of such a nature, and if the older asked the younger for anything, the latter would give it without always expecting a return' (Radcliffe-Brown, 1948, pp. 42-43).

B.1.3 *Eskimo* – Influence and prestige accrued to the North Alaskan Eskimo whale boat leader or caribou hunting leader at least in part by virtue of the stuff he doled out in ostensibly generous fashion (Spencer, 1959, pp. 144, 152 f, 210 f, 335-336, 351). Great men noted for their great generosity (pp. 154-155, 157). Stinginess as usual deplorable (p. 164).

B.1.4 *Carrier* – A big-man, slighted by a fur trader, boasts that he is just as good a chief as the trader: ' "When it is the proper season to hunt the beaver, I kill them; and of their flesh I make feasts for my relations. I, often, feast all the Indians of my village; and, sometimes, invite people from afar off, to come and partake of the fruits of my hunts . . ." ' (Harmon, 1957, pp. 143-144, cf. pp. 253-254).

B.2.0 *Melanesia* – I have elsewhere presented a general study of the economics of big-man leadership in western Melanesian societies (Sahlins, 1963). Generalized reciprocity is here the decisive 'starting mechanism' of ranking. A following is developed through private assistance to individuals, a tribal name (renown) through large-scale giveaways, often of pigs and vegetable foods. The wherewithal for his generosity comes initially from the aspiring big-man's own household from his nearest relatives: he capitalizes in the beginning on kinship dues and by finessing the generalized reciprocity appropriate among close kin. He often enlarges his household at an early phase, perhaps by taking additional wives – ' "Another woman go garden, another woman go take firewood, another woman go catch fish, another woman cook him – husband he sing out plenty people come kaikai" ' (Landtman, 1927, p. 168). A leader's career is well under way when he is able to link other men and their families to his faction, to harness their production to his ambition by helping them in some big way. He cannot, however, extend these people too far: some material benefits must accrue to followers on pain of encouraging their discontent and his downfall.

Most examples that follow are of big-man systems. The concluding cases are different: chiefdoms or protochiefdoms in which generalized reciprocity between ranks is apparent in a redistributive context.

B.2.1 *Siuai* – The most thorough exposition of Melanesian big-man economics is Oliver's (1955) study. The development of influence and prestige through generalized transactions is richly described. There are several peripheral features likewise of interest in the present context. Notable is the influence of rank on customary rates of balance in shell money dealings: 'One great advantage of being a leader lies in one's ability to buy things more cheaply ("When a mumi [big-man] sends out thirty spans of *mauai* to purchase a pig for a feast, the pig owner would be ashamed to send along a pig worth less than forty"). On the other hand, this commercial advantage of the leader is usually counterbalanced by the traditional exercise of *noblesse oblige*' (p. 342). So, 'the most praiseworthy thing a man can do is to exceed the transactional requirements of ordinary trade and kin relationships by paying generously (in goods) for all goods and services he receives, by giving goods to persons to whom he is not directly obligated, and by doing these things after the manner of great leaders of the past' (p. 456, cf. pp. 378, 407, 429-430).

Thurnwald writes of another Buin Plain people that *mamoko*, the reward given by a big-man to his followers, 'is considered an act of liberality, for which there is no obligation. Any gift of friendship is described by the same name. A surplus payment over the price agreed is also called *mamoko*. *Totokai* is the excess payment of a kitere [follower] to his *mumira* [leader] for ensuring his good will and his willingness to credit him with *abuta* [shell money] on another occasion. *Dakai* designates a payment for reconciliation or reparation between men of equal position' (Thurnwald, 1934-35, p. 135). The variation of reciprocity by rank difference is clear.

B.2.2 *'Gawa (Busama)* – Clubhouse leaders and, especially, outstanding village leaders are typical western Melanesian big-men. Hogbin writes: 'The man who is generous over a long period thus has many persons in his debt. No problem arises when these are of the same status as himself – the poor give one another insignificant presents, and the rich exchange sumptuous offerings. But if his resources are greater than theirs they may find repayment impossible and have to default. Acutely conscious of their position, they express their humility in terms of deference and respect. . . . The relation of debtors and creditors forms the basis of the system of leadership' (Hogbin, 1951, p. 122). The leaders were ' "men who ate bones and chewed lime" – they presented the best meat to others, leaving only scraps for themselves, and were so free with areca nuts and pepper that they had no betel mixture left. Folk-tales about legendary headmen of the past relate that, although these men had "more pigs than anyone could count and bigger gardens than are made now", they gave everything away' (p. 123, cf. pp. 118 f). The main run of clubhouse leaders were reluctantly placed in that position. The work was hard – ' "His hands are never free from earth, and his forehead continually drips with sweat" ' (p. 131) – and the material rewards nil. The principal big-man of the village, however, was ambitious. 'It is frequently insisted that the headmen were so jealous of their reputation that they went to the trouble of inventing excuses for giving food away' (p. 139). Low rank was the reward of stinginess, and he who is prepared to take advantage of others, 'He sinks to the bottom of the social ladder . . .' (p. 126).

B.2.3   *Kaoka* (*Guadalcanal*) – A main-run big-man economy (Hogbin, 1933-34, 1937-38). 'Reputation . . . is enhanced not by accumulating wealth in order to use it for one's self but by giving it away. Every event of importance in a person's life – marriage, birth, death and even the construction of a new house or canoe – is celebrated by a feast, and the more feasts a man gives, and the more lavish he is in providing food, the greater is his prestige. The social leaders are those who give away most' (Hogbin, 1937-38, p. 290)

B.2.4   *Kapauku* – Described by the ethnographer as sort of upland New Guinea capitalists. The big-man pattern, however, is an ordinary (sweet potato) garden variety. 'Loans' and 'credit' put out by Kapauku big men (*tonowi*, 'generous richman') are not interest bearing in the standard sense (see above A.2.4); they are means of developing status through generosity (Pospisil, 1958, p. 129). 'The society views its ideal man as a most generous individual, who through the distribution of his

203

fortune satisfies the needs of many people. Generosity is the highest cultural value and an attribute necessary for acquiring followers in political and legal life' (p. 57). The big-man's status sinks if he loses the wherewithal for generosity (p. 59); if he is excessively demanding he is likely to face an egalitarian rebellion – ' ". . . you should not be the only rich man, we should all be the same, therefore you only stay equal with us" . . . was the reason given by the Paniai people for killing Mote Juwopija of Madi, a *tonowi* who was not generous enough' (p. 80, cf. pp. 108-110). Wealth is not enough: '. . . a selfish individual who hoards his money and does not lend [*sic*] it, never sees the time when his word will be taken seriously and his advice and decisions followed, no matter how rich he may become. The people believe that the only justification for becoming rich is to be able to redistribute the accumulated property among one's less fortunate fellows, a procedure which also gains their support' (pp. 79-80). Big-men buy more cheaply than prevailing rates (p. 122). One big-man summed up well, if cynically, the rank-generating impetus delivered by generalized reciprocity. ' "I am a headman," ' he said, ' "not because the people like me but because they owe me money and are afraid" ' (p. 95).

B.2.5   *New Guinea Highlands* – The big-man pattern, here worked out in a segmented lineage context, is general in the Highlands.

'The Kuma "big men" or "men of strength" . . . who can command much wealth, are entrepreneurs in the sense that they control the flow of valuables between clans by making fresh presentations on their own account and choosing whether or not to contribute to others. Their profit in these transactions is incremental reputation. . . . The aim is not simply to be wealthy, nor even to act as only the wealthy can act: it is to be *known* to be wealthy. Further, a man does not really achieve his ambition until he can be seen to act as if wealth itself were of no account' (Reay, 1959, p. 96, see pp. 110-111, 130). There is also the usual Melanesian corollary of the big-man, the 'rubbish man': 'A man is a "rubbish man" of no consequence if he has not enough food to offer many friends and relatives as well as meet his personal requirements' (p. 23).

The use of generalized reciprocity as a mechanism of status differentiation in another Highland instance (Kyaka) is succinctly put by Bulmer: 'These supporters of a leader are normally in a state of mutual obligation with him, having been helped by him with bridewealth payment and the like, or expecting help of this kind. Such assistance obligates them to channel through him such pigs of their own as they are putting into the Moka [interclan pig-exchange]' (Bulmer, 1960, p. 9).

B.2.6   *Lesu* – 'A rich man might pay five *tsera* for a pig for which another man would pay four. The more he pays the more prestige the buyer has. Everyone then knows he is a rich man. On the other hand, the owner of a pig would gain prestige if he sold it for four *tsera* when he might have received five' (Powdermaker, 1933, p. 201).

B.2.7   *To'ambaita* (*N. Malaita*) – Another good description of a typical big-man order, conforming in all essential respects to those already discussed (Hogbin, 1939, esp. pp. 61 f; 1943-44, pp. 258 f).

B.2.8   *Manus* – The Manus have – or had, in their 'old lives' – a big-man pattern (Mead, 1934, 1937). Their clans, however, were also ascriptively divided into two ranks, *lapan* (high) and *lau* (low). This ranking was according to Mead not of great political significance, but its economic side is of interest nonetheless. 'Between *lapan* and *lau* there is a type of mutual helpfulness expected, not unlike a slight version of the feudal relationship – the *lapan* takes care of the economic needs of the *lau* and the *lau* works for the *lapan*' (Mead, 1934, pp. 335-336).

For discussion of other big-men systems see Sahlins 1963. Among the well-described ones are the Arapesh (Mead, 1937a, 1938, 1947), the Abelam (Kaberry, 1940-41, 1941-42), and Tangu (Burridge, 1960). Deacon struck the general note: 'Yet for all that the Malekulan is, as has been said, grasping and bourgeois in his attitude toward wealth, generosity and consideration for one's debtors are held up as virtues. . . . To be stingy is to sink in public esteem; to be openhanded is to acquire fame, honour, and influence' (Deacon, 1934, p. 200).

B.2.9   *Sa'a* – The generalized reciprocity principle in the context of a small scale redistributive system. 'The good chief and the commoners regarded one another as mutually dependent on each other, and the people loved a chief who by his feasts brought glory on the place, and one of the reasons why [the chief] Wate'ou'ou was called . . . "he who keeps the canoe on a straight course", was because he was good at feasts' (Ivens, 1927, p. 255). 'Stowed away safely in the lodge in bags is the chief's possession in money, which in a measure is what

Doraädi called the "panga", the "bank" of the village because it is drawn on for communal purposes such as feasts or the payments of blood money. The Sa'a chiefs were wealthy men owing to the contributions made to them on public occasions by the commoners' (p. 32). 'Chief and priest were exempted from the obligation to make a return for gifts received which held always in the case of commoners' (p. 8). 'Chiefs were said to *kuluhie hänue*, succour the land, to draw the people up who came to them for protection, and the word *kulu*, draw or lift up, appears in the compound *mänikulu'e*, glorious, a word associated with feasts and chiefs' (p. 129, cf. pp. 145, 147-148, 160 f, 221 f).

B.2.10 *Trobriands* – Generalized rank reciprocity organized as redistribution. The underlying ethic was reciprocal assistance between chiefs and people. Malinowski's many statements of the economic obligations of chieftainship include several which highlight the status implications of generosity. For example: '. . . to possess is to be great, and . . . wealth is the indispensable appanage of social rank and attribute of personal virtue. But the important point is that with them to possess is to give. . . . A man who owns a thing is naturally expected to share it, to distribute it, to be its trustee and dispenser. And the higher the rank the greater the obligation. . . . Thus the main symptom of being powerful is to be wealthy, and of wealth is to be generous. Meanness, indeed, is the most despised vice, and the only thing about which the natives have strong moral views, while generosity is the essence of goodness' (1922, p. 97). Again: 'Not in all cases, but in many of them, the handing over of wealth is the expression of the superiority of the giver over the recipient. In others, it represents subordination to a chief, or a kinship relation or relationship-in-law' (p. 175). '*Relationship between Chiefs and Commoners*. – The tributes and services given to a chief by his vassals on the one hand, and the small but frequent gifts which he gives them, and the big and important contribution which he makes to all tribal enterprises are characteristic of this relationship' (p. 193). The Trobriand chief's difficulties in holding on to his betel, and the little stratagems he employed to save some for himself, are famous anecdotes of the introductory anthropology course (Malinowski, 1922, p. 97).

B.3.0 *American Plains* – Plains Indian chiefs were local equivalents of Melanesian big-men. The pattern is much the same; the cultural idiom varies. Generalized reciprocity here again a decisive starting mechanism of leadership. Military honors were an important attribute of leaders, but influence rested as much or more on generous dispositions of horses, of loot, of meat, of help to the poor and widowed, and the like. The chief's faction was a roving band, a cluster of lesser and often dependent people, for whose well-being the chief felt responsible and upon whom he might draw economically. Wealth in horses was an ultimate necessity for a band chief: the loss of this fund of generosity was the loss of influence.

B.3.1   *Assiniboin* – 'The chief of a band is little more than the nominal father of all and addresses them as his children in a body' (Denig, 1928-29, p. 431). 'A chief must give away all to preserve his popularity and is always the poorest in the band, yet he takes good care to distribute his gifts among his own relatives or the rich, upon whom he can draw at any time he be in need' (p. 449, cf. pp. 432, 525, 547-548, 563; on the element of calculation in Assiniboin generosity, see pp. 475, 514-515).

B.3.2   *Kansa-Osage* – 'The chiefs and candidates for public preferment render themselves popular by their disinterestedness and poverty. Whenever any extraordinary success attends them in the acquisition of property, it is only for the benefit of their meritorious adherents, for they distribute it with a profuse liberality, and pride themselves in being esteemed the poorest man in the community' (Hunter, 1823, p. 317).

B.3.3   *Plains Cree* – ' "It is not an easy thing to be a chief. Look at this chief now. He has to have pity on the poor. When he sees a man in difficulty he must try to help him in whatever way he can. If a person asks for something in his tipi, he must give it to him willingly and without bad feeling" ' (Mandelbaum, 1940, p. 222, cf. pp. 195, 205, 221 f, 270-271).

B.3.4   *Blackfoot* – The same pattern, in essence (Ewers, 1955, pp. 140-141, 161 f, 188-189, 192-193, 240 f).

B.3.5   *Comanche* – The same (Wallace & Hoebel, 1952, pp. 36, 131, 209 f, 240).

B.4.0   *Polynesia* – I have elsewhere offered studies of the economies of Polynesian chieftainship (Sahlins, 1958, 1963). Redistribution is the transactional form, generalized reciprocity the principle. The few notes here highlight particularly the principle.

207

B.4.1   *Maori* – Firth's excellent analysis of Maori economics provides the *mise en scène* for considerations of rank-reciprocity in Polynesia. I cite two long passages: 'The prestige of a chief was bound up with his free use of wealth, particularly food. This in turn tended to secure for him a larger revenue from which to display his hospitality, since his followers and relatives brought him choice gifts. . . . Apart from lavish entertainment of strangers and visitors, the chief also disbursed wealth freely as presents among his followers. By this means their allegiance was secured and he repaid them for the gifts and personal services rendered to him. All payment among the Maori was made in the form of gifts. There was thus a continual reciprocity between chief and people. The chief also acted as a kind of capitalist, assuming the initiative in the construction of certain "public works" if the term may be so used. It was by his accumulation and possession of wealth, and his subsequent lavish distribution of it, that such a man was able to give the spur to these important tribal enterprises. He was a kind of channel through which wealth flowed, concentrating it only to pour it out freely again' (Firth, 1959, p. 133). 'The quantity and quality of . . . gifts received tended to increase with the rank and hereditary position of the chief in the tribe, his prestige, and the following which he was able to gather around him. But the relationship was by no means one-sided. If the income of a chief was largely dependent on his prestige and influence and the regard of his people, this in its turn was contingent upon his liberal treatment of them. There were constant calls upon his resources. His slaves and immediate dependents had to be fed, he was expected to assist those of his tribesmen who came to him in need, a crowd of relatives – and the Maori bonds of kinship stretched far – looked to him for a generous repayment of all the small social services they rendered him, and for an occasional *douceur* as a mark of appreciation of their loyalty. When presents of foodstuffs were made to him by people of other tribes his regard for his reputation required that he should distribute a considerable portion of them among his tribespeople. For all gifts made to him a return was expected, of equivalent or even greater value. . . . Again, the calls of hospitality were never ending. Entertainment had to be provided on a lavish scale for visiting chiefs and their adherents. . . . Moreover, on occasions of the birth, marriage or death of any people of rank in the village his personal resources were drawn upon to a serious extent, while the occasional provision of a large feast also drained him of food supplies. In this connection he seems to have exercised control of the communal stores of food which he commanded to be disbursed as required. If the chief's use of wealth be reviewed, then, it is seen that to the varied sources which provided him with his stores of goods corresponded a number of serious liabilities. The result was that a sort of equilibrium was maintained between income and expenditure. In general, at no time was the chief the possessor of enormous quantities of valuables, though the system of receipt and redistribution of goods allowed a great quantity of them to flow through his hands' (pp. 297-298, cf. pp. 130 f, 164, 294 f, 345-346).

B.4.2   *Hawaii* – Chiefs had extensive call on the labor, the resources and products of the underlying *makaainana* population, as well as control over certain specialists and enjoyment of certain sumptuary perquisites. The chiefdom, often embracing the whole of a large island, was an elaborate collection-redistribution apparatus. 'It was the practice for kings, i.e. paramount chiefs of individual islands, to build storehouses in which to collect food, fish, tapas [bark cloth], malos [men's loin cloths], pa-us [women's loin skirts], and all sorts of goods. These store-houses were designed by the Kalaimoku [chief's executives] as a means of keeping the people contented, so they would not desert the king. They were like the baskets that were used to entrap the *hinalea* fish. The *hinalea* thought there was something good within the basket, and he hung round the outside of it. In the same way the people thought there was food in the storehouses, and they kept their eyes on the king. As the rat will not desert the pantry . . . where he thinks food is, so the people will not desert the king while they think there is food in his storehouse' (Malo, 1951, p. 195). The tendency at the highest levels of chieftainship, however – and despite well meaning advice of counselors – was to press too heavily on the lesser chiefs and people, with the result that, as Malo puts it, 'Many kings were put to death by the people because of their oppression of the *makaainana* [commonalty]' (p. 195, cf. pp. 58, 61; Fornander, 1880, pp. 76, 88, 100-101, 200-202, 227-228, 270-271).

B.4.3   *Tonga* – A fine native statement of the chiefly economic ethic, attributed by Mariner to the chief Finau upon Mariner's explanation of the value of money: 'Finow replied that the explanation did not satisfy him; he still thought it a foolish thing that people should place a value on money, when they either could not or would not apply it to any useful (physical) purpose. "If", said he, "it were made of iron, and could be converted into knives, axes and chisels, there would be some sense in placing a value on it; but as it is, I see none. If a man," he added, "has more yams than he wants, let him exchange some of them away for pork or *gnatoo* [bark cloth]. Certainly money is much handier, and more convenient, but then, as it will not spoil by being kept, people will store it up, instead of sharing it out, as a chief ought to do, and thus become selfish; whereas, if provisions were the principal property of man, and it ought to be, as being both the most useful and the most necessary, he could not store it up, for it would spoil, and so he would be obliged either to exchange it away for something else useful, or share it to his neighbors, and inferior chiefs and dependents, for nothing." He concluded by saying "I understand now very well what it is that makes the Papalangis ["Europeans"] so selfish – it is this money!" ' (Mariner, 1827 i, pp. 213-214).

Conversely, the upward flow: '. . . the practice of making presents to superior chiefs is very general and frequent. The higher class of chiefs generally make a present to the king, of hogs or yams about once a fortnight. These chiefs, about the same time, receive presents from those below them, and these last from others, and so on, down to the common people' (p. 210; cf. Gifford, 1929).

B.4.4   *Tahiti* – From indications of the Duff missionaries, it looks as if Ha'amanimani, the Tahitian priest-chief, acted faithfully to the ideal expressed by Finau: 'Manne Manne was very urgent for sails, rope, anchor, etc. for his vessel, none of which articles we had to spare: on which account, though the captain gave him his own cocked hat and a variety of articles, he was still discontented; saying, "Several people told me that you wanted Manne Manne, and now I am come, you give me nothing." An observation similar to this he once made to the missionaries: "You give me," says he, "much parow (talk) and much prayers to the Eatooa, but very few axes, knives, scissars, or cloth." The case is, that whatever he receives he immediately distributes among his friends and dependents; so that for all the numerous presents he had received, he had nothing now to shew, except a glazed hat, a pair of breeches, and an old black coat, which he had fringed with red feathers. And this prodigal behaviour he excuses, by saying that, were he not to do so, he should never be a king, nor even remain a chief of any consequence' (Duff missionaries, 1799, pp. 224-225). For all this it is apparent from the Duff journal as well as other early reports (e.g. Rodriguez, 1919) that Tahitian high chiefs might accumulate considerable stocks of goods and especially that they had very considerable power to demand foodstuffs from the underlying population. The traditional counsel was the same as in Hawaii – 'Your household must not be accused of food hiding. Let not your name be associated with hidden foods or hidden goods. The hands of the Arii must be always open; on these two things rest your prestige' (Handy, 1930, p. 41) – but apparently Tahitian chiefs were inclined as it is said, to 'eat the powers of the government too much'. (Yet see also Davies, 1961, p. 87 note 1.)

B.4.5 *Tikopia* – A stream of gifts flow from below to the Tikopia chief, but then his obligation to be generous is at least as great as his ability to accumulate things. Generosity indeed was a jealously guarded chiefly prerogative: 'Chiefs are recognized as being proper persons to control large quantities of food, to have a number of valued objects stored away in their houses. . . . But the stocks which they accumulate are expected to be dispersed in a manner which will yield benefit to their people. Great accumulation by a conmoner must also be followed by a corresponding dispersal. But such a man would incur the charge from the chiefly families of *fia pasaki* "desiring to boast", and would be watched by them lest he attempt to usurp some of their privileges. According to precedent in Tikopia history they would probably take an opportunity either to seize his goods or to kill him' (Firth, 1950, p. 243). The Tikopia chiefs, in short, would not tolerate starting mechanisms. This is not true throughout Polynesia. In the Marquesas, for example, upward mobility through 'accumulating and dispensing wealth' was possible (Linton, 1939, pp. 150, 153, 156-157; Handy, 1923, pp. 36-37, 48, 53). (On other aspects of the reciprocity between Tikopia chiefs and people see Firth, 1936, pp. 382-383, 401-403; 1950, pp. 34, 58, 109 f, 172, 188, 190, 191, 196, 212 f, 321.)

B.5 *Miscellaneous.*

B.5.1 *Northwestern North America* – Generalized reciprocity permeated the political economy of the Northwest Coast

Indians, both in the potlatch giveaways between chiefs and in the internal relation of chiefs and their respective followers. The Nootka are a clearly described case in point. Chiefs acquired a variety of dues: from the first catch of salmon traps, early pickings of berry patches, from large catches of fish taken by their people, and the like (e.g. Drucker, 1951, pp. 56-57, 172, 255, 272, *et passim*). Conversely, ' "Every time a chief got a lot of food of any kind, he gave a feast to give it away to his people" ' (p. 370) (see also Suttles, 1960, pp. 299-300; Barnett, 1938; Codere, n.d.).

The Tolowa-Tututni political economy is the same in principle as that prevailing to the north, albeit a slighter version. Drucker characterizes the chief-follower relation as 'symbiotic' – 'The relationship uniting the rich-man and his kinsfolk was essentially a symbiotic one. It is said that some of the richest men never worked; their henchmen hunted and fished for them. In return the rich-man gave feasts, and in lean times would share his stores with his people. He bought wives for the young men, or at least contributed most of the payment; but it was also he who accepted and held the bride prices paid for their sisters and daughters. Perhaps most important of all; it was the rich-man who was obliged to pay compensation for wrongs his henchmen committed, to save them, and himself, from retaliation . . . he received a lion's share of any indemnities paid for injuries to one of them' (Drucker, 1937, p. 245; for indications of similar rank-reciprocity in California see Kroeber, 1925, pp. 3, 40, 42, 55; Goldschmidt, 1951, pp. 324-325, 365, 413; Loeb, 1926, pp. 238-239).

B.5.2   *Creek* – One of the prettiest descriptions of chiefly redistribution, again run on the underlying principle of generalized reciprocity, appears in W. Bartram's late eighteenth-century account of the Creek: 'After the feast of the busk is over, and all the grain is ripe, the whole town again assemble, and every man carries of the fruits of his labour, from the part [of the town field] first allotted to him, which he deposits in his own granary; which is individually his own. But previous to their carrying off their crops from the field, there is a large crib or granary, erected in the plantation, which is called the king's crib; and to this each family carries and deposits a certain quantity, according to his [apparently meaning "their"] ability or inclination, or none at all if he so chooses, this in appearance seems a tribute or revenue to the mico [chief], but in fact is designed for another purpose, i.e. that of a public treasury, supplied by a few and voluntary contributions, and to which every citizen has the right of free and equal access, when his own private stores are consumed, to serve as a surplus to fly to for succour, to assist neighboring towns whose crops have failed, accommodate strangers, or travellers, afford provisions or supplies, when they go forth on hostile expeditions, and for all other exigencies of the state; and this treasure is at the disposal of the king or mico; which is surely a royal attribute to have an exclusive right and ability in a community to distribute comfort and blessings to the necessitous' (Bartram, 1958, p. 326; cf. Swanton, 1928, pp. 277-278).

B.5.3   *Kachin* – 'In theory then people of superior class receive gifts from their inferiors. But no permanent economic advantage accrues from this. Anyone who receives a gift is thereby placed in debt (*hka*) to the giver.... Paradoxically therefore although an individual of high-class status is defined as one who receives gifts . . . he is all the time under a social compulsion to give away more than he receives. Otherwise he would be reckoned mean and a mean man runs the danger of losing status' (Leach, 1954, p. 163).

B.5.4   *Bemba* – A classic redistributive economy, a classic generalized reciprocity between chief and people. '. . . the distribution of cooked food is an attribute of authority, and therefore prestige, and . . . its reception puts a man under an obligation to return to the giver respect, service, or reciprocal hospitality' (Richards, 1939, p. 135). The paramount is most engaged in the distributive process, and this 'is of course necessary to the chief if he is to make gardens and conduct tribal business through his councillors. But it is more than this. The giving of food, as in most African tribes, is an absolutely essential attribute of chieftainship, just as it is of authority in the village or household, and the successful organization of supplies at the capital seems to be associated in the Bemba mind with the security and well-being of the whole tribe itself. . . . The whole institution of the *kamitembo* [the sacred kitchen and storehouse of the tribe] illustrates to my mind that close association between authority and the power to distribute provisions on which the tribal organization depends. The chief owns the food and receives tribute, and the chief

213

provides for his subjects and distributes cooked food to them. Both of these attributes are symbolized in the *kamitembo* house' (pp. 148, 150). 'I never heard a chief boast to another about the size of his granaries, but often about the amount of food brought to him and distributed by him. In fact chiefs particularly valued the fact that some of their food was brought to them and not grown in their gardens, for it gave them some kind of resource to fall back upon. The Bemba say: "We will shake the tree until it gives up its fruit", that is to say, we will nag the big man until he divides his supplies. If a chief attempted to dry meat and keep it for subsequent division his followers would sit and stare at it and talk about it until he was forced to give them some, but supplies brought irregularly from other villages provided constant fresh resources' (p. 214). 'The people still definitely prefer their ruler to have a big granary. It gives them, I think, a sense of security – a feeling of certainty that there will be food at the capital and a knowledge that they are working for a powerful and successful man. ... Besides this, a hungry man has technically the right to call upon his chief for help. I did not hear of this claim being made very often, but still, in a sense, the *umulasa* [tribute-labour] garden and *umulasa* granary are recognized as belonging to the people. A man can steal from the tribute garden of a chief, but not from those of his wives, and I have sometimes heard old natives speak with pride of "our" granary, adding, "It was we who filled it to overflowing". Thus the commoner got by his labour the sense of supernatural support, a personal approach to his chief, food in return for his work, support in time of starvation, and . . . leadership in economic pursuits. The chief in return got extra supplies of food to distribute, the means of supporting his tribal council, the necessary labour for tribal undertakings such as road-building, and last, but not least, prestige' (p. 261; cf. pp. 138, 169, 178-180, 194, 215, 221, 244 f, 275, 361-362).

B.5.5   *Pilagá* – Generosity is no starting mechanism, but it is a sustaining mechanism of rank. In Henry's tables (1951, pp. 194, 197, 214) it is the chief who gives more goods (and to more people) than anyone else. Henry comments regarding this: 'It will . . . be observed that in no case is the contribution of his [i.e. the chief's] family to any family equaled or exceeded by any other family. As a matter of fact, No. 28 [the chief] himself alone contributes on an average of 35% of the income, i.e. food received of each family. Thus the role of the chief and his family in Pilagá society is to support others. The chief and his family thus become *the unifying factor in the village*. It is this that gives meaning to the use of the father term for the chief and the child term for the members of the village. . . . The position of the chief, despite the "prestige" it carries also entails burdens. All the people are his children (*kokotepi*) for whom he is responsible. Hence the word for chief, *salyaranik*, signifies one who is heavy' (pp. 214-215).

APPENDIX C

Notes on Reciprocity and Wealth

Reciprocity and Wealth – The following notes mostly concern societies already considered in other contexts. The citations illustrate particularly the association between wealth differences and generosity (generalized reciprocity). That food is the item so often shared is significant. Examples that indicate sharing in favor of need between socially distant parties – those who would ordinarily enter balanced exchange – especially underscore the assertions of this section.

C.1.0   *Hunters and gatherers.*

C.1.1   *Andamans* – 'It has been stated above that all food is private property and belongs to the man or woman who has obtained it. Everyone who has food is expected, however, to give to those who have none. . . . The result of these customs is that practically all the food obtained is evenly distributed through the whole camp . . .' (Radcliffe-Brown, 1948, p. 43).

C.1.2   *Bushmen* – 'Food, whether vegetable or animal, and water are also private property, and belong to the person who has obtained them. Everyone who has food is, however, expected to give to those who have none. . . . The result is that practically all food obtained is evenly distributed through the whole camp' (Schapera, 1930, p. 148). Compare these last two quotations! It is an extremely rare fortune in anthropology, and fills one with humble awe, to enter the presence of a great natural law. Actually, the elided parts of these citations indicate some difference in manner of distribution. An older married man

215

Marshall D. Sahlins

among the Andamanese will share out food after he has reserved sufficient for his family; a younger man hands over the pigs to elders for distribution (see also Radcliffe-Brown, 1948, pp. 37-38, 41; Man, n.d., pp. 129, 143 note 6). The one who takes game or veldkos among the Bushman does the sharing out, according to Schapera.

The Andamanese who is lazy or helpless is still given food, despite the probability or certainty of no reciprocation (Radcliffe-Brown, 1948, p. 50; Man, n.d., p. 25). A lazy hunter fares badly among the Bushmen; a crippled one is abandoned by all save his nearest relations (Thomas, 1959, pp. 157, 246; see also Marshall, 1961, on Bushman sharing).

C.1.3   *Eskimo* – The Alaskan seal-hunter is often solicited for meat, especially in lean winter months, and these requests are very rarely refused (Spencer, 1959, pp. 59, 148-149). 'In times of food shortage, it was the successful hunter and his family who might go hungry, since in his generosity he gave away whatever he had at hand' (p. 164). Notable are the obligations of the fortunate toward non-kin in the camp: 'Generosity was a primary virtue and no man could risk a miserly reputation. Thus anyone in the community, whether inland or coastal, could ask aid of a man of wealth and it was never refused. This might mean that the men of wealth would be obliged to support an entire group in times of stress. Here, too, aid was extended to non-kin' (p. 153; presumably these non-kin might at other times enter balanced exchanges, as in the 'bidding game' – see A.1.7). Lazy people take advantage of a hunter's bounty, and do not necessarily reciprocate even if they have their own stores (pp. 164-165; see also pp. 345-351, 156-157 for give-aways in which poor stand to gain materially).

Generally among Eskimo large game is 'common property', though smaller animals are not, yet the hunter might in any case invite people of the camp to a meal (Rink, 1875, pp. 28 f; Birket-Smith, 1959, p. 146; see also Boas, 1884-85, pp. 562, 574, 582; Weyer, 1932, pp. 184-186).

Spencer's note of the reaction of Alaskan Eskimo to the Great Depression of the 1930s is of interest in the context of economic behavior during general shortage: 'More so than in a time of prosperity, the community sense of in-group consciousness appears to have developed. Those who did engage in hunting were obliged by custom to share their catch – seal, walrus, caribou, or any other game – with the less fortunate members of the community. But while this factor of sharing operated between non-kin, the economic circumstances of the period furthered the aboriginal family system as a cooperative institution. Families worked together and extended their joint efforts to the benefit of the community at large. The return to the aboriginal social patterns at a time of economic stress appears to have lent the family system a force which it still possesses. As may be seen, however, the cooperative arrangement between non-kin in the community tends to break down with the addition of new wealth' (Spencer, 1959, pp. 361-362).

C.1.4 *Australian Aborigines* – Local communities of Walbiri or of friendly tribes could drop in on neighboring Walbiri when in need. They were welcomed, even if the hosts' supplies were limited, but there was some degree of balance in the economic relationship. The requests of hungry communities 'often took the form of appeals to actual kinship ties and, couched in these terms, could hardly be refused. The suppliants, then or later, made gifts of weapons, hair-string, red ochre and the like to express their gratitude and, equally important, to rid themselves of feelings of shame or embarrassment' (Meggitt, 1962, p. 52). In lean seasons among the Arunta, everyone shared in available supplies, ordinary generation, sex and kinship-status considerations notwithstanding (Spencer & Gillen, 1927 i, pp. 38-39, 490).

C.1.5 *Luzon Negritos* – Large quantities of food are shared; whenever a good find is made neighbors are invited to partake until it is eaten up (Vanoverbergh, 1925, p. 409).

C.1.6 *Naskapi* – The same (e.g. Leacock, 1954, p. 33).

C.1.7 *Congo Pygmies* – A hunter cannot very well refuse – in view of public opinion – to share out game in the camp (Putnam, 1953, p. 333). Larger animals, at least, were generally shared through extended family groups; vegetables were not so distributed unless some family had none and then others 'come to their assistance' (Schebesta, 1933, pp. 68, 125, 244).

C.1.8 *Western Shoshoni* – Essentially the same customary sharing of large game, and of lesser family supplies in favor of need, in the camp (Steward, 1938, pp. 60, 74, 231, 253; cf. also pp. 27-28 on helping families whose traditional piñion haunts were not bearing).

C.1.9 *Northern Tungus (mounted hunters)* – The hunting spoil, by the custom of *nimadif*, went to the clan – 'in other words, the

217

fruit of the hunting does not belong to the hunter, but to the clan' (Shirokogoroff, 1929, p. 195). There was great readiness to assist clansmen in need (p. 200). Reindeer were allocated to the poor of the clan following epizootics, with the result that families holding over sixty deer were not to be seen (p. 296).

C.1.10 *Northern Chipewayan and Copper Indians* – Samuel Hearne notices an outbreak of 'disinterested friendship' among members of his crew as they prepare to attack some Eskimos: 'Never was reciprocity of interest more generally regarded among a number of people, than it was on the present occasion by my crew, for not one was a moment in want of anything that another could spare; and if ever the spirit of disinterested friendship expanded the heart of a Northern Indian, it was here exhibited in the most extensive meaning of the word. Property of every kind that could be of general use now ceased to be private, and every one who had any thing that came under that description seemed proud of an opportunity of giving it, or lending it to those who had none, or were most in want of it' (Hearne, 1958, p. 98).

C.2.0 *Plains Indians* – In many northern tribes there was insufficiency of good buffalo horses and unequal possession of them. Those without horses, however, did not suffer for food in consequence; the meat circulated to have-nots, in various ways. For example:

C.2.1 *Assiniboin* – Denig notes that in a large camp men who lacked horses, and the old and infirm as well, would follow the hunt, taking meat as they would but leaving the hide and choice parts for the hunter, and they got as much meat as they wanted (Denig, 1928-29, p. 456, cf. p. 532). When food was scarce people would spy out lodges that were better supplied and drop in at mealtimes, as 'No Indian eats before guests without offering them a share, even if it is the last portion they possess' (p. 509; cf. p. 515). The successful horse raider might be flattered so by old men upon his return from the raid that by the time he reached his lodge he ('frequently') had given all the loot away (pp. 547-548).

C.2.2 *Blackfoot* – The poor in horses might borrow from the wealthy – the latter thus adding to the number of followers – and people whose herds had been depleted by misfortune were particularly so helped by those more fortunate (Ewers, 1955, pp. 140-141). A person who borrowed a horse for a chase might return the owner the best of the meat taken, but this evidently was conditional upon the horse-owner's own supply (pp. 161-162). If borrowing was not possible, the man would have to rely on the 'rich' for meat and usually had to take the lean (pp. 162-163, but see pp. 240-241). A case cited of an amputee warrior thereafter supplied with a lodge, horses and food by his band (p. 213). Those who captured horses on raids were supposed afterward to share their loot with less fortunate comrades, but arguments were frequent here (p. 188; compare with Plains Ojibway generosity before the raid, C.2.5). Note how wealth differences generalize exchange: in intratribal trading, rich men paid more dearly for things than did others; the average man, for example, gave two horses for a shirt and leggings, the rich man three to nine horses for the same thing (p. 218). A man, in addition, frequently gave horses to the needy ' "to get his name up" ', and the poor might take advantage of the rich by giving small presents to the latter or simply praising them loudly in the hopes of a horse return (p. 255). Ewers thus summarizes the economic relation between rich and poor: 'Generosity was felt to be a responsibility of the wealthy. They were expected to loan horses to the poor for hunting and moving camp, to give food to the poor, and to give away horses occasionally. They were expected to pay more in intratribal barter than were Indians who were not well to do. If the man of wealth had political ambitions it was particularly important that he be lavish with his gifts in order to gain a large number of followers to support his candidacy' (p. 242).

The reaction to general shortage was heightened sharing. Lean winter periods were common: 'Then the wealthy, who had put up extensive winter supplies the previous fall, had to share their food with the poor' (Ewers, 1955, p. 167). The rank structure of the band was also engaged to organize relief: hunters had to turn over their bag to the band chief, who had it cut up and divided equally to each family. When game became more plentiful, this 'primitive form of food rationing' was discontinued and the chief stepped out of the central distributive role (pp. 167-168).

C.2.3 *Plains Cree* – The same inclination of those better off to share meat to people without horses, to give horses away on occasion – for which from the poor one received in return not meat but fealty (Mandelbaum, 1940, p. 195) – and other generosities found in the Plains in connection with wealth differences (pp. 204, 221, 222, 270-271; see also Wallace and Hoebel,

1952, p. 75 *et passim* on the Comanche; Coues on the Mandan (village Indians), 1897, p. 337).

C.2.4 *Kansa* – Hunter writes that if one party to an agreed exchange could not meet his obligations due to ill health or bad hunting luck, he was not dunned, nor did friendly relations with his creditors cease. But one who failed of his obligations for reason of laziness was a bad Indian and would be abandoned by his friends – such types, however, were rare (Hunter, 1823, p. 295). Moreover, '. . . no one of respectable standing will be allowed to experience want or sufferings of any kind, while it is in the power of others of the same community to prevent it. In this respect they are extravagantly generous; always supplying the wants of their friends from their own superabundance' (p. 296).

Generalized reciprocity apparently intensified during shortage. 'Whenever a scarcity prevails, they reciprocally lend, or rather share with each other, their respective stores, till they are all exhausted. I speak now of those who are provident, and sustain good characters. When the case is otherwise, the wants of such individuals are regarded with comparative indifference; though their families share in the stock, become otherwise common from public exigency' (p. 258).

C.2.5 *Plains Ojibway* – Tanner and his Ojibway family, destitute, reach a camp of Ojibway and Ottawa; the chiefs of the camp meet to consider their plight and one man after another volunteers to hunt for Tanner's people; Tanner's FaBrWi is stingy to them, but her husband beats her for it (Tanner, 1956, pp. 30-34). In similar circumstances, an Ojibway lodge insisted on silver ornaments and other objects of value in return for giving Tanner's family some meat one winter. This insistence on exchange struck Tanner as despicable, for his people were hungry – 'I had not before met with such an instance among the Indians. They are commonly ready to divide what provisions they have with any who come to them in need' (p. 47, see also pp. 49, 60, 72-73, 75, 118, 119).

During a period of epidemic and general food shortage in an Ojibway camp, Tanner and another hunter managed to kill a bear. 'Of the flesh of this animal,' he wrote, 'we could not eat a mouthful, but we took it home and distributed to every lodge an equal portion' (p. 95). On another similar occasion, an Indian who had shot two moose tried to get Tanner to secretly share them, keeping the meat from the rest of the camp.

Tanner, a better Indian than this, refused, went out hunting, killed four bears and distributed the meat to the hungry (p. 163).

On special economic behavior of the warpath: if a man of the war party was short of moccasins or ammunition he took out one of that object and walked about the camp before a person well supplied; the latter ordinarily gave over the thing desired without the necessity of anyone speaking, or else, the leader of the party went from man to man taking what was needed by the person who was short (p. 129).

C.3.0 *Miscellaneous.*

C.3.1 *Nuer* – See the citations in the text of this section. 'Kinsmen must assist one another, and if one has a surplus of a good thing he must share it with his neighbors. Consequently no Nuer ever has a surplus' (Evans-Pritchard, 1940, p. 183). Generalized reciprocity characteristic between haves and have nots, especially if close kin and neighbors, in the compact dry season camps, and during seasons of generally low supplies (pp. 21, 25, 84-85, 90-92; 1951, p. 132; Howell, 1954, pp. 16, 185-186).

C.3.2 *Kuikuru (upper Xingú)* – The contrast between the handling of the major crop, manioc, and the disposition of maize is an instructive illustration of the relation of sharing to supplies on hand. Kuikuru households are in general self-sufficient; there is little sharing between them, especially of manioc which is produced with ease and in quantity. But during Carneiro's stay, maize was planted by only five men of the village, and their harvest was divided through the community (Carneiro 1957, p. 162).

C.3.3 *Chukchee* – Despite an anthropological reputation something to the contrary, the Chukchee are remarkably generous 'toward everyone who is in need' (Bogoras, 1904-09, p. 47). This includes aliens, such as poor Lamut families who got sustenance from neighboring rich Chukchee without payment, and also starving Russian settlements in whose favor Chukchee have slaughtered their herds for little or no return (p. 47). At the annual fall slaughter, about one-third of the deer were given to guests, who need not make returns, especially if poor; neighboring camps, however, might exchange slaughtered beasts at this time (p. 375). At serious setbacks to herds, neighboring camps – these need not be related – might render assistance (p. 628). Tobacco is highly valued by Chukchee

221

but is not hoarded when scarce; '. . . the last pipeful be divided or smoked by turns' (p. 549, cf. pp. 615 f, 624, 636-638).

C.3.4 *California-Oregon* – The Tolowa-Tututni 'rich-man' was, as we have noted, a source of aid to his people (Drucker, 1937). Poorer people depended on the bounty of richer. 'Food was shared by the provident with the improvident within the village group' (DuBois, 1936, p. 51). Of the Yurok, Kroeber writes that food was sometimes sold, 'but no well-to-do man was guilty of the practice' (1925, p. 40), implying that the exchange would be generalized rather than balanced (selling) in this case. Similarly Kroeber remarks that small gifts among the Yurok were ordinarily reciprocated, as 'Presents were clearly a rich man's luxury' (p. 42, cf. p. 34 on the liberal disposition of fish by successful fishermen). Meat, fish and the like taken in large quantities by Patwin families went to the village chief for distribution to families most in need; a family, moreover, might demand food of fortunate neighbors (McKern, 1922, p. 245).

C.3.5 *Oceania* – The Melanesian big-man complex, wherever it exists, argues the prevalence of generalized reciprocity in exchange between people of different fortune.

The Duff missionaries' description of Tahitian generosity, especially of *richesse oblige*, is probably too good to be true, anyhow too good to be analytically adequate: 'All are friendly and generous, even to a fault; they hardly refuse anything to each other if importuned. Their presents are liberal, even to profusion. Poverty never makes a man contemptible; but to be affluent and covetous is the greatest shame and reproach. Should any man betray symptoms of incorrigible avariciousness and refuse to part with what he has in time of necessity, his neighbors would soon destroy all his property, and put him on a footing with the poorest, hardly leaving a house to cover his head. They will give the clothes from their back, rather than be called pēere, pēere, or stingy' (1799, p. 334).

Firth's discussion of Maori sharing in favor of need is more measured: 'At a time of shortage of provisions . . . persons did not as a rule keep to themselves the product of their labour, but shared it out among the other people of the village' (Firth, 1959, p. 162). It is as true in the forests of New Zealand as the savannahs of the Sudan that 'Starvation or real want in one family was impossible while others in the village were abundantly supplied with food' (p. 290).

Of interest in connection with responses to general scarcity is the development in food-poor Polynesian atolls of reserve lands administered in group interests, the products of which were periodically pooled by communities (e.g. Beaglehole, E. & P., 1938; Hogbin, 1934; MacGregor, 1937). The restudy of Tikopia by Firth and Spillius, however, provides probably the most comprehensive report of the reaction of a primitive society to prolonged and intense food shortage. The reaction proceeded far: while traffic in food did not develop, theft certainly did and contraction of foodsharing to the household sphere did too. These latter responses, negative reciprocity and diminution of the sector of generalized, were apparently progressive, increasing as the crisis deepened. It is impossible to do justice here to Firth's and Spillius' analyses, but it is at least useful to excerpt some remarks from Firth's summary of exchange behavior during the famine: 'In general it can be said . . . that while morals degenerated under the strain of famine, manners remained. At the times of greatest food shortage the ordinary modes of serving food were kept up. . . . But while in matters of hospitality all the *forms* of etiquette continued to be maintained throughout the period of famine, its *substance* radically altered. No longer was food actually shared with visitors. Moreover, after food had been cooked it was . . . concealed – sometimes even locked up in a box. . . . In this development kinship ties were affected, though not quite in the same way as the more general rules of hospitality. Kin who called in were treated as ordinary visitors; food was not shared with them. . . . In many cases if food was left in a house a member of the household remained behind to guard it. Here, it was stated to Spillius, the inmates were often not so much afraid of theft by strangers but of the inroads of kin who normally would have been welcome to come and take what they pleased. In the definition of kin interests that took place under the stress of famine there was some atomization of the larger kin groups on the consumption side and a closer integration of the individual household group. (This normally meant elementary family but often included other kin.) Even at the height of the famine it appeared that within an elementary family full sharing of food continued to be the norm. The atomization tended to be most strong where food was most desperately short – and it must be remembered that supplies varied considerably in different groups, depending on

223

their size and their wealth in land. But in one respect the strength of kin ties was manifested, in the common practice of pooling supplies, especially where food – though scarce – was not desperately short. Closely related households "linked ovens" (*tau umu*) by each drawing upon its own stock of food and then sharing in the work of the oven and in a common meal . . . the Tikopia avoided where possible their general responsibility or undefined responsibility for kin during the famine but showed no disposition to reject responsibility which had been specifically defined by the undertaking. What the famine did was to reveal the solidarity of the elementary family. But it also brought out the strength of other kin ties personally assumed . . .' (Firth, 1959a, pp. 83-84).

C.3.6   *Bemba* – High incidence of generalized reciprocity associated with differential food stocks, and also during general hunger seasons. Thus, 'If a man's crops are destroyed by some sudden calamity, or if he has planted insufficient for his needs, relatives in his own village may be able to help him by giving him baskets of grain or offering him a share in their meals. But if the whole community has been visited by the same affliction, such as a locust swarm or a raider elephant, the householder will move himself and his family to live with other kinsmen in an area where food is less scarce. . . . Hospitality of this sort is commonly practised in the hunger season, when families go all over the country "looking for porridge" . . . or "running from hunger". . . . Hence the legal obligations of kinship result in a particular type of food distribution, both within the village and the surrounding neighbourhood, which is not found in those modern communities in which a more individual domestic economy is practised' (Richards, 1939, pp. 108-109). 'The economic conditions under which [a Bemba woman] lives necessitate reciprocal sharing of foodstuffs, rather than their accumulation, and extend the individual's responsibility outside her own household. Plainly, therefore, it does not pay a Bemba woman to have very much more grain than her fellows. She would merely have to distribute it, and during the recent locust scourge the villagers whose gardens escaped destruction complained that they were not really better off than their fellows for "our people come and live with us or beg us for baskets of millet" ' (pp. 201-202).

C.3.7   *Pilagá* – Henry's *Table I* (1951, p. 194) indicates that all unproductive persons in the village studied – it was, recall, a period of very low supplies – received food from more people than they gave food to. The 'negative' balance of these cases – old and blind, old women, etc. – varies from − 3 to − 15 and the eight persons listed as unproductive make up more than half of those showing such negative balance. This is contrary to the general Pilagá trend: 'It will be at once clear from the tables that the Pilagá *on the whole* gives to more people than he receives from, but that, with the unproductive Pilagá the situation is reversed' (pp. 195-197). The negative balance of unproductive people shows as well in the number of transactions as in the number of people given to minus received-from (p. 196). In *Table III*, presenting the approximate ratios of food quantity received to food quantity given away, ten persons are listed as unproductive and for eight of these income exceeded out-go; six persons are listed as very or exceptionally productive and four had out-go over income, one had income over out-go and one had income = out-go (p. 201). I take these figures to mean that those who had food shared it out to those who had none, in the main.

NOTES

1. I am indebted to Eric Wolf for many suggestions concerning this paper, and to the Social Science Research Council (Washington, D.C.), which in it may finally see some return on a most generous Faculty Research Fellowship.

2. These materials appear as Appendices to the present volume, pp. 186-225.

3. For the present purpose 'economy' is viewed as the process of provisioning society (or the 'socio-cultural system'). No social relation, institution, or set of institutions is of itself 'economic'. Any institution, say a family or a lineage order, if it has material consequence for provisioning society can be placed in an economic context and considered part of the economic process. The same institution may be equally or more involved in the political process, thus profitably considered as well in a political context. This way of looking at economics or politics – or for that matter, religion, education, and any number of other cultural processes – is dictated by the nature of primitive culture. Here we find no socially distinct 'economy' or 'government', merely social groups and relations with multiple functions, which we distinguish as economic, political, and so forth.

That economy thus presents itself as an aspect of things is probably generally acceptable. That the emphasis be the provisioning of *society* may not prove so acceptable. For the concern is not how individuals go about their business: 'economy' has not been defined as the application of scarce available means against alternative ends (material ends or otherwise). From means to end 'economy' is conceived as *a component of culture* rather than *a kind of human action*, the material life process of society rather than a rational, need-

225

satisfying process of individual behavior. Our purpose is not to analyze entrepreneurs but to compare cultures. We reject the historically specific Business Outlook. In terms of controversial positions recently developed in the *American Anthropologist*, the stand adopted is much more with Dalton (1961; cf. Sahlins, 1962) than with Burling (1962) or LeClair (1962). Also, solidarity is here affirmed with housewives the world over and Professor Malinowski. Professor Firth upbraids Malinowski's imprecision on a point of economic anthropology with the observation that 'This is not the terminology of economics, it is almost the language of the housewife' (Firth, 1957, p. 220). The terminology of the present effort similarly departs from economic orthodoxy. This may be justly considered a necessity born of ignorance, but something is to be said as well for the appropriateness, in a study of kinship economies, of the housewife's perspective.

Economy has been defined as the process of (materially) provisioning society and the definition opposed to the human act of satisfying wants. The great play of instrumental exchange in primitive societies underscores the usefulness of the former definition. Sometimes the peace-making aspect is so fundamental that precisely the same sorts and amounts of stuff change hands: the renunciation of opposed interest is in this way symbolized. On a strictly formal view the transaction is a waste of time and effort. One might say that people are maximizing value, social value, but such is to misplace the determinant of the transaction, to fail to specify the circumstances which produce different material outcomes in different historical instances, to hold fast to the economizing premise of the market by a false assignment of pecuniary-like qualities to social qualities, to take the high road to tautology. The interest of such transactions is precisely that they do not materially provision people and are not predicated on the satisfaction of human material needs. They do, however, decidedly provision society: they maintain social relations, the structure of society, even if they do not to the least advantage the stock of consumables. Without any further assumptions, they are 'economic' in the suggested meaning of the term.

The reader familiar with recent discussions of primitive distribution will recognize my indebtedness to Polanyi (1944, 1957, 1959) on this score, and likewise the departures from Polanyi's terminology and threefold scheme of principles of integration. It is also a pleasure to affirm with Firth that 'Every student of primitive economics, in fact, gratefully builds upon the foundations which Malinowski has laid' (Firth, 1959, p. 174).

ACKNOWLEDGEMENTS

Thanks are due to the individuals and publishers concerned for permission to quote passages from the following works:

Allen & Unwin and Oslo University Press in respect of *The Nomads of South Persia* by Fredrik Barth; The American Sociological Association and Professor A. W. Gouldner in respect of 'The Norm of Reciprocity: A Preliminary Statement', *American Sociological Review*, Volume 25, by A. W. Gouldner; The Australian National University and Melbourne University Press in respect of *The Kuma* by Marie Reay; The Free Press of Glencoe in respect of *The Gift* by Marcel Mauss; The Government Printer, Wellington in respect of *Economics of* the *New Zealand Maori* by Raymond Firth; Harvard University Press in respect of *A Solomon Island Society by* Douglas Oliver; Her Majesty's Stationery Office in respect of *The Land Dyaks of Sarawak*, Colonial Research Studies No. 14, by W. R. Geddes; International African Institute and Mrs Lorna Marshall in respect of 'Sharing, Talking, and Giving: Relief of Social Tensions among !Kung Bushmen', *Africa*, Volume 31, by Lorna Marshall; Oxford University Press in respect of *Land, Labour and Diet in Northern Rhodesia* by Audrey I. Richards (published under the auspices of the International African Institute); Routledge & Kegan Paul in respect of *Transformation Scene: The Changing Culture of a New Guinea Village* by Ian H. Hogbin, *Argonauts of the Western Pacific* by Bronislaw Malinowski, and with Hillary House, *Primitive Polynesian Economy* by Raymond Firth; Martin Secker & Warburg and Alfred A. Knopf in respect of *The Harmless People* by Elizabeth M. Thomas (copyright 1958, 1959 by Elizabeth Marshall Thomas); Yale University Press in respect of *The Travels of William Bartram* by William Bartram (edited by Francis Harper) and 'The Philosophy of the Navaho Indians' by Clyde Kluckhohn in *Ideological Difference and World Order* edited by F. S. C. Northrop.

REFERENCES

BARNETT, H. G. 1938. The Nature of the Potlatch. *American Anthropologist* 40: 349-358.

BARTH, FREDRIK. 1961. *Nomads of South Persia*. London: Allen & Unwin (for Oslo University Press).

BARTRAM, WILLIAM. 1958. *The Travels of William Bartram*. Francis Harper (ed.). New Haven: Yale University Press.

BEAGLEHOLE, ERNEST & BEAGLEHOLE, PEARL. 1938. *Ethnology of Pukapuka*. Bernice P. Bishop Museum Bulletin 150.

BIRKET-SMITH, KAJ. 1959. *The Eskimos*. Second edition; London: Methuen.

BLACKWOOD, BEATRICE. 1935. *Both Sides of Buka Passage*. Oxford: Clarendon Press.

BLEAK, D. F. 1928. *The Naron*. Cambridge: Cambridge University Press.

BOAS, FRANZ. 1884-85. The Central Eskimo. *Smithson. Instn Bureau of American Ethnology Anthropological Reports* 6: 399-669.

BOGORAS, w. 1904-09. The Chukchee. *AMNH Memoirs*, 11, Parts I, II, III. F. Boas (ed.). New York.

BOHANNAN, PAUL. 1954. *Tiv Farm and Settlement*. Colonial Research Studies No. 15. London: H.M. Stationery Office.

—— 1955. Some Principles of Exchange and Investment Among the Tiv. *American Anthropologist* 57: 60-70.

BOHANNAN, PAUL & DALTON, GEORGE (eds.). 1962. *Markets in Africa*. Evanston, Ill.: Northwestern University Press.

Marshall D. Sahlins

BROWN, PAULA & BROOKFIELD, H. C. 1959-60. Chimbu Land and Society. *Oceania* **30**: 1-75.

BULMER, RALPH. 1960. Political Aspects of the Moka Ceremonial Exchange System Among the Kyaka People of the Western Highlands of New Guinea. *Oceania* **31**: 1-13.

BURLING, ROBBINS. 1962. Maximization Theories and the Study of Economic Anthropology. *American Anthropologist* **64**: 802-821.

BURRIDGE, KENELM. 1960. *Mambu: A Melanesian Millennium*. London: Methuen.

CARNEIRO, ROBERT L. 1957. *Subsistence and Social Structure: An Ecological Study of the Kuikuru Indians*. Ph.D. Dissertation, University of Michigan.

CODERE, HELEN. n.d. *Fighting with Property*. Monograph of the American Ethnological Society XVIII. New York: J. J. Augustin.

COUES, ELLIOT (ed.). 1897. *The Manuscript Journals of Alexander Henry and of David Thompson, 1799-1814*. New York: Francis P. Harper. 2 Vols.

DALTON, GEORGE. 1961. Economic Theory and Primitive Society. *American Anthropologist* **63**: 1-25.

DAVIES, JOHN. 1961. *The History of the Tahitian Mission 1799-1830*. C. W. Newbury (ed.). Cambridge: Cambridge University Press for the Hakluyt Society.

DEACON, A. BERNARD. 1934. *Malekula: A Vanishing People in the New Hebrides*. C. Wedgewood, (ed.). London: Routledge.

DENIG, EDWIN T. 1928-29. Indian Tribes of the Upper Missouri. *Smithson. Instn BAE-AR* **46**: 395-628.

DRUCKER, PHILIP. 1937. The Tolowa and their Southwest Oregon Kin. *Univ. Calif. Public. in Amer. Archaeol. and Ethnol.* **36** (4): 221-300. Berkeley: University of California Press.

—— 1939. Rank, Wealth, and Kinship in Northwest Coast Society. *American Anthropologist* **41**: 55-65.

—— 1951. *The Northern and Central Nootkan Tribes*. Smithson. Instn BAE. Bull. 144. Washington: U.S. Govt. Printing Office.

DUBOIS, CORA. 1936. The Wealth Concept as an Integrative Factor in Tolowa-Tututni Culture. *Essays in Anthropology Presented to A. L. Kroeber*. Berkeley: University of California Press, pp. 49-65.

DUFF MISSIONARIES. 1799. *A Missionary Voyage to the Southern Pacific Ocean Performed in the Years 1796, 1797, 1798 in the Ship Duff . . . etc.* London: T. Chapman.

228

ELKIN, A. P. 1952-53. Delayed Exchange in Wabag Sub-District, Central Highlands of New Guinea, with Notes on the Social Organization. *Oceania* **23**: 161-201.

—— 1954. *The Australian Aborigines: How to Understand Them.* 3rd ed. Sydney: Angus and Robertson.

EVANS-PRITCHARD, E. E. 1940. *The Nuer.* Oxford: Clarendon Press.

—— 1951. *Kinship and Marriage Among the Nuer.* Oxford: Clarendon Press.

—— 1956. *Nuer Religion.* Oxford: Clarendon Press.

EWERS, JOHN C. 1955. *The Horse in Blackfoot Indian Culture.* Smithson. Instn BAE Bull. 159. Washington: U.S. Govt. Printing Office.

FIRTH, RAYMOND. 1926. Proverbs in Native Life, with special reference to those of the Maori. *Folklore* **37**: 134-153, 245-270.

—— 1936. *We, The Tikopia.* London: Allen & Unwin.

—— 1950. *Primitive Polynesian Economy.* New York: Humanities.

—— 1951. *Elements of Social Organization.* London: Watts; New York: Philosophical Library.

—— (ed.) 1957. *Man and Culture: An Evaluation of the Work of Bronislaw Malinowski.* London: Routledge & Kegan Paul.

—— 1959. *Economics of the New Zealand Maori.* Wellington: R. E. Owen, Government Printer.

—— 1959a. *Social Change in Tikopia.* New York: Macmillan.

FORNANDER, ABRAHAM. 1880. *An Account of the Polynesian Race.* . . . London: Trubner. Vol. 2.

FORTUNE, R. F. 1932. *Sorcerers of Dobu.* New York: E. P. Dutton.

FREEMAN, J. D. 1955. *Iban Agriculture.* Colonial Research Studies No. 18, London: Her Majesty's Stationery Office.

GEDDES, W. R. 1954. *The Land Dayaks of Sarawak.* Colonial Research Studies No. 14, London: Her Majesty's Stationery Office.

—— 1957. *Nine Dayak Nights.* Melbourne: Oxford University Press.

GIFFORD, EDWARD WINSLOW. 1926. Clear Lake Pomo Society. *Univ. Calif. Public. in Amer. Archaeol. and Ethnol.* **18** (2): 287-390.

—— 1929. *Tongan Society.* Bernice P. Bishop Museum Bulletin 61.

GOLDSCHMIDT, WALTER. 1951. Nomlaki Ethnography. *Univ. Calif. Public. in Amer. Archaeol. and Ethnol.* **42** (4): 303-443. Berkeley: University of California Press.

GOULDNER, ALVIN W. 1960. The Norm of Reciprocity: A Preliminary Statement. *American Sociological Review* **25**: 161-178.

229

GRINNELL, GEORGE BIRD. 1923. *The Cheyenne Indians*. New Haven: Yale Univ. Press.

HANDY, E. S. C. 1923. *The Native Culture in the Marquesas*. Bernice P. Bishop Museum Bulletin 9.

—— 1930. *History and Culture in the Society Islands*. Bernice P. Bishop Museum Bulletin 79.

—— 1932. *Houses, Boats, and Fishing in the Society Islands*. Bernice P. Bishop Museum Bulletin 90.

HARMON, DANIEL WILLIAMS. 1957. *Sixteen Years in the Indian Country: The Journal of Daniel Williams Harmon 1800-1816*. Ed. by W. Kaye Lamb. Toronto: The Macmillan Co. of Canada.

HEARNE, SAMUEL. 1958. *A Journey from Prince of Wales' Fort in Hudson's Bay to the Northern Ocean, 1769, 1770, 1771, 1772*, ed. by Richard Glover. Toronto: The Macmillan Co. of Canada.

HENRY, JULES. 1951. The Economics of Pilagá Food Distribution. *American Anthropologist* 53: 187-219.

HENRY, TEURIRA. 1928. *Ancient Tahiti*. Bernice P. Bishop Museum Bulletin 48.

HOGBIN, H. IAN. 1933-34. Culture Change in the Solomon Islands: Report of Field Work in Guadalcanal and Malaita. *Oceania* 4: 233-267.

—— 1934. *Law and Order in Polynesia*. New York: Harcourt, Brace.

—— 1934-35. Native Culture of Wogeo: Report of Field Work in New Guinea. *Oceania* 5: 308-337.

—— 1934-35a. Trading Expeditions in Northern New Guinea. *Oceania* 5: 375-407.

—— 1937-38. Social Advancement in Guadalcanal, Solomon Islands. *Oceania* 8: 289-305.

—— 1938-39. Tillage and Collection: A New Guinea Economy. *Oceania* 9: 127-151.

—— 1939. *Experiments in Civilization*. London: Routledge.

—— 1943-44. Native Councils and Native Courts in the Solomon Islands. *Oceania* 14: 258-283.

—— 1951. *Transformation Scene: The Changing Culture of a New Guinea Village*. London: Routledge & Kegan Paul.

HOLMBERG, ALLAN R. 1950. *Nomads of the Long Bow*. Smithson. Instn Institute of Social Anthropology, Public. No. 10. Washington: U.S. Govt. Printing Office.

HOWELL, P. P. 1954. *A Manual of Nuer Law*. London: Oxford University Press.

HUNTER, JOHN D. 1823. *Memoirs of a Captivity Among the Indians of North America* (new edn.). London: Longmans.

IVENS, W. G. 1927. *Melanesians of the Southeast Solomon Islands.* London: Kegan, Paul, Trench, Trubner.

IZIKOWITZ, KARL GUSTAVE. 1951. *Lamet: Hill Peasants in French Indochina.* Etnologiska Studier 17, Goteborg: Ethnografiska Museet.

JOCHELSON, WALDEMAR. 1926. The Yukaghir and the Yukaghirzed Tungus, *AMNH Memoirs* **13** (1): 1-469.

KABERRY, PHYLLIS M. 1940-41. The Abelam Tribe, Sepik District, New Guinea: A Preliminary Report. *Oceania* **11**: 233-258, 345-367.

—— 1941-42. Law and Political Organization in the Abelam Tribe, New Guinea. *Oceania* **12**: 79-95, 205-225, 331-363.

KLUCKHOHN, CLYDE. 1959. The Philosophy of the Navaho Indians. In *Readings in Anthropology*, Vol. II, M. H. Fried (ed.). New York: Crowell.

KROEBER, A. L. 1925. *Handbook of the Indians of California.* Smithson. Instn BAE Bull. 78. Washington: U.S. Govt. Printing Office.

LANDTMAN, GUNNAR. 1927. *The Kiwai Papuans of British New Guinea.* London: Macmillan.

LEACH, E. R. 1951. The Structural Implications of Matrilateral Cross Cousin Marriage. *J. Royal Anthropological Institute* **81**: 23-55.

—— 1954. *Political Systems of Highland Burma.* London: Bell.

LEACOCK, ELEANOR. 1954. *The Montagnais' Hunting Territory and the Fur Trade.* Memoir of the American Anthropological Association 78.

LECLAIR, EDWARD E., JR. 1962. Economic Theory and Economic Anthropology. *American Anthropologist* **64**: 1179-1203.

LINTON, RALPH. 1939. Marquesan Culture. In Kardiner, A., *The Individual and his Society.* New York: Columbia University Press, pp. 137-196.

LOEB, EDWIN M. 1926. Pomo Folkways. *Univ. Calif. Public. in Amer. Archaeol. and Ethnol.* **19** (2): 149-409.

MACGREGOR, GORDON. 1937. *Ethnology of the Tokelau Islands.* Bernice P. Bishop Museum Bulletin 146.

MALINOWSKI, BRONISLAW. 1915. The Natives of Mailu. *Transactions of the Royal Society of South Australia* **39**: 494-706.

—— 1921. The Primitive Economics of the Trobriand Islanders. *Economic Journal* **31**: 1-16.

—— 1922. *Argonauts of the Western Pacific.* London: Routledge & Kegan Paul (3rd imp. 1950).

Marshall D. Sahlins

MALINOWSKI, BRONISLAW. 1935. *Coral Gardens and Their Magic.* Vol. 1. New York: American Book Co.

—— 1939. Anthropology as the Basis of Social Science. In Cattel, Cohen, and Travers (eds.), *Human Affairs.* London: Macmillan.

MALO, DAVID. 1951. *Hawaiian Antiquities.* (2nd edn.) Bernice P. Bishop Museum, Spec. Publication No. 2.

MAN, EDWARD HORACE. n.d. *On the Aboriginal Inhabitants of the Andaman Islands.* Reprinted from *JRAI*, 1885. London: RAI.

MANDELBAUM, DAVID G. 1940. The Plains Cree. *Amer. Mus. Nat. Hist.-Anthrop. Papers* 37 (2): 155-316.

MARINER, WILLIAM. 1827. *An Account of the Tongan Islands in the South Pacific Ocean.* (3rd edn., 2 vols.) John Martin (ed.). Edinburgh: Constable.

MARSHALL, LORNA. 1961. Sharing, Talking, and Giving: Relief of Social Tensions Among !Kung Bushmen. *Africa* 31: 231-249.

MAUSS, MARCEL. 1954. *The Gift.* Glencoe, Ill.: The Free Press.

MCKERN, W. C. 1922. Functional Families of the Patwin. *Univ. Calif. Public. in Amer. Archaeol. and Ethnol.* 13 (7): 236-258. Berkeley: University of California Press.

MEAD, MARGARET. 1930. Melanesian Middlemen. *National History* 30: 115-130.

—— 1934. Kinship in the Admiralty Islands. *American Museum of Natural History – Anthropological Papers* 34: 181-358.

—— 1937. The Manus of the Admiralty Islands. In M. Mead (ed.), *Cooperation and Competition among Primitive Peoples.* New York and London: McGraw-Hill.

—— 1937a. The Arapesh of New Guinea, In M. Mead (ed.), *Cooperation and Competition Among Primitive Peoples.* New York and London: McGraw-Hill.

—— 1938. The Mountain Arapesh I. An Importing Culture. *Amer. Mus. Nat. Hist.-Anthrop. Papers* 36: 139-349.

—— 1947. The Mountain Arapesh III. Socio-Economic Life. *Amer. Mus. Nat. Hist.-Anthrop. Papers* 40: 159-232.

MEGGITT, MERVYN. 1956-57. The Valleys of the Upper Wage and Lai Rivers, Western Highlands, New Guinea. *Oceania* 27:90-135.

—— 1957. Enga Political Organization: A Preliminary Description. *Mankind* 5: 133-137.

—— 1957-58. The Enga of the New Guinea Highlands: Some Preliminary Observations. *Oceania* 28: 253-330.

—— 1962. *Desert People: A Study of the Walbiri Aborigines of Central Australia.* Sydney: Angus & Robertson.

232

NILLES, JOHN. 1950-51. The Kuman of the Chimbu Region, Central Highlands, New Guinea. *Oceania* 21: 25-26.

OBERG, KALERVO. 1955. Types of Social Structure in Lowland South America. *American Anthropologist* 57: 472-487.

OLIVER, DOUGLAS. 1955. *A Solomon Islands Society*. Cambridge, Mass.: Harvard University Press.

POWDERMAKER, HORTENSE. 1933. *Life in Lesu*. New York: W. W. Norton.

POLANYI, KARL. 1944. *The Great Transformation*. New York: Rinehart.

— 1959. Anthropology and Economic Theory. In M. Fried (ed.), *Readings in Anthropology*, II. New York: Crowell.

POLANYI, KARL, ARENSBERG, CONRAD & PEARSON, HARRY W. (eds.). 1957. *Trade and Market in the Early Empires*. Glencoe, Ill.: The Free Press.

POSPISIL, LEOPOLD. 1958. *Kapauku Papuans and Their Law*. Yale Univ. Public. in Anthrop. No. 54, New Haven: Yale University Press.

— 1959-60. The Kapauku Papuans and Their Kinship Organization. *Oceania* 30: 188-205.

POWELL, H. A. 1960. Competitive Leadership in Trobriand Political Organization. *Journal of the Royal Anthropological Institute* 90: 118-145.

PRICE, JOHN ANDREW. 1962. *Washo Economy*. Nevada State Museum Anthropological Papers No. 6, Carson City: State Printing Office.

PROVINSE, JOHN H. 1937. Cooperative Ricefield Cultivation Among the Siang Dyaks of Central Borneo. *American Anthropologist* 39: 77-102.

PUTNAM, PATRIK. 1953. The Pygmies of the Ituri Forest. In Carleton S. Coon (ed.), *A Reader in General Anthropology*. New York: Henry Holt.

RADCLIFFE-BROWN, A. R. 1930-31. The Social Organisation of Australian Tribes. *Oceania* 1: 34-63, 206-256, 322-341, 426-456.

— 1948 [1922]. *The Andaman Islanders*. Glencoe, Ill.: Free Press.

READ, K. E. 1946-47. Social Organisation in the Markham Valley, New Guinea. *Oceania* 17: 93-118.

— 1949-50. The Political System of the Ngarawapum. *Oceania* 20: 185-223.

— 1959. Leadership and Consensus in a New Guinea Society. *American Anthropologist* 61: 425-436.

233

REAY, MARIE. 1959. *The Kuma*. Melbourne University Press.

RICHARDS, AUDREY I. 1939. *Land, Labour and Diet in Northern Rhodesia*. London, New York, Toronto: Oxford University Press, for the International African Institute.

RINK, HENRY. 1875. *Tales and Traditions of the Eskimo*. Edinburgh and London: Blackwood.

RODRIGUEZ, MAXIMO. 1919. Daily Narrative kept by the Interpreter Maximo Rodriguez at the Island of Amat, otherwise Otahiti, in year 1774. In Corney, B.G., *The Quest and Occupation of Tahiti by Emissaries of Spain . . . 1772-1776*, Vol. III. London: Hakluyt Society.

SAHLINS, MARSHALL D. 1958. *Social Stratification in Polynesia*. Monograph of the American Ethnological Society, Seattle: University of Washington Press.

—— 1960. Political Power and the Economy in Primitive Society. *Essays in the Science of Culture in Honor of Leslie White*. Dole and Carneiro (eds.), New York: Crowell.

—— 1961. The Segmentary Lineage: An Organization of Predatory Expansion. *American Anthropologist* **63**: 322-345.

—— 1962. Review, of *Sociological Aspects of Economic Growth* (B. F. Hoselitz), *American Anthropologist* **64**: 1063-1073.

—— 1962a. *Moala: Culture and Nature on a Fijian Island*. Ann Arbor: University of Michigan Press.

—— 1963. Poor Man, Rich Man, Big-Man, Chief: Political Types in Melanesia and Polynesia. *Comparative Studies in Society and History*. (In press.)

SAHLINS, MARSHALL, D. & SERVICE, ELMAN R. (eds.). 1960. *Evolution and Culture*. Ann Arbor: University of Michigan Press.

SCHAPERA, I. 1930. *The Khoisan Peoples of South Africa*. London: Routledge.

SCHEBESTA, PAUL. 1933. *Among Congo Pygmies*. London: Hutchinson.

—— n.d. *Among the Forest Dwarfs of Malaya*. London: Hutchinson.

SELIGMAN, C. G. 1910. *The Melanesians of British New Guinea*. Cambridge: Cambridge University Press.

SERVICE, E. R. 1962. *Primitive Social Organization*. New York: Random House.

SHARP, LAURISTON. 1934-35. Ritual Life and Economics of the Yir-Yiront of Cape York Peninsula. *Oceania* **5**: 19-42.

—— 1952. Steel Axes for Stone Age Australians. In E. H. Spicer (ed.), *Human Problems in Technological Change*. New York: Russell Sage.

SHIROKOGOROFF, S. M. 1929. *Social Organization of the Northern Tungus*. Shanghai: The Commercial Press.

SPENCER, SIR BALDWIN & GILLEN, F. J. 1927. *The Arunta*. 2 vols. London: Macmillan.

SPENCER, ROBERT F. 1959. *The North Alaskan Eskimo: A Study in Ecology and Society*. Smithson. Instn BAE Bull. 171. Washington: U.S. Govt. Printing Office.

STEWARD, JULIAN. 1938. *Basin-Plateau Aboriginal Sociopolitical Groups*. Smithson. Instn BAE Bull. 120. Washington: U.S. Govt. Printing Office.

SUTTLES, WAYNE. 1960. Affinal Ties, Subsistence, and Prestige among the Coast Salish. *American Anthropologist* **62**: 296-305.

SWANTON, JOHN R. 1928. Social Organization and Social Usages of the Indians of the Creek Confederacy. *Smithson. Instn BAE-AR* **42**: 23-472. Washington: U.S. Govt. Printing Office.

TANNER, JOHN. 1956. *A Narrative of the Captivity and Adventures of John Tanner*. Prepared for Press by Edwin James. Minneapolis: Ross & Haines.

THOMAS, ELIZABETH MARSHALL. 1959. *The Harmless People*. New York: Knopf; London: Secker & Warburg.

THURNWALD, RICHARD C. 1934-35. Pigs and Currency in Buin. *Oceania* **5**: 119-141.

TURNBULL, COLIN M. 1962. *The Forest People*. London: Chatto & Windus; Garden City: Doubleday Anchor and American Museum of Natural History.

VAN LEUR, J. C. 1955. *Indonesian Trade and Society*. The Hague and Bandung: W. van Hoeve.

VAN OVERBERGH, MORICE. 1925. Negritoes of Northern Luzon. *Anthropos* **20**: 148-199, 399-443.

VAYDA, A. P. 1954ms. Notes on Trade Among the Pomo Indians of California, mimeo., Columbia University Interdisciplinary Project: Economic Aspects of Institutional Growth.

—— 1961. A Re-examination of Northwest Coast Economic Systems. *Transactions of the New York Academy of Sciences* (Series II) **23**: 618-624.

VEBLEN, THORSTEIN. 1915. *Imperial Germany and the Industrial Revolution*. New York: Macmillan.

WAGNER, GUNTAR. 1956. *The Bantu of North Kavirondo*: Volume II: Economic Life. London: Oxford University Press for the International African Institute, 2 vols.

WALLACE, ERNEST & HOEBEL, E. A. 1952. *The Comanches, Lords of the South Plains*. Norman: University of Oklahoma Press.

WARNER, W. LLOYD. 1937. *A Black Civilization*. New York & London: Harper and Bros.

WEYER, EDWARD MOFFAT. 1932. *The Eskimos*. New Haven: Yale University Press.

WHITE, LESLIE A. 1959. *The Evolution of Culture*. New York, Toronto, London: McGraw-Hill.

WILLIAMSON, ROBERT W. 1912. *The Mafulu: Mountain People of British New Guinea*. London: Macmillan.

NOTES ON CONTRIBUTORS

EGGAN, FRED. Born 1906, Seattle, Washington; studied at The University of Chicago, B.A., M.A., Ph.D.

Harold H. Swift Distinguished Service Professor of Anthropology and Director, Philippine Studies Program, University of Chicago.

Author of *Social Organization of the Western Pueblos*, 1950; 'Social Anthropology and the Method of Controlled Comparison' (*American Anthropologist*, Vol. 56, 1954); 'Social Anthropology: Methods and Results' (in *Social Anthropology of North American Tribes*, 1955);

Editor of *Social Anthropology of North American Tribes*, 1937, Enlarged Edition, 1955.

GLUCKMAN, MAX. Born 1911, South Africa; studied at The University of Witwatersrand, B.A.; Oxford, D.Phil.

Anthropologist, Rhodes-Livingstone Institute, 1939-42; Director, 1942-7; Lecturer in Social Anthropology, Oxford, 1947-9; Professor of Social Anthropology, Manchester, 1949.

Author of *The Judicial Process among the Barotse of N. Rhodesia*, 1954; *Custom and Conflict in Africa*, 1955; *Order and Rebellion in Tribal Africa*, 1963; *Rule, Law and Ritual in Tribal Societies*, 1964; *The Ideas of Barotse Jurisprudence*, 1964. Editor of *Seven Tribes of British Central Africa*, 1951; *Closed Systems and Open Minds*, 1964.

GOODENOUGH, WARD. Born 1919, Cambridge, Mass.; graduated from The Groton School, 1937; studied at Cornell University, A.B.; Yale University, Ph.D.

Instructor in Anthropology, University of Wisconsin, 1948-9; Assistant Professor of Anthropology, University of Pennsylvania, 1949; Associate Professor, 1954; Professor, 1962; Visiting Professor of Anthropology, Cornell University, 1961-2; Fellow, Center for Advanced Study in the Behavioral Sciences, 1957-8.

Author of *Property, Kin, and Community on Truk*, 1951; *Cooperation in Change*, 1963; and editor of *Explorations in Cultural Anthropology: Essays in Honor of George Peter Murdock*, 1964.

Notes on Contributors

LEWIS, IOAN MYRDDIN. Born 1930, Scotland; studied at Glasgow University, B.Sc. (Chemistry); Oxford, B.Litt., D.Phil.

Lecturer in African Studies, University College of Rhodesia and Nyasaland, 1957; Lecturer in Social Anthropology, University of Glasgow, 1961; Lecturer in Anthropology, University College, London, 1963.

Author of *A Pastoral Democracy: A Study of the Political Institutions of the Northern Pastoral Somali*, 1961.

SAHLINS, MARSHALL D. Born 1930, U.S.A.; studied at University of Michigan, B.A., M.A.; Columbia University, Ph.D.

Lecturer in Anthropology, Columbia University, 1955-6; Assistant Professer of Anthropology, University of Michigan, 1957; Associate Professor, 1961; Professor, 1964; Fellow, Center for Advanced Study in the Behavioral Sciences, 1963-4.

Author of *Social Stratification in Polynesia*, 1958; *Moala: Culture and Nature on a Fijian Island*, 1962; and co-author of *Evolution and Culture*, 1960.

SCHNEIDER, DAVID M. Born 1918, U.S.A.; studied at Cornell University, B.S., M.A.; Harvard, Ph.D.

Lecturer in Anthropology, London School of Economics, 1949; Instructor in Department of Social Relations, Harvard, 1951; Lecturer, 1952; Assistant Professor, 1953; Fellow, Center for Advanced Study in the Behavioral Sciences, 1955-6; Associate Professor, University of California at Berkeley, 1956; Professor, 1959; Professor of Anthropology, University of Chicago, 1960; Chairman of Department, 1963 to date.

Joint author or editor of *The Micronesians and their Depopulation*, 1949; *Personality in Nature, Society and Culture*, 1953; *Marriage, Authority and Final Causes*, 1955; *Zuni Kin Terms*, 1956; *Matrilineal Kinship*, 1961.

WARD, BARBARA E. (Mrs H. S. Morris). Educated at Newnham College, Cambridge, M.A. (History); London University, Dip.Ed. and M.A. (Anthropology).

Lecturer in Anthropology, Birkbeck College, London University, 1949-50 and 1955 onwards; Visiting Professor, Cornell University, 1963-4.

Editor of *Women in the New Asia*, Unesco, 1963.